POLITICS OF ILLUSION

Studies in Cuban History

Series Editor: Louis A. Peréz Jr.

POLITICS OF ILLUSION

The Bay of Pigs Invasion
Reexamined

edited by

James G. Blight
Peter Kornbluh

LYNNE
RIENNER
PUBLISHERS

BOULDER
LONDON

Published in the United States of America in 1998 by
Lynne Rienner Publishers, Inc.
1800 30th Street, Boulder, Colorado 80301

and in the United Kingdom by
Lynne Rienner Publishers, Inc.
3 Henrietta Street, Covent Garden, London WC2E 8LU

Library of Congress Cataloging-in-Publication Data
Politics of illusion :   the Bay of Pigs invasion reexamined   /   edited by
    James G. Blight and Peter Kornbluh.
        (Studies in Cuban history)
        Includes bibliographical references and index.
        ISBN 1-55587-783-4 (hardcover   :   alk. paper)
        1. Cuba—History—Invasion, 1961.   2. Oral history.   I. Blight,
    James G.   II. Kornbluh, Peter.   III. Series.
    F1788.P575   1997
    972.9106'4—dc21   97-23213
                                                                              CIP

British Cataloguing in Publication Data
A Cataloguing in Publication record for this book
is available from the British Library.

Printed and bound in the United States of America

        The paper used in this publication meets the requirements
    ∞   of the American National Standard for Permanence of
        Paper for Printed Library Materials Z39.48–1984.

    5 4 3 2 1

To the memory of McGeorge Bundy,

for whom the Bay of Pigs provided on-the-job training,
who learned fast and helped his president to do likewise,
who later inspired a new generation of scholars
to follow his lead
in combining experience and analysis, people and documents,
and who knew, as Mary and Janet did,
the real significance of the 27 roses that late October day.

And to the memory of Enrique Baloyra,

who showed us the way toward the "hyphenated Fourth force,"
who introduced us to his "guys,"
and their documents,
and a few "Cuban barbershop counterfactuals,"
and thus greatly enlarged our view of these events.

Contents

Preface

This book, and the research process leading up to it, have been follow-ups to the Cuban missile crisis project, which was, like the Bay of Pigs project, a collaboration of Brown University's Thomas J. Watson Jr. Institute for International Studies, the National Security Archive, and various institutes and agencies in Cuba. The decision to approach the Bay of Pigs invasion and related events was made in 1995 jointly by the Watson Institute and the archive.

For various reasons, some relating to a nosedive in U.S.–Cuban relations in early 1996, preparations for a Havana conference on the Bay of Pigs were postponed. At that point, several members of the U.S. organizing team met to decide whether it would be possible to, in effect, take two interim steps at once: (1) to gather the U.S. participants for a conference to discuss new U.S. documents including, for the first time, documents from the anti-Castro resistance; and (2) to raise the odds of a subsequent conference in Cuba, via the generation of new information from the U.S. side. Their conclusion was in the affirmative.

T-shirts were distributed to participants on the first evening of the subsequent U.S. conference, meant to symbolize the larger goals of the project. On the front was a CIA aerial photograph of the Bay of Pigs battle in progress. On the back was the last stanza of the song "Playa Girón," by Cuban songwriter Sylvio Rodríguez:

> Que escriban la historia, su historia
> [todos] los hombres de playa Girón.

> Well, let them write the history, their story,
> [all] the men of the Bay of Pigs.

"Todos/all" was added to embrace the ultimate goal of the project, which is the participation of all sides from the Bay of Pigs events, so as to enrich the historical record.

*   *   *

First and foremost, we would like to express our gratitude to our Cuban counterparts for playing an important role in advancing the historical record. The project on the Bay of Pigs originated in our conversations with them.

This project and book would not have happened without the support of Kimberly Stanton of the MacArthur Foundation, whose brainchild the project was at the outset; and Janet Shenk of the Arca Foundation, whose support of U.S.–Cuban collaborative projects is legendary and who successfully lobbied her board on our behalf for the use of the Arca conference center at Musgrove Plantation, St. Simons Island, Georgia. On 1 March 1996, our small group met in Janet's office in Washington, and two hours later, what became the Musgrove Conference on the Bay of Pigs was approved. Soon after that, the Musgrove staff, headed by Wayne and Nieta Carver, with Anne Judge as liaison in Washington, got in gear with very short notice and did their usual flawless job come conference time.

With only three months to do work that can sometimes take a year or more, our operations team had to perform beyond the call of duty. As usual, janet Lang of the Watson Institute assumed overall responsibility for organizing the conference. She did her usual marvelous job, under less than ideal conditions, and not only by playing "Dr. No" for JGB. janet was assisted by a competent staff of assistants. We particularly thank John White at the National Security Archive and Brenda Menard of the Watson Institute. Brenda was the virtual "desk officer" in charge of the project's logistics from beginning to end, and she also transcribed the tapes of the Musgrove discussions. At the archive, John led a team that included Mary Burroughs, Sue Bechtel, and Robin Rone, who worked on organizing the documents for the briefing notebook. We also thank Jon Elliston and Hugh Byrne for assistance with the chronology of U.S. decisionmaking.

For various kinds of assistance at the Watson Institute, we thank Sheila Fournier, Richard Gann, Leslie Baxter, Mary Esser, and Jean Lawlor. Our (then) undergraduate assistant, Andrew Goodridge, translated the documents from the Cuban resistance and acted as interpreter for us during interviews in Cuba. We are also grateful to Thomas Biersteker, director of the Watson Institute, and P. Terrence Hopmann, director of the Global Security Program at the institute; and Thomas Blanton, executive director of the archive. They gave us carte blanche to make this project happen. In addition, Terry and Tom Blanton participated actively in the conference itself.

We thank Stephanie Fawcett and Mary Kennefick of the John F. Kennedy Library for assistance with the documents. We also thank Warren Kimball, chairman of the advisory board of the State Department's Office of the Historian, and the historian himself, William Z. Slaney, for making key documents available prior to the publication of the FRUS series. Brian Latell and Mike Warner of the CIA's Center for the Study of Intelligence are also to be commended for making high-level CIA documents available for the FRUS series.

In addition to logistical challenges, the nature of the events under investigation—painful for veterans of the episode to recall, even with the distance of several decades—made it necessary to get something close to instant and iron-clad commitments for the conference, and to master the material to be distributed in advance of the conference. Especially helpful in making our case to various veterans of the events were Enrique Baloyra, Don Bohning, and Richard Helms.

For valuable assistance in seeing the book into print, we thank Lynne Rienner, Steve Barr, and Sally Glover at Lynne Rienner Publishers; and Fred Fullerton, Amy Langlais, George Potter, and Nancy Hamlin Soukup at the Watson Institute. We also owe a debt of gratitude to Mitchell Kaplan, proprietor of Books & Books in Coral Gables, Florida, and president of the Miami Book Fair, for featuring *Politics of Illusion* at the November 1997 fair; and to Don Bohning (again) and Richard Bard of the *Miami Herald* for coverage of both the Musgrove Conference and the publication of the book.

We dedicate this book to Mac Bundy, who died suddenly during its preparation. Before critical oral history, there was Mac, with his constructive criticism, vivid testimony, and rigorous scholarship. He was the embodiment of what we now try to practice as we seek to get a little closer to understanding what it was really like. We also dedicate it to Enrique Baloyra, who died as the book was going to press. It was Quique who first saw how critical oral history might be applied to the story of the Cuban resistance and exiles, and who worked so creatively to make it happen.

J. G. B.

P. K.

A Note on Declassified Documents

All declassified documents cited in this book are either included in Appendix 5 and presented in the order of appearance by chapter or are available from the National Security Archive at George Washington University, the Gelman Library, Suite 701, 2130 H Street, NW, Washington, D.C. 20037 (Telephone: 202-994-7000; Fax: 202-994-7005).

Dramatis Personae

The participants in the Musgrove Conference on the Bay of Pigs invasion were a diverse group of former officials of various agencies of the U.S. and Soviet governments and several Cuban exile and resistance organizations; and scholars who are among the most knowledgeable specialists on Cuba, U.S.–Cuban relations, Cold War crises, and governmental decisionmaking. As is obvious in the sketches that follow, however, the distinction between former officials and scholars is partly one of convenience. Several former officials and former members of the anti-Castro resistance have also written extensively and well about U.S.–Cuban relations in the period of the Bay of Pigs invasion.

Veterans

From the Kennedy White House

Arthur Schlesinger Jr. Special assistant to President John F. Kennedy, with oversight of (among other issues) all Latin American initiatives, including the Alliance for Progress and, during the Bay of Pigs crisis, liaison with the Cuban leadership in exile. Alone among Kennedy's close advisers, Schlesinger opposed the invasion throughout the first months of the administration. He wrote several memoranda warning the president not to move ahead with the invasion, though he did not argue his case in high-level meetings, much to his later regret. Arthur Schlesinger Jr. is also one of the most eminent historians of the post–World War II era, having won the Pulitzer Prize twice and having written best-selling biographies of both John Kennedy (*A Thousand Days,* 1965) and Robert Kennedy (*Robert Kennedy and His Times,* 1978).

From the State Department

Wayne S. Smith. A political officer in the U.S. Embassy in Havana, from 1958 to January 1961, when the United States broke relations with Cuba and the embassy was closed. During the first two years after Fidel Castro came to power in Cuba (1959–1960), he was in close touch with both the CIA station in Havana and members of the anti-Castro Cuban underground. After the Bay of Pigs invasion, he became executive assistant to Adolf Berle, White House Latin American liaison. Later, when the United States and Cuba partially reestablished relations during the presidency of Jimmy Carter, he was director of Cuban affairs in the State Department, and later chief of the U.S. mission in Havana. Wayne Smith is also the author or editor of many books and articles on contemporary U.S.–Cuban relations, including a scholarly memoir of U.S.–Cuban relations in the Castro years (*The Closest of Enemies,* 1987).

From the Central Intelligence Agency

Jacob L. Esterline. A veteran of the forerunner of the CIA, the OSS, he commanded Burmese guerrillas behind Japanese lines during World War II. After the war, he joined the CIA. He was the Washington director of Operation PBSUCCESS, which resulted in a successful coup in 1954 against Guatemalan leader Jacobo Arbenz, and later became CIA station chief in Guatemala and in Venezuela, from which he was recalled to Washington in early 1960 to direct the project that would ultimately result in the Bay of Pigs invasion. A specialist in guerrilla warfare, he designed the initial projected intervention of Cuban exiles—a clandestine airdrop to take place in the Escambray Mountains near the Cuban town of Trinidad, on the south coast, a plan that was rejected by President Kennedy. During the period before the Bay of Pigs invasion, he tried in various ways to get the operation canceled, foreseeing the failure that ultimately occurred. He later became CIA station chief in Miami in the late 1960s, before retiring and moving first to the Caribbean, then to North Carolina, living "under cover" and using the name "Jake Engler" to avoid possible reprisals by Cuban agents.

Samuel Halpern. A veteran of the forerunner of the CIA, the OSS, he joined the CIA after World War II and worked his entire career in the Directorate of Plans, specializing in covert operations, mostly in Asia, where he was working when he was called back to Washington in 1961 to help organize a covert operation against Cuba. (The operation, code-named MONGOOSE, was led by Gen. Edward Lansdale in the Defense Department and William K. Harvey at the CIA.) He was also involved later on in other operations involving Cuba, run from CIA-sponsored facilities in Central America. Since retiring from the CIA, Samuel Halpern has become one of the leading figures in opening up the secret history of the Cold War, writing about his own experiences and cooperating with others writing about some of the legendary people he worked for, including Lansdale, Harvey, Desmond FitzGerald, Richard Bissell, and Richard Helms.

From the Defense Department

Col. Jack Hawkins. A retired Marine Corps officer, he was a specialist in amphibious operations, having participated in the planning of the U.S. invasion of Okinawa in 1945 and the Inchon landing during the Korean War. After Korea, he became an instructor at the Marine Corps school in Quantico, Virginia, from which he was recalled in 1960 to help redesign the CIA operation against Cuba. Hawkins's task was to work with Jacob Esterline to transform what had initially been an airdrop of CIA-trained Cuban anti-Castro guerrillas into an amphibious landing at the Bay of Pigs of a fighting force of approximately fifteen hundred Cuban exiles, who had been trained by the CIA in a camp in Guatemala. Like Jacob Esterline, he sensed that the political leadership in the Kennedy administration did not fully understand the requirements for a successful landing at the Bay of Pigs. He joined Esterline late in the process in an effort to get Richard Bissell, overall director of the operation, to cancel it, but to no avail. Colonel Hawkins was unable to travel to Musgrove for the conference, but he was in daily contact by phone during the conference, and he sent a long memo to the participants prior to the conference that figured importantly in the Musgrove discussions. His memo "Covert Actions Against the Castro Government of Cuba, January 1960–April 1961" (Document 4.3) was his first statement for the public record since the failed invasion 35 years before.

From Brigade 2506

Rafael Quintero. He joined the anti-Batista underground in Cuba in the late 1950s, after being falsely accused of subversion and jailed by members of Batista's security forces. After Batista was overthrown, he joined a literacy campaign organized by the Catholic Church, but was expelled for refusing to join the Communist Party. He then joined the Movement to Recover the Revolution (MRR) and traveled to the United States, seeking assistance and training for forces intending to overthrow Fidel Castro. One of the first to enlist in Brigade 2506, he helped build their training camp in Guatemala before returning to join the Cuban resistance on the island. Following the Bay of Pigs invasion, he escaped, rejoined the resistance, and worked with Robert Kennedy in the effort to ransom the members of the brigade captured at the Bay of Pigs. Following their release in December 1962, Rafael Quintero joined Manuel Artime and Félix Rodríguez in a CIA-sponsored anti-Castro operation in Central America. Following the close of that operation in 1964, he returned to the CIA and later worked for them on many diverse assignments, and was intimately involved during the 1980s in efforts to train and supply the Nicaraguan Contras.

Alfredo G. Durán. An early enlistee in Brigade 2506, he received guerrilla training and, later, after the plan of the invasion changed, training as an infantryman with the invasion force. Following the defeat of the brigade, he escaped, but was captured 30 days later, taken to Havana, and imprisoned. He remained in prison until the fall of 1962. Most brigade members returned to the United States in December 1962 under the terms of an agreement between the U.S. and Cuban governments. Alfredo Durán is a past president of the Veteran's Association of Brigade 2506, from which he was expelled by its members for reasons associated with his participation in the Musgrove Conference, and for his public statements prior to the conference indicating his willingness to go to Havana to discuss the history of the Bay of Pigs invasion with Cuban President Fidel Castro and his colleagues. He is a former chairman of the Florida Democratic Party and a leader of several organizations of Cuban exiles dedicated to peaceful reconciliation with Cubans who have remained in Cuba.

From the Movement to Recover the Revolution (MRR)

Lino B. Fernández. Trained in Cuba as a physician, he eventually specialized in psychiatry, and he was a medical school classmate of Manuel Artime, a founder of the anti-Castro resistance and later the political chief of Brigade 2506. He was a member of the anti-Batista resistance, and soon after Fidel Castro came to power, he became a leading figure in the formation of the Movement to Recover the Revolution, second in command to its charismatic leader, Rogelio González Corzo, better known by his underground name, "Francisco." Lino Fernández, known in the underground as "Ojeda," was the military commander of the MRR by late 1960, working closely with both "Francisco" and with Artime. He was captured in February 1961 and spent the next 17 years in Cuban prisons on the Isle of Pines, at La Cabaña Fortress in Havana, and elsewhere. He was released, along with approximately three thousand other political prisoners in 1978, in accordance with the terms of an agreement between the Carter administration and the Cuban government, following which he and his wife rejoined their children in South Florida, where he currently practices medicine.

From the Students' Revolutionary Directorate (DRE)

Enrique A. Baloyra. After joining the anti-Batista underground while still a high school student in Havana, he became involved with several organizations connected to the Catholic Church that emphasized community service. Soon after Fidel Castro came to power, he joined the DRE, working in its intelligence unit. Following a government crackdown in the wake of the failed Bay of Pigs invasion, he left Cuba to join the anti-Castro movement in exile, and remained with the DRE until 1964, when the CIA ceased to fund its operations against the Cuban government. Enrique Baloyra was professor of political science at the University of Miami's Graduate School of International Studies, and its former associate dean. He wrote widely on civil-military relations and transitions to democracy in Latin America, and coedited the recent *Conflict and Change in Cuba* (1993). He was active in many organizations in South Florida seeking a peaceful transition to democracy in Cuba.

The View from Moscow

Oleg T. Daroussenkov. After graduating from the Soviet Foreign Ministry's School of International Relations, he became the first specialist on Cuba to be sent by the Soviets to Havana, where he joined the embassy staff in the summer of 1961. For over a year following his arrival in Cuba, he was a special assistant to Ernesto ("Ché") Guevara, Cuban minister of industries. He also served as interpreter for many Soviet officials visiting Cuba at that time. For the next 30 years, he was the Soviet Union's top specialist on Cuba, dividing his time between the embassy in Havana and his post as director of Cuban affairs in the International Department of the Central Committee of the Communist Party of the Soviet Union. He retired in 1993 as Russian ambassador to Mexico.

Scholars

Thomas Blanton. Executive director, The National Security Archive at George Washington University.

James G. Blight. Professor of international relations (research), The Thomas J. Watson Jr. Institute for International Studies, Brown University.

Philip Brenner. Professor of international politics and foreign policy, School of International Service, The American University.

Malcolm Byrne. Director of analysis, The National Security Archive at George Washington University.

Jorge I. Domínguez. Clarence Dillon Professor of international affairs and director, Center for International Affairs, Harvard University.

Piero Gleijeses. Professor of U.S. foreign policy, The Paul H. Nitze School of Advanced International Studies, Johns Hopkins University.

James G. Hershberg. Assistant professor of history, George Washington University.

P. Terrence Hopmann. Professor of political science and director, Program on Global Security, The Thomas J. Watson Jr. Institute for International Studies, Brown University.

Peter Kornbluh. Senior analyst, The National Security Archive at George Washington University.

Thomas Skidmore. Carlos Manuel de Céspedes professor of the history of modern Latin America and director, Center for Latin American Studies, Brown University.

1. OBJECTIVE. The purpose of the program outlined herein is to bring about the replacement of the Castro regime with one more devoted to the true interests of the Cuban people and more acceptable to the U.S. in such a manner as to avoid any appearance of U.S. intervention.

> CIA
> *Program of Action Against the Castro*
> *Regime, 16 March 1960*
> *[Document 2.1]*

An illusion is not the same thing as an error; nor is it necessarily an error. . . . What is characteristic of illusions is that they are derived from human wishes. . . . You have to defend [an] illusion with all your might. If it becomes discredited . . . you feel betrayed; there is nothing left for you to do but to despair of everything until, perhaps, education and reason shall free you from your burden.

> *Sigmund Freud,*
> The Future of an Illusion

What is set down below implies no criticism of particular individuals; if that were the object the writer would begin with himself. . . . Hope was the parent of belief. . . . In prolonged balancing and rebalancing of marginal elements of this operation, all concerned managed to forget—or not to learn—the fundamental importance of success in this sort of effort. Limitations were accepted that should have been avoided, and hopes were indulged that should have been sternly put aside. Many of the lesser mistakes or failures . . . can be explained largely by the failure to recall this basic rule.

> *McGeorge Bundy,*
> *Memorandum to President John F. Kennedy,*
> *24 April 1961 [Document 6.2]*

Prologue: "John Wayne's" Betrayals

———

The Wayne hero could be calm, in a time of the empire's dominance. His self-discipline was counted on to awe or attract others. The mature Wayne was lightly weaponed—a rifle or one pistol, and he often did not have to use that. He faced down foes. The villain in the "shoot-out" is undone by Wayne's stride as he comes down the street.

> *Garry Wills,* John Wayne's America: The Politics of Celebrity

In those days, the Cubans thought of the Americans in what I call the "John Wayne syndrome." . . . We thought the Americans worked the way John Wayne worked in his movies. Of course, this was naive, but this was the way most of us felt. I mean: the Americans hated communism and, like John Wayne, they never lost—ever.

> *Rafael Quintero, 31 May 1996*

Shortly after midnight on 17 April 1961, approximately 1,400 commandos began to arrive at Playa Girón (Girón Beach) from Bahia de Cochinos (Bay of Pigs), on the southern coast of Cuba. Trained in Guatemala by the CIA of the United States, which also supplied arms and munitions, their goal was to go ashore, establish a beachhead, and hold it against the expected counterattack by the army and militia of the Cuban government led by Fidel Castro. In time, the men of Brigade 2506, as the invasion force was called, hoped to link up with their comrades—the anti-Castro rebels in the Escambray Mountains some 80 miles away. They also expected assistance from the U.S. Armed Forces at the Bay of Pigs, which many in the brigade believed would lead to a large-scale U.S. military intervention, the overthrow of the government, and its replacement with rebel leaders living in exile in Miami.

Instead, the invaders were defeated within 72 hours by Cuban militia forces in fierce fighting at Playa Girón. Trapped without the expected control of the air over the beach and surrounding area, the *brigadistas* were

1

pounded by surviving remnants of Fidel Castro's small air force before, during, and after the landing. The U.S. Armed Forces did not intervene, either in the air or on the ground. The invaders could not link up with their comrades in the Escambray Mountains; the internal resistance to the government was crushed throughout Cuba as a result of the invasion; the socialist character of the Cuban Revolution was proclaimed by Fidel Castro; and the new U.S. administration of President John F. Kennedy was humiliated. The invaders who survived were imprisoned, the Cuban Revolution was consolidated, and the U.S. administration that had trained and supplied the rebels was in disarray.

This event, more than any other, sowed the seeds of decades of bitter enmity between the United States and Cuba. It made plausible, perhaps even necessary, the theretofore unlikely alliance between Cuba and the Soviet Union, leading to a series of crises involving the three countries, including the Cuban missile crisis of October 1962. And Playa Girón/Bay of Pigs became the fundamental historical point of contention for the bitterest of enemies: the government of Fidel Castro, for which the event proved its ability to defend itself against the United States, and the Cuban exile community, for whom the event symbolized their betrayal by the U.S. government, from whom they had mistakenly expected whatever military support might prove necessary to win.

First Cut, 1961–Present: Multiple Betrayals

From the moment it became clear that Brigade 2506 was going to be defeated, the accusations of betrayal began to fly. On 20 April, following a difficult, acrimonious press conference, President Kennedy famously said to his aide, Theodore Sorensen: "All my life I've known better than to depend on the experts. How could I have been so stupid, to let them go ahead?"[1] Embedded in this typically self-deprecating remark was deep bitterness toward the officials at the CIA, the principal U.S. agency in the operation, especially Director Allen Dulles and Deputy Director for Plans Richard Bissell. Both would be fired by Kennedy before the year's end. Kennedy also took aim at his military advisers on the Joint Chiefs of Staff and would soon bring in Gen. Maxwell Taylor, who would conduct Kennedy's personal investigation of the Bay of Pigs and then become chairman of the Joint Chiefs.

The feeling of betrayal was mutual at the CIA. Allen Dulles would later say that he felt Kennedy had never been really committed to the project to unseat Castro, as President Eisenhower had been.[2] Everyone involved in the project at the CIA believed that an American president simply would not—and could not—let such an operation fail. And in fact, it was the patently unbelievable, almost surreal quality of the events—a small, backward country with a new, beleaguered government had beaten the most powerful nation on earth—that led those intimately involved, notably those in the CIA, to turn to one conspiracy theory or another in order to "explain" its outcome. It is not necessary to buy into the Oliver Stone paranoia about how a shadow government, led by CIA operatives outraged over betrayal by the White House at the Bay of Pigs, ultimately killed Kennedy. One can reject Stone's conspiracy theory but still appreciate how broad and deep the resentment in the CIA was toward the young president, for the episode had ruined careers, deflated morale, and left the agency a legacy of public distrust it lives with even now.

The feeling of betrayal felt by both the CIA and the White House was, if anything, even more viscerally felt by the anti-Castro Cubans, both those who fought at the Bay of Pigs, and those who were rounded up and imprisoned or exiled in the aftermath of the failed invasion. In the North Americanized vernacular of many Cubans of that era: How was it possible that they could lose with "John Wayne" on their side? The Cuban exiles, by and large, did not develop complicated conspiracy theories to account for the defeat of the brigade, and the de facto loss of their country to Fidel Castro and to communism. The most often heard accounting was that Kennedy and his fellow gringos simply lacked *cojones* (balls).

For many Cuban exiles, the bitterness of having felt betrayed remains, after 35 years or more, even though most have become successfully integrated into the mainstream of U.S. society.[3] This was brought home to us as we were recruiting participants for the conference whose proceedings make up the bulk of this book. Early on, our expectation was to proceed directly to a conference in Cuba, with the participation of Fidel Castro, on the model of a similar conference we organized in Havana in January 1992 on the Cuban missile crisis.[4] We had received word that one of the Cuban participants would be José Ramón Fernández, who in April 1961 was the commander of the victorious militia forces at the Bay of Pigs. The senior surviving commander of Brigade 2506 is Erneido Oliva, who recently retired as a major general from the U.S. National Guard. We invited him to participate. After expressing his adamant opposition to participation, he said this:

> You mentioned the Bay of Pigs "fiasco." I think a better word is "betrayal." It is well documented that the Cuban freedom fighters, under my command, performed their combat duties courageously and well. Yet, the United States government did not honor its commitment to the leaders of the exile forces . . . I believe that if we had received the promised military support during the invasion, we could have defeated the rebel army.[5]

It is now clear that Kennedy never promised U.S. military support to anyone, under any circumstances, at the Bay of Pigs. But it is also clear how the bitterness of defeat-by-betrayal felt by Cuban exiles like Erneido Oliva is as powerful now as it was in April 1961.[6]

And so it has been: to study the events known in shorthand as "the Bay of Pigs" is to encounter layer upon layer of bitterness and blaming. To analyze it is, for the most part, to categorize and try to evaluate the various accusations. From April 1961, through Peter Wyden's landmark *Bay of Pigs: The Untold Story,* down to our own work in the adjacent events of the missile crisis: on the Bay of Pigs, time has seemed to heal no wounds at all.[7]

A Reexamination, Using Critical Oral History

Against this backdrop of accusations of betrayal, we decided to try to gather representatives of the key U.S. institutional players in these events, and representatives of both Brigade 2506 and the underground anti-Castro resistance. What was the objective in bringing these disparate elements together? It was to try to do better than our predecessors at reaching relatively objective, data-based, informed conclusions—from the points of view of the various anti-Castro perspectives—about how this tragedy could have occurred. We felt three factors favored such an attempt:

- The experience in the Cuban missile crisis project showed that even representatives of countries that are currently deeply adversarial— the United States and Cuba—can engage in civilized discussions that advance historical scholarship.
- The end of the U.S.–Soviet Cold War has resulted in the availability of people who have not previously spoken for the public record— especially those from intelligence agencies—and also the availability of newly declassified and revealing documents on the foreign policy of the Kennedy administration.
- We speculated that in the new, post–Cold War circumstances, some key people in the events surrounding the Bay of Pigs might wish to come forward and get their views on the record and into the informed discussion of that period and these events, rather than take their secrets to the grave.

As we envisioned it, the Bay of Pigs project would make use of a research method called "critical oral history," which we jointly developed in the course of the Cuban missile crisis project. The method requires the simultaneous interaction of documents bearing on the paper trail of decisions for issues and events under reexamination, memories of those who participated in the decisions, and scholars, whose business it is to know the relevant aspects of the written record.

As formerly secret documents become available, we begin to understand more clearly than before the way events unfolded. Yet documents have a weakness of their own; they do not supply their own context. To a large extent, the memories of the participants can help supply the missing context to the documents, and the documents can supply many of the facts that human memories distort or forget. And in concert, several people's memories may test and correct each individual's memory, so that errors in recollection or egregious distortions can be reduced—all the more so if the parties to a discussion are known to have divergent views of the event. (This is especially true, as one would expect, in the case of former adversaries, whose views of an event are usually not just discrepant, but often contradictory. And despite their common anti-Castro roots, many have taken an adversarial stance toward the people or agencies believed to have been guilty of betrayal regarding the outcome at the Bay of Pigs.) In a properly designed conversation, therefore, in which key participants discuss the event among themselves and with knowledgeable scholars, a more accurate picture can be reconstructed than would be possible if we relied solely on recollections alone.

This is why the method is called critical oral history. Unlike conventional oral history, in which people merely tell their stories, critical oral history subjects these stories to multidimensional criticism. Thus a particular story—not only a policymaker's recollection of his experience but also, perhaps, a scholar's favorite theory—must answer to three judges: the documentary record, the expertise of specialists in the field, and the recollections of those who lived through the event in positions of official responsibility.[8]

Second Cut, 31 May–2 June 1996: Multiple Illusions

From 31 May to 2 June 1996, representatives of the key U.S. institutional players in these events, and representatives of Brigade 2506 and of the anti-Castro underground resistance, gathered at Musgrove Plantation conference center, St. Simons Island, Georgia, to reexamine the events. In preparation, the participants acquainted themselves with old and new scholarship on the events, with newly declassified documentation from the CIA and, for the first time, with documents from the anti-Castro underground resistance in Cuba between January 1959 and July 1961 (see Appendix 3 and Appendix 4 for the chronology and selected documents from the resistance).

Several of the veterans of those events chose to participate only after considerable reflection and discussion with the organizers. Some questioned the wisdom of having certain others participate. (Words like "betrayal" and "apologist" were not uncommon in these preliminary conversations.) In truth, we did not know what to expect from people who had, more or less, refused for 35 years to sit down with one another to discuss the Bay of Pigs. At the very outset of the discussions, Philip Brenner, one of our participating scholars, merely stated what everyone was feeling when he said that we had gathered "a group of people who can be characterized as having felt betrayed by some of the others, or really by the agencies of some of the others, at this table. The potential for tension among your participants is really quite extraordinary."9

In the event, there was plenty of emotion—as is obvious in the text—but there were no recriminations, no accusations. Instead, there was a remarkable degree of self-criticism. "John Wayne," who came up literally and figuratively in the discussions—that is, representatives of the various U.S. agencies involved at the time—admitted to holding all sorts of illusions. Likewise for the members of the anti-Castro groups such as former *brigadista* and underground resistance fighter Rafael Quintero, who admitted to having a "John Wayne complex," naive though he was at the time. We have tried to highlight some of these transformations in the epigraphs to the six chapters by contrasting views from 1961 and from the 1996 conference.

For each session (and its corresponding chapter in this book), a scholar led off by anchoring the conversation in the declassified documents and other materials that were read in preparation for the conference. This helped to steer the conversation in productive directions, but only because all the participants, without exception, came prepared to reexamine their own beliefs, their long-held views regarding whom they felt had betrayed them. In retrospect, one must marvel at the mental flexibility of some of the participants, and their courage, in showing a readiness to alter views that were so deeply held, for such a long time.

A final note: the appendices—the chronologies and documents—were inextricably involved in the discussions that follow. The degree to which the participants refer to the documents, and in which the documents drive the discussion, is unprecedented in our experience of critical oral history conferences. The reader should, we believe, follow suit and be prepared to refer to the documents and chronology far more often than is usual with appendices. (Documents in Appendix 5 are identified by chapter and order of appearance in the discussion within that chapter. When mentioned in either the text or endnotes, they are identified in this way—as in [Document 1.1], which directs the reader to the first section of Appendix 5, first document, "MRR Strength in Northern Oriente.") Indeed, the discussions may be somewhat difficult to follow unless the effort is made to coordinate the discussions with the chronologies and documents. We believe the reader will conclude, however, along with our participants at Musgrove, that the effort will have been worth the trouble.

Notes

1. Theodore C. Sorensen, *Kennedy* (New York: Harper & Row, 1965), p. 309.
2. See Arthur Schlesinger Jr., *A Thousand Days: John F. Kennedy in the White House* (New York: Fawcett, 1965), pp. 239–240. See also Allen Dulles, "My Answer on the Bay of Pigs," unpublished ms., 20 (box 244), Allen Dulles Papers, Mudd Library, Princeton University; cited in Piero Gleijeses, "Ships in the Night: The CIA, the White House and the Bay of Pigs," *Journal of Latin American Studies* 17, pt. 1 (February 1995): 1–42.
3. See David Rieff, *The Exile* (New York: Farrar Straus & Giroux, 1992) for a fascinating account of the liveliness of the events of April 1961 in the minds of Miami's Cubans, and even in their conversations.
4. See James G. Blight, Bruce J. Allyn, and David A. Welch, *Cuba on the Brink: Castro, the Missile Crisis and the Soviet Collapse* (New York: Pantheon/ Random House, 1993).
5. Erneido Oliva to James Blight, 6 November 1995. One of the most recent accounts of the Bay of Pigs is by Evan Thomas, *The Very Best Men, Four Who Dared: The Early Years of the CIA* (New York: Simon & Schuster, 1995). Thomas calls his second chapter (of two) on the Bay of Pigs simply "Fiasco" (pp. 261–272), and emphasizes the "screw-ups," of which there were many. Perhaps the limiting case of such analyses was by Thomas Thompson, who called it "a black comedy excursion into a world of spooks, liars, gangsters and idiots" (quoted on the back cover of Peter Wyden, *Bay of Pigs: The Untold Story* [New York: Simon & Schuster, 1979], from a review in the *Los Angeles Times*). But as the letter from Oliva makes clear, this is a rather superficial rendering of the meaning of these events.
6. During the Cuban missile crisis project, the organizers received, on a regular basis, threatening messages from various exile groups seeking to use the scholarly conferences as a forum to press their views and agendas. Just prior to the conference immediately preceding the January 1992 Havana conference—in Antigua, in January 1991—a "proposal" was received from an exile group seeking to participate. Having heard that two former members of the Kennedy administration, Robert McNamara and Arthur Schlesinger, would participate, they "offered" to begin the conference by conducting a posthumous "war crimes trial" against President Kennedy (and presumably his former associates, McNamara and Schlesinger). If we refused their "offer," they said, they would come to Antigua and see to it that our conference would not be held. Fortunately, this was a bluff, but the bitterness underlying such a proposition struck us as entirely real.
7. Peter Wyden, *Bay of Pigs: The Untold Story* (New York: Simon & Schuster, 1979).
8. The outstanding contribution of the Cuban missile crisis project was probably to bring that pivotal and supremely dangerous event back to life, so that a new generation of scholars and officials can consider anew its significance. Since the initiation of the project in 1987, over 50 books (in a dozen languages), hundreds of articles, and many widely viewed television documentaries on the missile crisis have appeared, spurred directly by the project. Dissertations and theses once again are being written on the events of October 1962, but in a new vein, using much information that was formerly unavailable, and applying it to the post–Cold War world. As the director of one contributing U.S. foundation said, "The missile crisis is once more a fit subject of informed conversation." For surveys of the new literature, see Len Scott and Steve Smith, "Lessons of October: Historians, Political

Scientists, Policymakers and the Cuban Missile Crisis," *International Affairs* 70, no. 4: 659–684; and James G. Blight and janet M. Lang, "Burden of Responsibility: Reflections on the Critical Oral History of the Cuban Missile Crisis," *Peace and Conflict: Journal of Peace Psychology* 1, no. 3: 225–264.
    9. Philip Brenner, Chapter 1 in this volume.

1

The Anti-Castro Resistance
Meets the CIA

The role of the U.S. is to prevent communism, disguised as Fidelism, from becoming the expression of the present revolutionary feeling in Latin America. . . . Mr. President, we want to state that our hope lies with you.

Alberto Müller to John F. Kennedy,
24 January 1961 [Document 1.7]

We called for help. . . . [But] the CIA tried to do everything themselves. . . . From then on, the CIA headquarters did everything. It was like a "one-man show."

Lino Fernández, 31 May 1996

James G. Blight: Okay. . . . While participating in these conferences, we expect to enjoy ourselves, we expect to meet old friends and get introduced to new friends.[1] Yet, for me personally, much of what we are about to discuss is difficult, even tragic, and still the subject of contentious debate. The missile crisis, for example, was the great tragedy that almost, but didn't quite, come to pass. The tragedy that is the subject of this conference did come to pass. Dick Goodwin says, in his memoir, that making decisions in the White House is difficult, but bleeding and dying on a beach is a lot more difficult than that.[2] I [repeat] that to let those of you know, who really did suffer in various ways because of these events, that the chairman here is very much aware that we are entering on difficult, serious ground.

I've asked some of our distinguished scholars here to try to kick us off in the right direction by giving some of their impressions of the relevant documents and by posing a few questions to those of you on the other side of the table who participated in the events. Session I is on "The Anti-Castro Resistance and Initial Contacts with the CIA." I've asked Jorge Domínguez to get us going. I have asked Jorge to go first in part because he is so knowledgeable, and in part because he never goes over the time limit.

9

[Laughter.] He is the only academic that I have ever met who doesn't go over time limits. In that sense, I hope he serves as a role model for any of you who tend to be delinquent in this respect. Jorge?

Jorge Domínguez: That's an intimidating way to introduce me. I thought that we should begin by recalling at least one of the reasons why the goals of the resistance, as well as the goals of the Bay of Pigs invasion and the U.S. government, turned out to be so difficult to accomplish. So I will quote from then vice president Richard Nixon's note on his conversation with Fidel Castro. Nixon concludes—it is April of '59—

> The one fact that we can be sure of is that he has those indefinable qualities which make him a leader of men. Whatever we may think of him, he is going to be a great factor in the development of Cuba and very possibly in Latin American affairs generally. He has the power to lead.[3]

It is worth noting just how perceptive Richard Nixon was.

There are at least two questions that connect the issue of the Cuban Resistance to the question of U.S. policy regarding the Bay of Pigs invasion. One is: Would there be a revolt in the wake of the invasion? Here is the second one: Was time on Fidel Castro's side? If there was to be no revolt following the invasion, then the plan was flawed in its conception. But if time was on Fidel Castro's side, then it was urgent to invade immediately.

One of the things that I learned in the Cuban missile crisis project is that many of the things that I thought I knew at the beginning proved to be incorrect or at least incomplete. Let me tell you what I thought I knew about the Cuban Resistance before reading these documents. It was growing in strength well before the Bay of Pigs invasion. It was already large and it was becoming larger and powerful. I am talking about most of 1960 and early 1961. And it would remain powerful later on. From the Cuban government's own records at the time, it is clear that the insurgency threatened the new revolution. It operated in all of the provinces. The Cuban government counted 179 different groups of insurgents in the mountains, in the lowlands, and in the cities. The number of battlefield deaths that the Cuban government acknowledged was 500 for the government and about 2,000 to 2,500 for the insurgents. Remember: these are battlefield deaths. These are not people killed in a traffic jam, these are not casualties of injured and captured. These are people killed in battle and it is, I would suggest, a large number by international standards.

Fidel Castro's 1996 anniversary speech and Richard Bissell's memoirs (in your briefing notebook of secondary sources) remind us that by late 1960, in the Escambray Mountains alone, there were about 1,000 people under arms.[4] Another measure of the dimensions of the resistance is Hugh Thomas's estimate that in the days just before, or just after, the landing of the invasion force, about 100,000 people were arrested.[5] Now, Thomas does not say how he got that number, but one confirmation that it may well have been of that magnitude is that, in 1965, Fidel Castro told Lee Lockwood that there were still 20,000 political prisoners in Cuban jails.[6] Presuming that some people were arrested only for a short period of time, it is possible, therefore, to imagine that tens of thousands of people might have been arrested around the time of the invasion at the Bay of Pigs. Moreover, the documents that we have here before us indicate these were people of vision, of talent, of commitment, of courage, who were ready to work for the long run and who had already been at it for a long time. Why? Because they knew what Richard Nixon discovered in April of 1959: that their adversary was a very tough adversary indeed.

But having said all that, I believe that despite the size and the power of the resistance, it was implausible that armed opposition in Cuba had the organizational and military capacity in April 1961 to launch a revolt of the sort envisaged by planners in Washington and in Miami. It was simply too soon and, consequently, my judgment would be, subject to revision, that the invasion plan was flawed in its conception. It was simply not possible.

Now, as to the second policy issue that I raised: whether time would or would not be on the side of the Cuban government. It is, frankly, hard to tell. In one sense, time was working for the Cuban government because of its growing alliance with the Soviet Union. This alliance rapidly strengthened the government's capacity to control the population and repress the opposition. On the other hand, the economic conditions were deteriorating fairly rapidly, protest over the evolution of the political regime was also developing, and there would be renewed willingness to revolt even after the invasion.

Within this issue of whose side time was on, there are at least two very different problems. One was a problem within the resistance itself. As I've read these documents—and I realize there may very well be more documents I am unaware of—the impression that I had from reading these documents is that the rebels had a very militarized conception of their tasks. I would put this question to Lino, and to the other former members of the resistance at the table. Nearly all of these documents are concerned with guns, other weapons, munitions, and the like. Getting to Alberto Müller's January 24, 1961 [Document 1.7] letter was a great relief because it was the first time the United States is told that there is a political task that needs to be undertaken.[7] Müller's letter to President Kennedy has, in my reading, much eloquence and vision. But if it was characteristic of the resistance to think of its task as purely a battlefield task, then I doubt they would have succeeded, in any event.

There is a second reason why I think it is doubtful that the government could have been overthrown, even if there had been more guns. It was the effect of the invasion itself. The invasion decapitated the opposition, it destroyed their first rank of leadership. Many were captured. Some were shot. Many served out very long prison terms. Others sought political asylum, while still others, eventually, thereafter emigrated and by their emigration assisted the Cuban government to export its opposition and consolidate the regime. So I believe that the invasion plan as conceived, given that it was connected to the resistance, could not have succeeded. This is not because the resistance was not big, strong, committed, and visionary, but because the invasion came too soon and also because, given both the militarized conception of the resistance and the effects of the invasion itself, time turned to out to be on Fidel Castro's side.

Blight: Thanks Jorge. I wonder if it would be appropriate at this time for Lino [Fernández], Quique [Baloyra], and Rafael [Quintero] to say a few words in response. Jorge has put some provocative propositions on the table.

Lino Fernández: Well, when I decided to come to this meeting, I was wondering if it was going to be necessary to try to prove that I was a member of the resistance—to prove that I ever existed. I was very worried about it.

Blight: Excuse me, Lino. Did you say you imagined you would have to prove that you ever existed?

Fernández: I was worried that it would not be believed by others. I have been living in the United States for almost 18 years. It seems to me that most of the literature written about the Bay of Pigs invasion, about the Cuban situation, about the Cuban past, always forgets to mention what was really happening inside Cuba. As a psychiatrist—I am a psychiatrist, that is my medical specialty—one of my main concerns from the very beginning of my encounter with this literature was: Why can't the United States tell what really happened at that time? And I thought—as a psychiatrist—that maybe it is because of the severe trauma of the Bay of Pigs invasion.

It was really a humiliation for the Kennedy brothers. In 72 hours the brigade was captured. After that, a lot of things were written: what happened in this event, what happened on this date, what happened to that aircraft. And so on. Lots of details about the invasion. So I think that for many years something has been very clear, and that is that in this preoccupation with all these details about the invasion, there is also a tendency to ignore what was going on inside Cuba. It was a tendency then, on the part of

American leaders and the American people; and it is a tendency now. We believe that what happens inside Cuba must be somehow forced on Cuba from the outside, from the United States, or from the Soviet Union, or from somewhere else. It is as if there is no reality that is Cuban, by itself. . . .[8]

Why was the internal resistance concerned with military issues? We were trying to organize an opposition to the government, but we didn't find any political solution to the problems. Why? Because the Cuban government did not recognize the opposition, they did not give the people a chance politically, or as you may say, democratically—the normal way of solving such problems in this country. We were unable, we Cubans were unable, to solve our problems inside our country politically, by ourselves. We were not able to do that at that time.[9]

And so we did call for help. We called for help. And some organizations appointed new resistance leaders from outside Cuba. But somehow the outsiders did not trust our autonomous forces opposing the Cuban regime. And others thought: the United States won't permit a communist country 90 miles away from its shores. And from that I think came another very, very, very—I would say—dangerous idea. That idea was to put our hopes and faith in the CIA. The idea of calling the internal resistance and giving us control of the Cuban fight was inconceivable to the CIA, no matter what they said. The CIA tried to do everything themselves, once they contacted the resistance. From then on, the CIA headquarters did everything. It was like a one-man show.

It was almost—again I speak as a psychiatrist—pathological. The CIA tried to invent, to fabricate, an opposition inside Cuba, at the same time—just as Jorge was now saying—there was already a growing resistance movement inside the country. From the time the CIA headquarters started fabricating an organization or making their own resistance, they proved they did not understand the basic facts: *the opposition has to be from the inside, and it has to grow inside!* The same situation exists today. Nobody from the outside can "save Cuba." The only sensible policy then, and now, would be "hands off Cuba." Right now, the situation is depressing. Hands should be off Cuba, and in the future should be out of Cuba, because that is the only way of finding solutions to the real problems that Cuba has. . . .

When I think about the Bay of Pigs invasion, I can still hardly believe it. I mean, look at any map of Cuba. There is no way that invasion force could get to the Escambray, or that we could get to them. Unbelievable. Thirty-six years ago I was mad, really mad. And I am still mad, because, I mean, I think that there were so many real possibilities of helping the Cuban people, but the CIA chose that one. I agree with Jorge Domínguez. That invasion came too soon. If it had come later, the invasion would still have failed, but our resistance might have survived.

Blight: Thank you, Lino, for those eloquent remarks. I have Tom Blanton first on my response list.

Thomas Blanton: I have a question to Lino based on something that Jorge asked. One of the documents that you showed me at lunch was the list of the first 20 or so members of the brigade, of whom 11 came from the resistance.[10] I think this directly reinforces Jorge's point about the militarized focus of the resistance. To you and Quique I would ask: Is it correct to say, in retrospect, that there was too militarized a concept driving the resistance? And, if so, did that derive simply from the experience that you had just lived through, in the sense that the revolution itself was a militarized concept and therefore it was the most available model at hand? What were the sources of that? Is this a correct assessment of a core problem of the resistance?

Fernández: I think so.

Alfredo Durán: I just want to add to Tom's question something that was implied, but not directly stated: Whether the resistance was too dependent or absolutely dependent on the CIA? Did the CIA create the resistance or were there, as Lino implied, two different resistances?

Fernández: The resistance tried to create itself—its own self. The CIA tried to create *another* internal resistance without taking the trouble to find out what was already there, in Cuba. The CIA put their hands inside Cuba and they failed to produce a resistance full of people loyal primarily to them. This fact was the rationale of Richard Bissell's conclusion that there was an insignificant internal resistance, and therefore the CIA would sponsor an invasion.[11] They did not have houses, they did not have safe houses, they did not have the ways of communicating inside Cuba, going from the internal resistance fronts to the outside. They did not know how to put somebody outside and train him to work successfully in the Escambray with fighters who were inside. The reality is that they did not have those kinds of capabilities.

I want to make something clear. We did *not* call them [the CIA]. I never called. The CIA men, they approached me several times, and I had a lot of conversations with them, a lot of conversations. What did we talk about? The CIA men wanted to put in our hands the Batista people—members of the army. We didn't like that. We were against Batista. We were fighting against Batista for seven years and we were not fighting Castro at the time, only later, as you know. There was no *way* we were using the Batista army. That was very clear from the very beginning and [the CIA] didn't like that one bit. . . .

Rafael Quintero: I want to answer this question about the creation and control by the CIA of the resistance. This is a misconception. There was a resistance long before the United States government decided to overthrow Fidel Castro. The resistance came first and then later the United States destroyed it. The United States wanted the Cuban situation to conform to Guatemala or whatever. I left Cuba in 1959, after working with the Cuban government on the agrarian reform. But I never came to the United States to get the United States to help the resistance. I came to the United States to get help *somewhere,* to help the resistance. The United States decided to send me to a camp, first. Second, when the CIA decided to open camps in Guatemala the first recruits were taken from the resistance in Havana, Cuba, and were sent from Cuba to the United States.

Long before anybody even thought about the invasion, we already had an organization in Cuba. I saw this when I went back to the infiltration camps in January 1960. There were a great amount of—of highly motivated people with one big problem—they didn't have the means to do anything against the government.

Blight: Quique, would you like to add something to that?

Enrique Baloyra: Yes, Jim, when you were talking about this Bay of Pigs project, I said, "No, I can't do this." I mean there is going to be all the whining of the right, that we were betrayed, and the lack of leadership, and blah, blah, blah—it was a short-sighted policy and so on.[12] So I began trying to find something there, some angle from which it might be useful. But then I remembered a speech by Fidel Castro to the first Party Congress of the Communist Party in 1975, and he was talking about the spirit of the young people at the time, and of the purity of their intentions in early 1959, their desire to build a country, to do right, to put a wedge between what had not worked up to there and what was going forward.[13] I was teaching in Chapel Hill at the time, and I thought to myself: I used to know people like this! The only problem is that they all fought against Mr. Castro.

I think that part of the frustration that we feel after all these years is that history has been written by the victors. In this case, however, there is also a long appendix written mainly by sore losers, or people who are trying to—you know—dissemble the whole thing, put a spin on it, rationalize it, or whatever. So I thought: well, maybe this is worthwhile because we can put something important on the record, the force of all those young people, idealistic people who because of number one, religious convictions, and number two, because they were evicted from the revolutionary coalition, decided to take up arms against the government. They did so simply to give an account of themselves before they would be crushed like coal.

I don't think that there was a hell of a big chance in April of 1961 for us to be ready to overthrow the government. I am sorry, but I cannot blame the Americans for failure there. I am not here to blame the Americans for a damn thing, by the way, in that sense. It was not your responsibility to liberate Cuba. It was ours. I *can* blame you for getting into a fight and then trying to take over, and then diverting the fight and not allowing for the maturation of the indigenous resistance. . . .

I think it is important that you read the resistance chronology [Appendix 4].[14] The resistance chronology begins with people being expelled from a literacy campaign in early 1959. And people like Rafael Quintero were told that they have to abandon their efforts to help with the agrarian reform because they are not politically correct. They were trying to organize precedents, to elect their own leadership, so that they could run the co-ops, but the orders from above said that there are some people who are more politically correct than you, and they are going to take over this place—co-ops and everything else. Bye, and thanks, and we will call you, don't call us. Okay?

I think that the revolutionary coalition on the other hand had a blueprint. They knew what they wanted to do and they just went ahead, and they were going to do it, whether a minority in the coalition liked it or not. They all believed that everything in Cuban history justified a single body, a single leader, a single way of doing things. That being the case, and absent an option to give up being Cuban, we had no choice but to fight. Whether it was in January of 1959 or '60 or '61 it didn't matter. It probably didn't matter.

I hope that in reading the chronology you ask yourself: Where did these people come from? In many cases, from the government. In many cases from a very strong religious conviction. I am one of the people who criticize those who write about Cuba because they presume Cuban exceptionalism—which is, as you know, also a problem in American history—American exceptionalism. And, in comparative terms, we were not ready to make a frontal attack. The CIA and its plans just accelerated the tempo and exposed everybody at a time when they were still very vulnerable. And then the U.S. government/CIA way of doing things: you guys made up your minds that you would work with only one Cuban rebel organization. Not finding the one you wanted, you tried to create one organization. The effect of this was to increase the capacity of the Cuban government to smash the whole thing. It was tragically put together for them at a meeting in a house on the outskirts of Havana in March 1961, where "Francisco" and the others were captured.[15]

So therefore, yeah, it was our fault. Your fault was to get into the fight, to set it up in a way that would accomplish *your* objectives with *our* means, not *our* means with *our* objectives. I think the United States was also at fault for backing out of the plan you did decide upon. The United States disregarded the resistance and the brigade, and everybody and their uncle. That's your fault. But we never sent them away. That was our fault. We all thought: this is going to be John Wayne, with the Nelson Riddle Orchestra, and we don't even need Desi Arnaz here. [Laughter.] . . . .

Blight: We of course now know about the eventual massive dimensions of Soviet involvement in Cuba, a level of support scarcely imaginable to many in 1959–1960. Let's say the CIA didn't exist. Given the maturation of the regime and its Soviet connections, how did the time issue appear around the time Kennedy came to office? I don't want to leave this session without addressing that. . . . Wayne?

Wayne Smith: We were in contact with the opposition, the resistance. At least some of the organizations, in our view, were quite cohesive and effective. Our conclusion, however, was that the internal resistance never had the capability of overthrowing the government, nor was it likely to [ever] have that capability, even in the long term. In that sense, our conclusion at the embassy was that time was certainly on the side of the government, which was beginning to consolidate its power, and it was, as Jim just said, establishing its link with the Soviet Union—it was beginning to receive Soviet military assistance and its militia were being trained. . . .

We knew there was dissatisfaction with the government's movement to the left. *We* didn't like that either, as you will recall. There was Castro's decision to associate with the Soviets and also, as he announced at the Bay of Pigs—or on the eve of the Bay of Pigs—that the Cuban Revolution was a socialist revolution. There was unhappiness with that, no question about it. But our judgment was that the overwhelming majority of Cubans remained with the government. It was fundamentally a force for good, as they saw it. So, yes, time was certainly on Castro's side. But my God, this should not have led the CIA to the conclusion that, therefore, we must invade *now,* for all the reasons that Lino and Quique went into. . . .

Philip Brenner: I want to start by saying [that] the potential for tension among your participants is really quite extraordinary. Really, we are very lucky and privileged that all of you are willing to talk civilly to each other now, even though it is obvious that a good deal of tension still exists, after all these years. . . .

My first question is to Oleg Daroussenkov. It follows up the discussion about Soviet aid to Cuba. Jorge said at the outset—and Wayne agreed in his follow-up—that time was on the Cuban government's side partly because of steadily increasing Soviet aid. And yet, we had understood from our earlier conferences that Soviet aid was withheld in the period we are discussing because Khrushchev and his colleagues in Moscow were unsure, to say the least, about the leadership of Fidel Castro and his revolution. I thought that it was only *after* the Bay of Pigs that the Soviets made a major commitment to Cuba.[16]

. . . .

Arthur Schlesinger Jr.: One of the issues raised by [CIA Director] Allen Dulles, in arguing for the urgency of the Bay of Pigs invasion, was the alleged expected delivery of MiG aircraft to Cuba, supposedly by May 1. I don't know whether this was fantasy, but he seemed persuaded that such a delivery would take place, and that the sort of invasion the CIA was planning could not be undertaken after the Cubans had received the MiGs.

Blight: Oleg, do you understand what Arthur is saying?

Oleg Daroussenkov: Something about the aircraft. [Alfredo Durán translates Arthur Schlesinger's remark into Spanish for Oleg Daroussenkov, and then translates Daroussenkov's response into English for the group.] Yes, I understand the question. Really, the first negotiation between the Soviet Union and Cuba about arms was in May, if I remember correctly, of '60. This was at the time of Raúl Castro's visit to the Soviet Union. There were some basic principles established of military cooperation, but at that moment there was nothing concrete given by the Soviet Union to Cuba. I think there was only some little token support to the Cubans, very little really—I don't remember exactly—but some artillery, some tanks, and a few MiG fighters to be delivered later.

Jacob Esterline: You were training Cuban pilots at that time and that was a great concern to us.

Daroussenkov: But really at that time, the Cubans had no pilots to use.

Esterline: Whether the military aid was Czechoslovakian or Russian, it was a problem that Mr. Dulles and other people at the agency became very concerned about.

Blight: It is interesting how often this concern about the MiGs appears in the U.S. documents.

Smith: There may have been "very little" aid, but tanks and artillery were already starting to arrive in 1960. They were there. And they were used at the Bay of Pigs—the tanks and artillery. Jake is right: pilots were being trained, and planes were on their way. This, in my mind, reinforces the assessment that Soviet military aid was beginning and that time, therefore, was on the side of Castro. He was going to be able to consolidate his position with Soviet support of the type we are discussing. I don't see how it can be argued otherwise.

Samuel Halpern: Some of my friends who have been looking at some of the Soviet archives—before they were closed up again—will be coming out with a book some time next year that touches on this topic. They indicate that at least small arms, ammunition, and supplies were given to Castro and his people by the Soviets while they were in the Sierra Maestra. Not that they were all Russian arms. They could have been Czech, they could have been Bulgarian, they could have been Polish. At least they came out of the [Eastern] bloc. And so, with Castro receiving supplies and equipment—in small numbers, but even before he came out of the Sierra Maestra—we get a more accurate picture of Castro's real state of mind, and the Soviets', even before his movement came to power.

Blight: Sam, these are Soviet documents?

Halpern: These are Soviet documents.

Peter Kornbluh: Sam, is this the book by Fursenko and Naftali?[17]

Halpern: Yes, exactly.

Blight: I think we have closure on this issue. Phil, you are the one who started this. As I recall, the question about Soviet arms was the first of three you wanted to pose.

Brenner: My second question concerns the extent to which there was an internal opposition in Cuba. What are the true numbers of the resistance? Are the numbers in your documents inflated? In real numbers, how large was the active opposition that the internal resistance could really count on to oppose the government, no matter what?

Fernández: In March of 1960, a CIA man asked me the same question in Havana. At the beginning of April and May 1960, we were organizing all over the country. I told him we had about 5,000 fighters.

Brenner: Who is "we"?

Fernández: The MRR [Movement to Recover the Revolution]. A second organization formed in November 1960 was the 30th of November

Movement. The MRP [People's Revolutionary Movement] came late in the year of 1960. And, there were not many other people inside who were well organized. Not many.

When I was locked up in prison in 1961, I could judge the size of the resistance by the number of the people who were in prison—those who had been organized. In every prison, about 10 percent of the prisoners were from the MRR. And I found that we were about 6,000 fighters strong when I was sent to the biggest prison, on the Isle of Pines. I am talking about June or July of 1961.

There were also people who were fighting but who did not belong to any organized opposition. And that does not mean that they were not important in numbers. I can say that the internal resistance in Cuba was huge, huge. From the very beginning of the revolution, there was much opposition. I mean in 1960 there was constant activity of people who were organizing themselves.[18]

Many were farmers—farmers from everywhere, but mainly in the Escambray. But from August 1960 onward, most of the people who were fighting in the Escambray became trapped. That is why we decided to send the first commander, Plinio Prieto, and his men to help the Escambray fighters, who were being surrounded.[19] In less than two or three months after May 1960, there were more than 3,000 guerrilla fighters in the Escambray. . . .

Baloyra: Phil, you have several ballpark estimates about—at the time of the invasion—how many people were under arms or had use of arms against government personnel. The ballpark figure is more or less 2,500, I would say. On the other hand, the government picks up between April 16 and April 18 [1961], in Havana alone, 50,000 people, and incarcerates them in theaters, in colonial fortresses, in schools, in warehouses. These were not necessarily people who had actively engaged in violence. Over 50,000 people in Havana alone. I was there. I ran intelligence for the DRE [Revolutionary Students' Directorate] at the time. If we take the country as a whole, the number is maybe 100,000. You can make a third estimate by adding up the number of people tried by revolutionary courts—tried, and then convicted. When Lino fell prisoner there were 400 people with him. These were not a lot of what the FMLN [Farabundo Martí National Liberation Front] used to call "masses" or "camp followers."[20] But these were simply peasants who showed up waiting for a drop that never came, were encircled and captured. . . .[21]

But there is of course a big problem in trying to measure the strength of the resistance, especially in the early period. The problem is that a large portion of the resistance is "exported" immediately after Bay of Pigs. The regime has always been able to export the resistance. So there is an airlift that goes up to and beyond (more or less) the missile crisis, which is the second wave of exiles. And of those in Havana—and this is just purely intuitive, there is nothing precise, no scientific [rigor] here—but I would wager that around 50,000 people were picked up in Havana on the eve of the Bay of Pigs. Most of them were out of the country by the time of the missile crisis. Do not ask me if 80 percent or 70 percent or 60 percent or 51 percent were out by then. But I am sure most of them were. These were simply our people—the people whom we mixed with. I will talk later about this business of exporting the resistance. I would like, also later, to pose a question about the landing site to Jake.

I may be a little hot under the collar, I mean, on this business of time. I mean, what are you going to do with time? Why was time against us in Cuba? I frankly don't see it. If a pilot is going to defect, he is going to take a helicopter or a MiG with him. If he is going to blast you then it makes a hell of a difference whether he has a B-15 or a MiG. But we were not contemplating confronting the MiGs at all, to be honest. Historically I am aware that, with the exception of Afghanistan, no socialist regime has been overthrown where the rebels made a go of it. Okay? So I admit that is a very big "counterfactual," but counterfactuals are the stuff of life in Cuban barber shops in Miami. [Laughter.] You know, I have been hearing this stuff—these fantasies—all of my adult life and I am sick and tired of it. But what I can tell you, honestly, is that we were not ready to overthrow the government, true enough. But I do not see why time was against us. We were a committed group of people. We were reasonably intelligent and capable of "learning on the job." Given enough time to prepare, we might have made it.

Blight: Let's combine a couple of things here. Let's hear from those of you who want to speak to either one of Quique's main points: One is, how strong was the resistance—what were the numbers? The other issue is time—on whose side was time, the government or the resistance? . . .

Thomas Skidmore: If I were in the Cuban resistance in 1960, or if I were Fidel's mistress in 1960, I would be saying that any day now the Yankees are coming. Because the one thing I know from Cuban history is that as soon as there is an attempt at reform in Cuba, the marines show up. We have seen this again and again and again in Cuban history. I think '33 was the first act in this repetitive play, you might say.[22] So, my question is: To what extent did you in the resistance think that the Americans might arrive—not in some guerrilla fashion, but as an actual invasion force as had been done in the past in Cuba?

Quintero: One of the biggest problems that the resistance had to face all the time—this applies not just to the resistance at the time, but to most of the political problems in Cuba—was based on the fact that Cuba is 90 miles from the United States. Nobody ever in Cuba—nobody, not a Cuban in Cuba—believed that there was a possibility of having a communist island 90 miles away from the United States of America. This fact worked totally against the underground. We couldn't get support from the people who were most against Castro because they said, "You just keep complaining. You want to keep fighting like in the Batista time. You like that. You just like to fight, that's all. We will never have a communist country because the gringos are 90 miles away." . . .

Skidmore: And they won't allow it!

Quintero: Exactly! The gringos won't allow it. That is the first point. Second, in those days, the Cubans thought of the Americans in what I call the "John Wayne syndrome." What we thought about the Americans was what we have seen as little kids in the movies of John Wayne. We thought that the Americans worked the way John Wayne worked in his movies. Of course, this was naive, but this was the way most of us felt. I mean, the Americans hated communism and, like John Wayne, they never lost—ever. That was important. In the beginning, defeat was never in our minds. And that worked against us. There was this attitude of, why do anything? The Americans will take care of it. This made it difficult to organize the people.

But there is something else you have to understand about this question of how strong was the resistance—what were the numbers. It is this. When we are talking here about support, or the number of people who were in the resistance, let me tell you, maybe the resistance was 2 percent of the population in Cuba. I can tell you that 90 percent of the rest of the population were the people who were in the middle, trying to see who was going to win this fight. [Several participants hold up one finger, as if to determine which way the wind is blowing.] Yes, exactly—to see from where the wind blows. One of my sources was a captain in the rebel army in charge of communications. He was giving us information for a year—information we were sending, intelligence we were sending. On April 19, 1961, I met my contact. He says to me, "I'm sorry, you guys are losing. You are under arrest, because I cannot meet with a loser. I've got to be with the winner." I would say 90 percent of the population had the same attitude. Almost everybody in Cuba was waiting to see who was the winner. The only "uprising" in the minds of those people was a landing of American marines—they were waiting for the marines to land. They had been waiting for the marines to land, they had been waiting since 1902. [Laughter.]

And, that was what basically happened. There was this big change in the minds of the people after the invasion. They felt betrayed. They went with Castro because the United States—our big friend, our big paternalistic friend—has betrayed us.

Blight: Jake, what was your estimate, at the time, of the strength of the resistance? . . .

Esterline: About Castro, and about my own perceptions of the situation after Castro came to power—

I was chief of station in Guatemala for three or four years after that successful coup [in 1954]. At that time Pérez Jiménez was "on the throne" in Venezuela and the station in Caracas was pretty much destroyed.[23] So they sent me down there to build it back up. During that time, Fidel made his famous trip to Venezuela. That was where I first saw Fidel and saw the power of his charisma. It made a very profound impression on me. . . .[24]

Anyway, Nixon was coming to Venezuela.[25] The chief of security, a wonderful guy, was a friend of mine in Venezuela. We had mapped out all the things that the resistance might try to do, including killing the vice president, if possible. I could see right away that we were in trouble. I did everything I could to stop Nixon's party from coming. I pleaded with the ambassador to let me put more out on the thing that I had. He told me to go visit Colombia, where Nixon was visiting before he was to come to Venezuela. I tried, but I needed permission to leave, which was denied. So, I couldn't do it. Well, to make a long story short, they damn near *did* get him. Before that, I had been informed in very direct terms by one of Nixon's aides: "This is a political decision and keep your damn nose out of it." So I did. And the next time I crossed with the Nixon people was when I stumbled onto stuff related to Watergate. And that didn't score any points either. [Laughter.]

It seemed to me that something like a chain reaction was occurring all over Latin America after Castro came to power in Cuba. I saw—hell, anybody with eyes could see—that a new and powerful force was at work in the hemisphere. It had to be dealt with. So, when J. C. King called me from CIA headquarters and said, "Jake, do you want to come back and try this?"—I said, "Sure." So I returned to Washington about the beginning of '60. The Castro problem looked just as tough from a desk in Washington. I looked at it and looked at it, and I thought well, okay. So I said: "J. C., I will try to do something on this Cuba problem." I agreed to do this, even though I didn't know much about Cuba. I had been to Cuba a few times, but I was not intimately familiar with it. Not at all. Not even close.

That was my basic thought. This is a totally different situation than I've ever seen before. Basically, I agree with what was said earlier about Fidel Castro: he was something different, something more impressive, in a way, and definitely harder to handle than anyone we had ever seen in Latin

America. He was tightening his grip on the island. The only way we can go about this with any hope of success, I thought, is to isolate an area where there is a possibility of meeting up with the anti-Castro resistance. Now, at that point we still had a station in Havana. Information was good and very clear. We knew, therefore, that there was extensive and organized resistance to Castro in several areas of Cuba. So that was the number-one thought in my own mind. We have got to get some trained people into Cuba in such a manner that they can feed into the resistance forces that are already operating.

Now, as to specifics. Having looked at the problem for some time, I decided that I wanted to parachute our forces into the Escambray Mountains, and also via Trinidad, on the south coast of the island. My proposal at that time required the training of no more than 600 people. But they had to be *highly* trained. I thought they should probably go in by air. I suppose that was because I was familiar with airdrops, going all the way back to the war. That was the idea: put them in and see if they can survive—see if they become viable. In the process, we would also see if there was enough internal resistance that could combine with our more highly trained guerrillas. . . .

Blanton: I have just one question. Here you are, Jake, you are talking about dropping highly trained teams into the Escambray. And here is Lino and 5,000 organized people in Cuba with presumably networks and safe houses. Where was the disconnect?

Esterline: These trained guerrillas would have been their link with us. The guerrillas were to have become part of their organization. They would become a part of *the* organization. And if they survived and looked viable, then you would go to whatever the situation might call for next. . . .

Smith: But the decision was taken to move to a military invasion. And there was no link at all, in that plan, with the internal resistance.

Esterline: Right.

Blanton: But wasn't that decision to move to a military invasion also informed by intelligence feedback that said the resistance was declining—that Fidel was rounding them up and that the resistance was doomed to fail?

Esterline: My point is this, if we don't do something like what I was suggesting—the drop into the Escambray—how are we supposed to know whether the resistance can make a go of it or not? . . . The answer, to my way of thinking, was to try something that could not have a catastrophic result, like the airdrop, and see what happened.

Piero Gleijeses: May I say something? In an interview I did with [CIA Deputy Director for Plans Richard] Bissell, and also on the basis of those documents I have seen, it seems to me that the decision to shift from infiltration of guerrillas to an amphibious operation was made in October 1960. It was based on Bissell's view that the resistance against Castro in Cuba was too weak to succeed. The only way to overthrow Castro, therefore, was by invasion of some sort.

Let me make another point, on the issue of time—was time in favor of Fidel Castro or of the anti-Castro resistance? Well, it all depends on what you mean by "the resistance." By early 1961, for the government of the United States, the resistance was the brigade and time was definitely against the brigade. And time was against the brigade for two reasons, which Bissell argued in a very eloquent way. First of all because the government of Guatemala was becoming unstable. Ydígoras had been terrorized by the Nationalist Revolt of November 13, 1960, and the major reason for the revolt was the presence of this foreign force in Guatemala.[26] And the second point that Bissell kept mentioning was this: the morale of the brigade was fragile and would at some point collapse altogether. So from the point of view of the government of the United States, by early 1961 the resistance was the brigade and, for reasons mentioned by Bissell, time was against them.

Esterline: As a matter of fact, when the Bay of Pigs was picked as the landing site, I was not there. I was in Guatemala executing a secret base-rights agreement with Ydígoras Fuentes. This allowed us to keep the soldiers there, and keep our airplanes there, and keep things going. He was mad because the ambassador wouldn't talk to him. He had put in a desperate call. Since I had known Fuentes for some years, I was sent down, and we executed the agreement. Sure, the brigade's presence was driving people crazy at that time. But they couldn't throw us out, even if they had wanted to, as was proved in 1954.

. . . .

Blight: I call on Tom Blanton for the . . . documentary interjection.

Blanton: This is in your packet. [Holds up packet of material.] This is Jack Hawkins's statement, which he sent to Jim [Blight], after deciding he could not attend the conference. If you look at page 6 you will see how the Bay of Pigs was actually selected. It may answer a lot of questions. They were staying up all night, they were searching a map of the coast of Cuba, and there was only one airstrip to be found that might be big enough to land B-26s, and was also near where an amphibious landing might take place. They came up with this virtually overnight—staying up all night, a little like cramming for a college exam. That is how they picked it. They recommended the site because it was the "quietest" place they could find that satisfied the two requirements given to Hawkins: (1) must have an airstrip capable of handling B-26s; and (2) must be near to where an amphibious landing can take place. That's how the Bay of Pigs was chosen.[27]

Halpern: Was it Bissell's staff who did that?

Blanton: Hawkins's memo reads as follows:

> Pursuant to Mr. Bissell's verbal instructions to me, the paramilitary staff spent the next two days, and most of the nights, in an intensive study of the entire coast of Cuba in an effort to find a landing area that would meet the president's requirements.[28]

And chief among "the president's requirements" was that it not be "noisy"—so that the U.S. role in it could be plausibly denied.

Gleijeses: The proposal was submitted to the committee under the Joint Chiefs of Staff, which was commanded by General [David W.] Gray. And this committee chose between four different options presented. Their recommendation was then ratified by the Chiefs.

Halpern: And nobody looked at a map long enough to notice the difference between going from Trinidad to the Escambray Mountains, and going from a place called Bahia de Cochinos to the Escambray Mountains?

Gleijeses: Yes, but we are talking about this letter from Hawkins. This letter shows the operational implications of the new orders from the president. This is not the fault of the CIA, it is the fault of the White House and the State Department, who issued the new orders.

Blight: We are talking about the resistance, its strength, its possibilities, and so on. That is where we would like to end up. Peter.

Kornbluh: I'd like to go back quickly to Quique Baloyra's question: Why the rush? Specifically, was the issue the morale in the camps and the need to get these guys going, as opposed to just letting them sit there? Some members of the brigade had been there for months already doing various things. Piero cited Bissell as being deeply worried about the morale in the camps. But we also know that Jack Hawkins sent a report—a glowing report—which Bissell immediately took to President Kennedy. The report said, basically, that the brigade is ready to go, that they are an extraordinary fighting unit, and that they are bound to succeed [Document 3.6].[29] So the question arises: What *was* the situation in the camps? Was it good or bad, getting better or worse, as D-Day approached?

A second question concerns the conversation between Wayne Smith and Jake Esterline. It strikes me as the height of irony that, sitting here today, is one of the birds in the nest of spies in the Havana Embassy that Fidel thought that he had to close. . . .

Blight: That was obviously before Wayne became a fuzzy-headed liberal.

Smith: Events like the Bay of Pigs should turn us all into fuzzy-headed liberals. [Laughter.]

Kornbluh: As I was saying, it would seem to me appropriate, because of the people here, to open up a conversation specifically about what the embassy was doing at that point in terms of the resistance, in terms of the work inside Cuba, towards countering Castro, and the information that was coming back from the station. Jake, you just referred to the role of the station chief. What can you tell us about this network?

Blight: Thank you, Peter. Those are two large questions. Would someone like a quick shot at one or both of them?

Quintero: Yes, let me answer part of it. I was in the camps from the beginning. As a matter of fact before I went to Guatemala, I went first to Useppa Island.[30] So I knew the situation from May 1960 to November, when I was taken out of the camps to be sent to Cuba. When I left the camps in November, there were less than 300 persons in the camp. Those people were overtrained, definitely. The morale was too high and could not be sustained. Now I am talking about a very small piece of the whole brigade group.

From November on, I know much less. But I knew some things. I knew that there were lots of problems in the camps. People had been there too long, food was very bad. We had to build the camps—some people don't know this. There was nothing there. Nothing. We had to build camps in Guatemala, in Retalhuleu. Yes, then we went from Useppa to Retalhuleu. We built the camps and there was training plus work plus terrible food. So all of those three things together really put the people in a very bad mood. Then from November on I don't know what happened.

Durán: I think that the brigade had a very high morale, which was surprising, because of the terrible conditions in those camps. The food was bad, it was constantly raining, there was mud all over the place, the facilities to eat and to bathe were not good. And yet the morale was very, very high. The people there were well trained, and even more than well trained. We had a feeling that we were going into an adventure that we could not lose; we were going to win. I remember that I was on board the ship *Atlantico,* which was a rickety old merchant ship, on the dawn of April 17, looking at the shoreline of Cuba where I was going to disembark in a few minutes. My thoughts were—we are going to win this, we are going to bring democracy back to Cuba. The worst that can happen is that I might die, but we are going to win. I was very surprised to find that we lost and that I was alive. [Laughter.] I don't know if the decision was good that we were sent, but we wanted to be sent, we wanted to go in.

Blight: Wayne, would the embassy like to speak for itself?

Smith: I have already talked about that. We were in close contact with the resistance. We should have been. You have to know what's going on in the country to which you are assigned. I didn't run any explosives in the trunk of my car, or violate my diplomatic status too much. . . . [Laughter.]

Now about this issue of "what was the hurry?" Well, because the brigade was there, sure. But once the brigade was there, the most important decision had already been made: to try to solve the Castro problem with that kind of invasion. I don't know if Bissell was surprised by the fact that the brigade, being overtrained as Rafael said, had to be deployed quickly. But he shouldn't have been surprised.

Finally, on the other time issue: Quique and I are on opposite sides, in one sense. Quique thinks that maybe time was on their side. I don't think it was. But on the other hand, the best thing that we could have gotten done, it seems to me, would have been to follow Jake's original plan: send in the guerrillas, have them join with the internal resistance, and see what happens. If nothing happens with a group such as Jake had in mind, then we could have been reasonably sure that nothing would have happened without them either.

Baloyra: First, I was an internal resistance organizer. Any experience growing up in a Cuban family will tell you that when you fight a stronger oppressor, you do it the guerrilla way. [Laughter.] In what Lino was referring to before, there was a lot of spontaneity. In the internal resistance in the cities, we were a mainly a military organization [Documents 1.1, 1.3, 1.4]. But there was a propaganda section, a propaganda branch, and there were people who were running intelligence.[31]

How far along were we when we lived in Havana under the threat of

being captured by Batista's people? The bombing campaigns were organized to make noise. Batista was arbitrary and brutal. When we would have
success against him, he would pick up anyone on the streets and have him
murdered or maimed or beat up. In a way, this is the way that Rafael
Quintero got recruited against Batista in the '50s in Cuba—being beat up
by the police in his town because a bomb went off and they couldn't find
the person who did it. So they beat *him* up.

By the time of the Bay of Pigs invasion we have the operational capability to make that noise in Havana every night, and have that sort of psychological pressure on the government of having ten or fifteen really large
firecrackers detonate in defiance of censorship control and that type of
thing. What we did not have was the operational capability to fight in large
units. And we could not train people in Cuba to do that. This is the reason
why the guys had to go out, to learn to fight in formation. Because we had
no territory in which to do that. The problem was that once they went out,
many of them never returned. In the case of the Bay of Pigs, they were
trained for the Anzio-type landing that had nothing to do with the objectives or capabilities of the resistance.

Finally, what kind of struggle was the leadership of the internal resistance preparing for? Lino can answer that better than I. But in all honesty,
nobody read a damn thing, nobody prepared any battles in detail, no one
had any idea. Nobody knew anything about Mao's tactics or Lenin's or
anybody's. We were just making it up as we went along.

Alfredo is right about the feeling of invincibility—that we were going
to win this struggle. We all believed this. Why? Because we had just seen a
dictatorship—Batista's—crumble that before had looked invincible. All of
a sudden it was just falling apart. I will admit that, by April 1961, the
momentum was not with us yet. We had not sufficiently demoralized the
guy [Fidel Castro]. He was shooting a lot of people, trying to stay ahead of
us. He would have been exposed—this is my opinion—from the time that
he was perceived by the majority of Cubans as losing the fight. Would that
have been sufficient to beat him? I cannot guarantee you that. I do not on
the other hand think that the overwhelming majority were committed to
him. There was a very solid bloc that was firmly engaged against him and,
believe me, there was still a group in the middle who didn't know exactly
what to think of the whole thing. These people were not in any mood to be
martyrs. So it came down to this, too soon, in April 1961: you were for the
Americans or for Fidel. The Americans lost, and so we lost too.

Notes

1. The "reunion" atmosphere that permeated the first conference of the
Cuban missile crisis is captured nicely by J. Anthony Lukas, "Class Reunion:

Kennedy's Men Relive the Cuban Missile Crisis," *New York Times Magazine,* 30 August 1987, pp. 22–27, 51, 58, 61.

2. Richard N. Goodwin, *Remembering America: A Voice from the Sixties* (Boston: Little, Brown, 1988), p. 185.

3. Richard M. Nixon, "Memorandum of Conversation with Fidel Castro," 25 April 1959, p. 5. (Unless otherwise noted, this and all other formerly classified documents referred to in this book are available from the National Security Archive, Washington, D.C.)

4. Fidel Castro, "The Socialist Character of the Revolution, the First Great Salvo in Response to the Aggression." Speech marking the 35th anniversary of the victory at the Bay of Pigs, given on 16 April 1996, in Matanzas, Cuba. *Granma International* (the weekly edition of the Cuban Communist Party daily, *Granma*), 1 May 1996, pp. 4–7. The speech was remarkably forthcoming about the strength of the internal resistance, and the great difficulties the revolutionary government had in eliminating it, especially in the Escambray Mountains.

Richard M. Bissell Jr., *Reflections of a Cold Warrior: From Yalta to the Bay of Pigs* (New Haven: Yale University Press, 1996), pp. 160–161.

These materials were contained in a briefing notebook of secondary sources, memoirs, and academic analyses. This notebook, a larger notebook containing formerly classified material from the U.S. government, and also formerly secret material from the Cuban resistance, were distributed to all participants in advance of the Musgrove Conference.

5. Hugh Thomas, *Cuba, the Pursuit of Freedom* (London: Eyre & Spotiswoode, 1971).

6. Lee Lockwood, *Castro's Cuba, Cuba's Fidel* (Boulder, Colo.: Westview, 1990), p. 247.

7. Letter from Alberto Müller Quintana, secretary general of the Revolutionary Students' Directorate, to President John F. Kennedy, 24 January 1961 [Document 1.7]. This remarkable document begins with, "Dear Mr. President: In the long history of the world, only a few generations have been granted the role of defenders of Freedom in their most perilous hours," and concludes with an extended and moving reference to Lincoln's Gettysburg Address.

8. Lino Fernández adds: "The memoirs of Richard Bissell [*Reflections of a Cold Warrior*], Chapter 7—'Cuba'—is a case in point."

9. See, on the military preparations, Documents 1.3 and 1.4. They provide heretofore missing insight into the actual objectives of the resistance forces, and their plan for achieving them. An insurrection of large proportions was planned, probably for sometime in the summer or fall of 1961, beginning in the far western province of Pinar del Rio, where "Francisco" (Rogelio González Corzo) was to take personal charge of the offensive that, in the outline provided in these documents, is suggestive of the Tet Offensive in South Vietnam of January-February 1968, in ambition, if not in scale.

10. Musgrove participant Rafael Quintero is listed as number 27 on the list to sign up.

11. See, for example, Bissell, *Reflections of a Cold Warrior:* "A top priority [of the CIA] was to provide the citizens of Cuba with political alternatives, and a program was created to build up a 'responsible, appealing, and unified Cuban opposition to the Castro regime'" (p. 153).

12. The original conception called for a conference in Cuba on the Bay of Pigs, without benefit of a conference of former U.S. government and members of the Cuban resistance and Brigade 2506. A controversy broke out in the Miami Cuban exile community from the moment its members learned of a possible confer-

ence in Cuba on the Bay of Pigs. The prospect was first made public by Don Bohning in "Revisiting Bay of Pigs Invasion," in the *Miami Herald,* 25 January 1996. Following Bohning's announcement, the *Herald* invited four members of the community, all veterans of the Bay of Pigs, to respond. Alfredo G. Durán's piece— "Si me invitan voy . . ." ("If They Invite Me, I Will Go . . ."), *El Nuevo Herald* (the Spanish-language daily edition of the *Miami Herald*), 5 February 1996—was answered in the same edition by three others: Ramón B. Conte, "Convocatoria de criminales" ("The Meeting of Criminals"); Miguel Guitart, "Para sanar heridas" ("In Order to Heal Wounds"); and Juan Antonio Figueras, "Seguiremos combatiendo" ("We Will Continue Fighting"). Later, Gen. Erneido A. Oliva, the senior living commander of the Bay of Pigs veterans, responded with a scathing piece, "No viajaré a Cuba" ("I Will Not Go to Cuba"), *El Nuevo Herald,* 18 February 1996, in which he took the view that the proposed conference should occur only in a "free Cuba"; otherwise, it would aid the "indefinite stay of tyranny." The controversy was then analyzed in two thoughtful pieces by Horacio Ruiz Pavon, in "Llaman 'farsa' a reunión sobre Girón en Cuba" ("Conference on Girón in Cuba Is Called a 'Farce'"), *Diario Los Americas,* 11 February 1996; and by Miguel González Pando, "Controversia sobre Bahía de Cochinos" ("Controversy over the Bay of Pigs"), *El Nuevo Herald,* 26 February 1996; and also in a bizarre piece in the *Miami Herald* by J. Rafael Montalvo, "Brigade 2506 Never Surrendered." But due to circumstances having partly to do with the crisis in U.S.–Cuba relations following the 24 February shootdown by Cuba of two unarmed U.S. planes, the conference in Cuba had to be postponed. See Don Bohning, "Havana Meeting on Bay of Pigs Invasion Pushed Back," *Miami Herald,* 8 March 1996.

13. See, for example, Fidel Castro Ruz, "Report of the Central Committee of the CPC [Cuban Communist Party] to the First Congress (Havana, 1977)": "Innumerable sons and daughters of the Cuban nation belonging to various generations have had to sacrifice their lives. Many have given their lives for the noble cause of independence, justice and the dignity and progress of our people" (p. 5).

14. The briefing notebooks distributed to participants in advance of the conference included a "Chronology of Cuban Resistance," the principal items of which were also in the overall chronology of events from which the conference participants worked and to which they often referred. This subchronology was constructed by Enrique Baloyra, Lino Fernández, and Rafael Quintero from extant resistance documents. It is included in this book as Appendix 4.

15. "Francisco" was the underground name for Rogelio González Corzo, a Cuban agricultural engineer, the acknowledged organizational and inspirational leader of the MRR. On 18 March 1961, he was captured in a raid in the Miramar section of Havana, along with several other leaders of the underground resistance. All were arrested, tried, convicted, and, on 19 April, they were executed by the government. Both Enrique Baloyra and Lino Fernández believe that the creation of the Revolutionary Democratic Front (FRD), although ostensibly easier for the CIA to work with outside Cuba because it was a single body with a single leadership, was not under CIA command inside Cuba. This is the reason the CIA headquarters tried to create in December 1960 a super-unity under the name Unidad Revolucionaria. This pretentious and factitious super-organization created the conditions in which a disaster such as the one that occurred on 18 March 1961 became virtually inevitable. Although "Francisco" and the others knew that it was unsafe to meet in a relatively large group in Havana, the condition of the CIA pressing a joint leadership on him under his control made it necessary to have this meeting in order to maintain the autonomy of the resistance. See Document 1.5.

16. See, for example, the record and analysis of the Havana conference on the

missile crisis: James G. Blight, Bruce J. Allyn, and David A. Welch, *Cuba on the Brink: Castro, the Missile Crisis, and the Soviet Collapse* (New York: Pantheon/Random House, 1993), pp. 54–63, for Gen. Anatoly Gribkov's authoritative description of Soviet military assistance to Cuba in the early 1960s.

17. Alexander Fursenko and Timothy Naftali, *One Hell of a Gamble: Khrushchev, Castro and Kennedy, 1958–1964* (New York: Norton, 1997).

18. Lino Fernández adds: "The penalization of ideas and the centralization of power in a few hands was the detonator that triggered the internal resistance. At the time of the Bay of Pigs invasion there were some 30 guerrilla groups in just three provinces. In Las Villas and the Escambray alone there were 82 armed groups with approximately 3,000 men. Before the end of 1959, approximately 1,900 men had been shot by firing squads. According to a Cuban government source, 4,000 guerrillas died in a six-year war. In the Escambray alone, more than 8,000 guerrillas fought during a five-year period. Fifteen thousand farmers were transferred from their villages. By the middle of 1961, there were more than 30,000 political prisoners. Close to 150,000 people were rounded up and detained during the raids of April 1961, and approximately 200,000 went into exile. It is unknown how many went underground at that time." See Noberto Fuentes, *Nos impusieron la violencia* (Havana: Editorial Letras Cubanas, 1986); *Condenados del condado* (Buenos Aires: Centro Editor de America Latina, S.A., 1968); and *Caza-bandidos* (Montevideo: Arca Editorial, 1970). See also Ariel Hidalgo, *Disidencia: Segunda revolución Cubana?* (Miami: Editorial Universal Miami, 1994); Carlos Franqui, *Vida aventuras y desastres de un hombre llamado Castro* (Barcelona: Editorial Planeta, 1988); Lino B. Fernández, Alberto Müller, Alfredo Isaguirre et al., *A las naciones y hombres libres* (25,000-word document sent from the Isle of Pines Prison in 1963 to the United Nations; available from the National Security Archive, Washington, D.C., or from Lino B. Fernández).

19. In August 1960, Commander Plinio Prieto of the OA (Organización Auténtica) returned from the training camps and led a detachment of guerrillas. At this time, the MRR decided to support the Escambray guerrilla groups to alleviate the pressure exerted by the increasing number of regular troops that encircled the area. This is what the Cuban government called "the first sweep of the Escambray," between August 1960 and March 1961. See Appendix 4.

20. The Farabundo Martí de Liberación Nacional (Farabundo Martí National Liberation [Front], the leftist insurgency in El Salvador during the 1980s).

21. Former Cuban intelligence official Domingo Amuchastagui estimates that as many as 250,000 were rounded up as a result of the Bay of Pigs invasion, effectively breaking the back of all components of the resistance movement. He also maintains that without the invasion itself, and Fidel Castro's use of it as a rallying point for patriotic Cubans, the government would never have contemplated such a roundup, at least at that time, for fear that it would backfire. See "Cuban Intelligence Assessment," in David A. Welch and James G. Blight, eds., *Intelligence Assessment in the Cuban Missile Crisis* (London: Frank Cass, 1998).

22. In July 1933, U.S. Assistant Secretary of State Sumner Welles was sent by President Roosevelt as ambassador to Cuba to "mediate" a dispute between Cuban despot Gerardo Machado and a wide range of opposition groups. Actually, this was a ruse to get Machado to resign and, after some initial resistance, he left the country under the threat of armed U.S. intervention to remove him.

23. Marcos Pérez Jiménez, the brutal dictator of Venezuela, was overthrown in January 1958. Pérez Jiménez settled in the United States following his ouster.

24. Fidel Castro's first trip abroad after assuming power in Cuba was to

Venezuela. Arriving on 21 March 1959, he was received like a conquering hero to throngs of Venezuelans who greeted him in the streets of Caracas. See Tad Szulc, *Fidel: A Critical Portrait* (New York: Morrow, 1986), pp. 171–172. On Esterline's fascinating career, see the very useful and long-overdue piece by Don Bohning: "The Cold Warrior," *Tropic,* the Sunday magazine of the *Miami Herald,* 14 January 1996, pp. 6–12.

25. Vice President Richard Nixon visited Venezuela in May 1958, a little less than a year before Castro's visit. Nixon's car was attacked, its windows smashed, he was spat upon, and President Eisenhower ordered contingency plans for the U.S. military to extricate him from Caracas. See Thomas G. Paterson, *Contesting Castro: The United States and the Triumph of the Cuban Revolution* (New York: Oxford University Press, 1994), pp. 151–152.

26. Miguel Ydígoras Fuentes, the president of Guatemala, was strongly anti-communist and a favorite of the CIA station in Guatemala City.

27. The entire memorandum from Hawkins to Blight is available from the National Security Archive. Excerpts from it appear as Document 4.3 in Appendix 5. Hawkins later published a piece on the Bay of Pigs: "Classified Disaster," *National Review* (31 December 1996): 36–38. See also the interesting biographical piece by Don Bohning: "Did Site Doom Bay of Pigs?" *Miami Herald,* 5 January 1997, pp. 1, 18A.

28. Hawkins, "Covert Operations Against the Castro Government of Cuba," p. 6. This portion of the Hawkins memorandum to James Blight, 10 May 1996, was not included in the documents for the book. See note 27.

29. The report was sent by Hawkins to Esterline from the Guatemala training camp on 13 April 1961. See Peter Wyden, *Bay of Pigs: The Untold Story* (New York: Simon & Schuster, 1979), pp. 168–169. The text of Esterline's cable to Hawkins and Hawkins's reply were "leaked" in a special issue of *Life* devoted largely to the story of the brigade. See *Life,* 10 May 1963: 34.

30. Useppa Island, off the southwest coast of Florida, was the first training site for what later became Brigade 2506. The first group arrived in May 1960 to be trained as radio operators before being infiltrated into Cuba.

31. See, for example, Document 1.6, a Revolutionary Students' Directoate (DRE) broadcast of 20 January 1961, on "Trinchera Radio." Note that the broadcast not only provides the perspective of the resistance forces—that a virtual civil war was breaking out all over Cuba—but it also was used as a means of conveying specific messages, in this case to DRE Secretary General Alberto Müller. There is also mention of "Francisco" (Rogelio González Corzo), who had already, by January 1961, obviously achieved considerable notoriety as an inspirational leader of the underground in Cuba.

2

The CIA Calls the Shots

The purpose of the program outlined herein is to bring about the replacement of the Castro regime with one more devoted to the true interests of the Cuban people and more acceptable to the U.S. in such a manner as to avoid any appearance of U.S. intervention.

> *Jacob Esterline and Richard Drain,*
> *A Program of Covert Action*
> *Against the Castro Regime,*
> *16 March 1960 [Document 2.1]*

So my reaction as a Cuban is: fine, I don't ask that you think in terms of Cuban interests. You have your own American interests. No. It's our fault for listening to you, or believing you.

> *Enrique Baloyra, 31 May 1996*

Blight: Now, obviously one of the great guessing games in almost everybody's calculations about Cuba in the late 1950s and early 1960s is this: What *was* Cuba's relationship like with the Soviet Union? What was the Soviet commitment to Cuba? What are the terms under which the relationship evolved, and who set these terms? How far was the Soviet Union willing to go, before the missile crisis, to guarantee the security of the Castro government? Jorge raised the issue in his introductory remarks. Whether time is regarded as on the side of the government, or on the side of the resistance, depends to a considerable extent on one's view of the Soviet commitment to Cuba. . . .

I would like Oleg Daroussenkov, who worked on Cuba for 30 years as a Soviet and Russian analyst and diplomat, to get on the record an outline of what that relationship was about. When Oleg is finished, and with his remarks about the Soviet commitment to Cuba as background, I would like to turn next to Jake Esterline to pick up where he left off in session I—on the connections, and disconnects, between the CIA and the Cuban resistance.

Smith: Oleg spent 30 years of his life cultivating a relationship between his country and Cuba, and I have spent about 35 years of my adult life trying to cultivate a relationship between Cuba and the United States. I would therefore ask this learned group to consider the question: Which of us—Daroussenkov or Smith—has been the greatest failure? [Laughter.]

Daroussenkov: This is a very difficult question. [Laughter.] . . . Let me begin with the early days of the 1950s. I want to say, since it was mentioned here that there were Soviet arms in the Sierra Maestra—I can say with assurance that there was not one single Soviet arm, nor even a single bullet for those arms, in the Sierra Maestra.[1] Soviet military aid to the 26th of July movement did not exist. It is a fiction.

Let me explain why it *has* to be a fiction. In the Soviet Union at that time, there was no clear idea about the revolutionary movement led by Fidel Castro. On the contrary, there was a good relationship between the Communist Party of the Soviet Union and the Socialist Party of Cuba, at that time. And between the Socialist Party of Cuba and the 26th of July Movement, there were lots of misunderstandings. Sometimes, I would say, even deep antagonism. It was logical that, in the absence of reliable information, the Soviet Union would have some strange ideas about the character of the 26th of July Movement. Unfortunately I cannot remember the exact date, but I believe it was in 1958—I think about the middle of 1958—a small delegation of the Cuban Socialist Party visited Moscow. And I remember exactly what the leader of that delegation was saying. Very soberly, he said that Fidel Castro was an agent of the American Embassy! [Laughter.] That is exactly what he said.[2]

The revolution begins. The first Russian who appeared in Havana was Vassily Chichkov, the correspondent of *Pravda* in Mexico. Later he wrote a small book about Cuba. I met that man, who unfortunately has already died. He was a veteran of the Second World War and he was a writer. He had nothing to do with the KGB. In those days, not all *Pravda* correspondents worked for the KGB, though many did. Therefore, the first reports to Moscow were more or less truthful. They were very interesting, very hopeful. That was in January 1959.

Several months went by without any contact at all between the Soviet and Cuban governments. The first official contact, if I am not mistaken, happened when the first vice president of the Council of Ministers, [Anastas I.] Mikoyan, was approached by a Cuban, in Mexico. Mikoyan was in Mexico because of a Soviet exposition. I don't remember the month exactly, but it was about February of 1960. Unexpectedly, a very young man appeared there who looked as young as Andy Goodridge [gestures toward interpreter Andrew Goodridge]. He carried a message from Fidel Castro that the Cubans were interested in the Soviet exposition and, when it was finished in Mexico, would the Soviets bring the exposition to Havana? The idea was accepted and in March of 1960, Mikoyan went to inaugurate the exposition in Cuba.

I remember that by that time, many things were already being done to try to eliminate the Cuban Revolution. I believe that there were two persons who played very important parts in the future of developments of the circle: Vice President Nixon and Vice President Mikoyan. First, Fidel was received by Nixon and Nixon concluded that he was a communist. At that time, the confrontation with the Soviet Union and the ideological battle of the Cold War was at its most intense. The American government decided, therefore, to take every possible step to try to eliminate that revolution. On the other hand, Mikoyan, when he was in Cuba, realized the real situation—the firm backing that Fidel had in the country. This made a great impression on Mikoyan, who had fought in the Bolshevik Revolution decades before. . . .

When he returned to Moscow he was able to convince Nikita Khrushchev that it was really a deep revolution and that it had a great deal of support. Mikoyan told Khrushchev that they (the Cubans) were being harassed by the United States, that they are trying to find some support. At that moment the Soviet Union was feeling particularly threatened by the United States and the West. Military bases were all around. Long-range aviation was threatening all parts of the Soviet Union. In that situation, any opportunity to put the United States at risk was of interest to the Soviet Union, naturally.

But there was still no real understanding of the Cuban Revolution and not a great deal of trust in Fidel. Diplomatic relations were established in May 1960 with a single official visit by the Cubans, in May 1960. That was by Raúl Castro . . . Raúl went to Moscow and the conversations were started with the Soviet military. And it was the first time that the conversations talked about the possibility of sending Soviet arms directly to Cuba. . . .

And in reality, the real cooperation of the Soviet military with Cuba begins after the Bay of Pigs. In a way, the Bay of Pigs invasion speeded up everything immensely. There was a big hurry to arm the Cubans before the Americans invaded.

Esterline: When you were second secretary, were you ever a member of the KGB? Were you ever coopted by them?

Daroussenkov: I never had anything to do with the KGB.

Esterline: The reason I ask is because if you weren't involved with the KGB, then I don't think you would have known very much about what the KGB was really doing. So, it is entirely possible there could have been things going on in the Sierra Maestra—such as Soviet supply of weapons and ammunition—that you would not have known about.

Daroussenkov: The answer is very simple. I did not know about the KGB at that time while I was working in the embassy. But when I worked at the Central Committee of the Party—well, it is like the White House here. We had there all of the information. All things—economic information, everything.

Halpern: But not operations?

Daroussenkov: No, not operations.

. . . .

Blight: Now, I have asked Peter, and Peter has consented, to stimulate our conversation concerning the main topic for session II: "The CIA and the Anti-Castro Resistance." So, Peter, may we have a few leading questions and provocations, please?

Kornbluh: Well, the title of this session may not completely capture what we want to cover—the evolution of invasion planning from 1959 to 1960. The main question, it seems to me, for this session is: How and why did the Bay of Pigs plans evolve? I stress the plurality of plans, since there is more than one. How did these evolve during the last two years of the Eisenhower administration? Of course it is commonplace to try and begin at the beginning. But when you are talking about the Bay of Pigs, it is hard to say conceptually where the beginning was. Where did Operation Zapata, as we formally know it—its military code name was Operation Bumpy Road—come from? Where did that actually start? Where do we start when we talk about it?

Do we start with Richard Nixon's memorandum of conversation with Fidel Castro that Oleg just referred to, and Jorge Domínguez quoted at the opening of session I? I would just like to point out that Oleg's characterization of Nixon's conclusions about Castro aren't quite what he says in the conclusion of his memo. "My own appraisal of him as a man is somewhat mixed," Nixon concluded. Nixon then observes: "He seems to be sincere but he is either incredibly naive about Communism or already under Communist discipline—my guess is the former." Nixon goes on: "But because he has the power to lead to which I have referred, we have no choice but at least to try to orient him in the right direction."[3] Now Nixon, after he wrote this letter, became, by his own admission, one of the primary advocates of overthrowing Castro. It would be important if we could address the role of Nixon in the evolution of the plans to overthrow Castro during this period.

But back to chronology. Do we start with the original project proposal that is in your briefing books, primarily drafted by Jake Esterline—the March 17, 1960, proposal that Eisenhower approved [Documents 2.1 and 2.2]?[4] We have a unique opportunity with you being here, Jake, it seems to me, to go through the genesis of this particular document, the debate that took place in your office over what it should say. Or do we start with Richard Goodwin sitting down at his typewriter on 19 October 1960, and banging out the Kennedy press release urging support for the "freedom fighters" in Cuba?[5] This may have locked Kennedy into that hawkish position during the debate with Nixon on October 21.[6]

A new CIA publication just came out two weeks ago called "CIA Briefings of Presidential Candidates." It records this curious episode where Nixon realized in August of 1960 that Kennedy might be briefed about the Cuba operation. Nixon took Dulles aside and asked what Kennedy had been told. And he wanted to know what Lyndon Johnson had been told about covert action projects, specifically those related to Cuba. Dulles, according to the CIA, "gave a carefully crafted answer," to the effect that Kennedy was being told a little but not too much. According to another CIA official who was present, Nixon reacted by saying, "don't tell Kennedy anything that could be dangerous." In the end, without Kennedy even being told much about the operation, he took a strongly anti-Castro position and Nixon felt forced by the format of the debate to take the contrary position.

Or does the Bay of Pigs really begin in Guatemala? Do we go back six or seven years and start with the Guatemala operation, PBSUCCESS? Was it a kind of blueprint for the Bay of Pigs operation? That is something that we want to ask you, Jake. What was the experience that you brought to the drafting of the initial plan for the Cuba operation of March 17, 1960?

What *experience* was brought to the decisions that were made to launch the Cuba project? What *attitudes* were brought to the project during the late Eisenhower period, and in the CIA itself towards the issue of overthrowing Castro? In one of the first meetings that took place in the National Security Council after the Castro revolution, in early February 1959, Allen Dulles said to Eisenhower, "The new leadership in Cuba are like children. They have to be led." Was a similar attitude played out in the difficulties the CIA had in dealing with the internal resistance in Cuba? Is it possible that the CIA treated *all* the Cubans like "children," to their everlasting regret?

What about the politics of the 1960 election? We are in another presidential season right now. Cuba has been a hot political football in every presidential campaign since 1960. I'd like to get Arthur Schlesinger to say something about the way he believes electoral politics drove Cuba policy in the early Kennedy administration.

Finally, we should recall McGeorge Bundy's testimony before the Taylor Commission after the fiasco.[7] Bundy goes through various "what ifs" associated with the operation. What if Kennedy hadn't reduced the first air strikes from 16 planes to 8 planes, and then canceled the second air strike? What if the plan for overthrowing Castro hadn't changed from an infiltration plan to an invasion plan? Bundy rejected these counterfactuals by asserting: "I don't think the failure was because of the want of a nail.[8] I think that the men who worked on this got into a world of their own." Of course, Bundy was in that world, too. Some of you at the table were part of that world. I hope you will tell us about that world in this session.

Blight: So, gentlemen, where did it begin? How did it evolve? What were its components? I would like to focus all of us on Peter's last, very insightful admonition: tell us what it was like.

Esterline: I will try to start it. I think maybe it goes back to the Second World War, and the period right after it, when we, as a country, had to lead the Free World in the struggle against the Soviet Bloc. We kept a kind of war-period mentality. By this, I mean, just as in wartime, we did not ask questions of our superiors. I think we stayed with the mentality that if you are told to do something, you do it. . . .

I see that Peter wants to talk about Guatemala. Personally, I think the 1954 operation succeeded partially because of what the agency did, sure. But it was the "psychological" actions of the invasion force that were significant. And the actions of that bastard [Ambassador John] Peurifoy and Station Chief John Doherty were really key. So, Guatemala was a success, I guess. But to those of us who knew it, and knew about it, we didn't really think it was very much of a success. But it got Arbenz out, that's for sure.[9]

Blanton: Why was it not considered such a success by those of you who were closely involved with it?

Esterline: As a military success? Well, look, there really was hardly any fighting. And, of course, Castillo Armas was not very effective at all compared to Brigade 2506. It was a different kind of thing—more of a political action in my judgment that made it a success. It was not military action. We won more because of incompetence on the other side than anything else.

Let's see, what else was on Peter's mind? Well, when I was called back for the Cuba thing, we drafted this general umbrella paper with a lot of discussion among us. We did not have our military fellows there at that point, however.

Kornbluh: Who did that besides you?

Esterline: Richard Drain. I think it was just the two of us for the most part, as I recall. But here again we were sort of marching according to our marching orders from Ike. I think at that point we should have asked some questions about where the thing was going, about what the ultimate objective was going to be. But we didn't. In those years you were given an order and you did it. I have thought back so many times I have lost count: How did this thing start to steamroller and get away from us? How did we get pushed into this business of more people, more people, always more people? How did it happen? More to the point: How did we *let* it happen?

Blanton: Your response to the Guatemala experience was that it wasn't really a military success. So in your own case, it wasn't any kind of "model" for the Cuba operation. But does this apply to the others? What do you think Bissell or Eisenhower or Dulles believed or took as lessons from Guatemala? Is it possible that they thought it would be easy to pull this thing off?

Esterline: I don't think that they thought that this would be easy. But they thought that we could utilize an operation that would avoid the kind of mistakes that were made in Guatemala. And that is what we did try to do. And that is what we *did* do, up to a point, up to the point where the thing started to steamroller and get out of control.

Gleijeses: I would like to address the point of the Guatemala operation. I would agree that in hindsight the Guatemala operation was a very poorly conducted operation. It only succeeded because of the immense imbalance of power. But it is my very strong impression that the CIA thought it was a great success. When the operation succeeded they were so elated they forgot the many ways that they knew it could have gone wrong. So in the culture of the CIA, in the world of the CIA, what remained was a tale of a great success without any awareness of how flawed the operation had been.

Halpern: This reminds me of Operation Ajax—the overthrow of Mossadegh in Iran in 1953. This also left people with the impression that you can do this with mirrors. Because again in 1953, Kermit [Kim] Roosevelt didn't have anything but a mob in the street. But he was able to pull it off at the last minute with a bunch of circus people and money. So it was concluded that with plenty of cash, plenty of money to throw around, everything will turn out fine. I think Piero is right. It became part of the legend that you could do this kind of stuff without any trouble. And the higher up you went the hazier the view was. And if you balance the truth, like with Jake, or me in MONGOOSE later, you know it is not true. . . .

Smith: Well, yes, it's all part of the ambiance of the time. The United States, let's face it, up until the Cuban Revolution, up until its failure at the Bay of Pigs, didn't really take Latin America very seriously. It certainly didn't take Central America and Caribbean countries seriously. These were little countries that we wanted to do what we wanted them to do and if they didn't, well, we would get something going like the operation in Guatemala and that would take care of it. I didn't talk with Bissell, as Piero did, but I did know Dave Phillips, who was part of the operation in Guatemala. Dave was in Havana undercover, and said one night before he left—before we all left—he said: "The only difference between handling this situation and handling Guatemala is that this time our boys"—he didn't come right out and say the CIA—"this time our boys will come in by sea and last time they had to cross the land frontier. But otherwise, it will be just as easy." I mean there was this sort of hubris everywhere, and the mythology of the Guatemala operation was part of it. Fundamentally, we didn't take this country seriously. We just didn't take Cuba seriously.

Esterline: Well, *I* took Cuba and Castro very seriously. Seeing him in Caracas, it was obvious we were dealing with a different kind of leader. I still take it seriously, too seriously, according to my wife. Believe me, this last month, these six weeks, since I have started reading these documents, have been very difficult. My wife said the other day, "Your hair is getting even whiter than it was before." [Laughter.] I said, "Well I am getting nightmares again. I wake up kicking myself, you know where, for letting this thing steamroller away from me."

Now I read these reports from Cuba and I sat there in my office at CIA and I said goddammit! I hope Bissell has enough guts to tell John Kennedy what the facts are. And Lord, if I'd been there he might not have changed anything but he would have had the facts. I don't know if Kennedy ever got the facts or not. . . .

Halpern: That wouldn't have helped, Jake. Even later on in MONGOOSE, Dick Helms got the facts from me. I almost got fired but I didn't, but it was the same thing as with Jake. Nobody on top would listen.

Blight: I wonder if I am alone in feeling that Richard Bissell is the deus ex machina of this conference. We have his memoir in front of us. At lunch a month or so ago, Mac Bundy described Bissell as one of the most articulate, bright, energetic, creative people he'd ever met. And yet, in some way, all of this talent seemed to work to his disadvantage in the Cuba project. I wonder, Arthur, could you tell us a little about Richard Bissell: about how he created his own ambiance perhaps, or about how he fit into this, or how he fell into a trap, perhaps of his own making.

Schlesinger: Bissell was an economist who graduated from Groton in 1928 and Yale in 1932. I think Mac Bundy had a class with him at Yale. I got to know him after the war. He was a great friend of Joe Alsop's and Joe was a great friend of mine. In 1948 when the Marshall Plan was set up, Dick became deputy for Paul Hoffman in Washington. Averell Harriman asked me to go to Paris with him as a special assistant, and I got to know Bissell better.

He had extraordinary gifts of exposition, which I saw at the table in those meetings leading up to the Bay of Pigs. He gave a very dispassionate, quasi-objective account of what the plans were. Bissell would show the president the map and say that, if there is some trouble with the landing, they can go through here and get into the Escambray.

Unidentified Voice: Through the swamps?

Schlesinger: I believe he discovered only later that the "passage" to the Escambray was all swampland. He left a very strong impression on the president and on McNamara. He told the JCS [Joint Chiefs of Staff] that there would be uprisings behind the lines and defections from the militia. As Mac Bundy said later, "The trouble with Dick is he is so emotionally involved with this project that he has changed from an analyst to an advocate." And what we saw was a superb, well-organized, very effective advocacy. He talks about all this in his memoirs.[10] Since we all had the impression of him as a man of incredible intelligence, it was more convincing than it might otherwise have been. I was not convinced by it, but I had been in the OSS [Office of Strategic Services] during the war and had some background in intelligence operations and dealing with—this was in Europe—dealing with resistance groups. I worked with Bill Casey and Frank Wisner and others, and I just was not persuaded by Dick's otherwise very persuasive advocacy. But I think the fact that he was a social friend of many of us also must have had the effect of blunting the kind of criticism he might otherwise have gotten.

The other thing, of course, is that we were all inexperienced. It must be remembered that Kennedy came into office on January 20, and the Bay of Pigs took place just three months later. Here we were, a bunch of ex-college professors sitting around faced by this panoply of the Joint Chiefs of Staff, Allen Dulles, a legendary figure, and Dick Bissell, the man who invented and promoted the U-2. It was rather difficult even to open one's mouth sometimes, in the face of these guys.

Esterline: You know we really had almost turned into a broken record when this thing got moved down the line and we got to the critical point. We never composed our own air force. I predicted they would never let us have our own air force. So time and time again, we said to Dick [Bissell], "If you don't want a disaster, we absolutely *must* take out *all* of Castro's air force."

Dick promised, but he didn't deliver. For example, after one of the cancellations of air strikes that were so critical, we still knew where every Cuban plane was. Every plane. We knew that we had to destroy them before the landing at the Bay of Pigs and we knew where they were. And he promised us before the raid—there had been a diminution already of planes involved—this time he said, "I promise you that this time I'll get the things from the president for you." Well, he didn't. We didn't get those planes, and then that's when Hawkins and I walked out of the office. We went out in the parking lot for an hour or two. I said, "Jack, I've really never walked away from anything in my life, but I don't think I can continue." And he said, "I can't either." He said, "This is out of our control. We can't do this." So I called Dick and I said, "Dick, you are going to have to get two different people; we just can't go on with this the way it's going." [Dick said], "Don't do that." Well, he got us over to his house and we talked for two or three hours and he convinced us that even if we left, that wouldn't stop it at that point. So he talked us into continuing but he said, "I promise you that there will be no more reductions of air raids." He led us right into the mouth of disaster, because the raids were cut again, leaving our brave men like sitting ducks on that damn beach.[11]

Schlesinger: Part of the problem was that we assumed in the White House that the full weight of the agency was behind this operation. It was only later, after the collapse, that Bob Amory, who was an old friend of mine, told me that the intelligence branch had never been even officially notified of the operation, and had never been asked for an assessment—for example of the probability of uprisings behind the line.

Halpern: That was Allen Dulles's decision.

Esterline: Is that right? Arthur, a friend of mine heard that I was involved in this and he sent word to me, he said, "Dick is not very practical." He said, "Be careful of what you are getting into." But we were into it at that point.

P. Terrence Hopmann: The thing that struck me when I read Bissell's memoirs is that he seems to express greater doubt about the operation here than he apparently did in the various debates within the White House. The question that kept occurring to me is: as changes were made for political reasons, he seems never to have doubted that these changes would undermine the tactical chances of success. And yet in the end he acquiesces. Why? Secondly, whether or not some of his memoir is a rewriting a history, why wouldn't he at least have expressed these doubts—especially if the success of the operation was so important to him?

Esterline: He was the driving force to keep it going. Dick always wanted to keep it going.

Hopmann: Even if he thought the changes would ruin the operation—turn it into a fiasco? I mean, he mentions here for example, that again, during the period after the election but before the Kennedy administration takes office, that the program

> underwent a metamorphosis. The administration's determination to deal with Castro remained strong, and when efforts to establish a guerrilla organization proved fruitless, our reliance shifted to the invasion force being trained in Guatemala.[12]

But he never explains why that shift occurred, even though, as we were discussing earlier this afternoon, the first kind of activity—a guerrilla war—had a far greater chance of success than the World War II–style invasion. Yet this appears to be one of these major shifts in policy that seems suddenly to occur. Then he passes over it in one sentence. But if, as Jake has said, these changes spelled doom for the operation, and if Bissell knew they spelled doom for the operation (which he seems to have understood), then the mystery remains: Why did he not make a stand at the White House to prevent the disaster, either by arguing hard for the air strikes, or by canceling the operation?

Esterline: I think you will find that all these things were forced on us by the Special Group, which decided we needed more people. So, we really never had a chance to test the numbers that we were working on.

Blanton: You never had a chance to test the infiltration mode that you had been building for, did you?

Esterline: No, we were pushed beyond that.

Quintero: Based on what facts?

Halpern: There are no facts. Based upon guts, inside gut reactions. You know.

Quintero: Was it a one-man decision?

Halpern: A couple-of-men decision. And you will see this more and more when we get to MONGOOSE.

Esterline: You know, well . . . Let me just finish this off about Bissell and myself. When I read his memoirs I was amused because he almost wrote me out of it. That is good because at the time that he refused to go to see the president at the 11th hour, he sent General Cabell over and I almost went to jail for strangling that four-star general. Bissell and I never spoke again. Never. And he knew why to the day he died. And I knew why because I felt that I had never been so thoroughly deceived in my life. And I guess I will really have to apologize to General Cabell's family for the way that I treated him that night. Because he was just being a good soldier, although a pretty dumb one. I mean, how could a man with four stars not know that we desperately needed that air support that was part of the plan.

Baloyra: Two very quick contrasts. One, it seems to me that there is a great deal of continuity here. In Havana—in the middle levels of the bureaucracy between '56, '58, and '60—there are similarities, in the sense that particularly after Frank País and José Antonio Echeverría get killed in 1957, that Fidel begins to throw his weight around, giving the impression that he believes he is the center of the universe.[13] It was at that time that apprehension starts building up in the rebel movement. After the failure of the April '58 strike there was the idea that Fidel had to be stopped, somehow.[14] That is the thinking of the State Department bureaucracy, on the one hand.

On the other hand, the American Ambassador Smith was going around with a magnifying glass trying to find evidence that Fidel's a communist. Of course, he is not going to find anything. Forget it, because he is not. I am sorry for sounding like an academic looking, groping for a bureaucratic politics explanation, or whatever—but, anyway, the result is inaction, inertia. Nothing happens. John Foster Dulles is ill. Eisenhower is not interested in Cuba.

Things are drifting, and then there is an attempt at last-minute improvisation in November and December, they send [William D.] Pawley, of all people. They—imagine the mentality—they think that a magistrate of the Supreme Court and a guy flown from the Isle of Pines into Havana on December 30 of '58 constitute political competition for Fidel Castro. I don't know where their heads were, or who thought of this. But evidently we were not dwelling on the same planet. Okay. But I mean: here was one of the most formidable politicians of the Western Hemisphere coming to office—to power. And, to oppose this juggernaut, they would have a 68- or 75-year-old magistrate of the Supreme Court who was tainted, guiltily tainted, and a guy who was asked and invited to lead an army that didn't exist.[15]

Fast-forward the date. Okay, a very similar cast of characters are casting about to do these things. On the one hand, the presidential adviser is writing that the problem with the operation is that the less the military risk the greater the political risk and vice versa.[16] I mean, the die is cast here. And this is one parameter—the tension between political and military risk—that spelled doom for the operation. The second parameter is that there is the political figure of the new president, John Kennedy. There are high hopes in the group Kennedy has consciously gathered around him. They definitely do not want to sacrifice this man to another typical, you know, Cold War operation that fails.

And then they have the operational details. Now politically, moral force was not on our side at the Bay of Pigs. Something had to be done so that if this means, or this measure, was going to be pushed forward, then that alternative—the practical alternative to Mr. Castro that had to prove itself on a day-by-day basis—must be set up. You could not do that by seizing territory at the Bay of Pigs, or anywhere else. So, the final judgment of Kennedy is: well, let them show us what they've got. If this concept flies, then there will be a popular insurrection. And if not, then no harm done to the New Frontier, to Camelot.

But here is the total disconnect between the Cuban mentality and the mentality in the Kennedy White House. Kennedy put on the constraint of "low noise," no obvious American involvement, in order to limit his political risks. He thinks that by doing this, he can manage his political risks. But here this approach comes into direct contact with the Cuban mentality. The Cuban mentality of the time only wants to know who is winning. As Rafael said, 90 percent of the Cuban people only wanted to know—or mostly wanted to know—who is winning? After the Bay of Pigs, these Cubans conclude: these guys don't have a chance. So, the insurrection that was not very likely—maybe 5 percent tops, you know, the popular uprising, 5 percent tops, was cut to maybe 1 percent as a result of all of this subsequent rigmarole we call the Bay of Pigs.[17]

So my reaction as a Cuban is: fine, I don't ask that you think in terms of Cuban interests. You have your own American interests. No. It's our fault for listening to you, or believing you. But on the other hand, something *was* going to be done, and there *had* to be deniability but if, in spite of all this, the full prestige of the United States was going to be put on the

line. So—I know I sound like a broken record—why—why did you not go
for the Isle of Pines?[18]

Halpern: We will talk about that when we get to the MONGOOSE
Operation.

Baloyra: It would not have been your problem anymore after that. You
would have had more deniability—all you wanted—in an uprising of people who are there supported by two or three hundred who came from the
outside. I know, I know, it is not a perfect solution, necessarily, but it does
combine deniability with *doing* something. Of course, from the Isle of
Pines, we couldn't get to Cuba, but then Cuba couldn't get to us, because
Fidel didn't have a navy. And in terms of accumulating moral force and
political credibility for that "government" that you guys were thinking
about recognizing—well, at the Bay of Pigs, we don't have a hell of a
chance in 10,000 of pulling it off. On the Isle of Pines, there might have
been some chance. It is the only thing I can think of that would satisfy
Kennedy's requirement of low political risk and the Cuban requirement of
winning, winning something, even if it is only the Isle of Pines to start
with.

This is the only Cuban barbershop counterfactual that I will
allow myself this weekend. [Laughter.] But it is one that would have
allowed the American government to say: okay, you guys want to have your
country? You want to fight and die for it? Okay, here is a level playing field
called the Isle of Pines. You will not be 1,200 against 200,000. You will be
1,200 against whoever shows up in a skiff, or in some kind of makeshift
boat.

Blight: Rafael, do you want to add something to Quique's barbershop
counterfactual about the Isle of Pines?

Quintero: No, I want to ask a question to Jake and Sam. I still don't understand very well the kind of coordination—maybe Wayne can answer this
question—the kind of coordination, if there was any, and I doubt it,
between these different centers: the embassy in Cuba, the field agents in
Miami, and the CIA headquarters in Washington. Oh, I forgot to mention
the camps in Guatemala. Was there any coordination? I mean was there
anyone in charge of that coordination?

Esterline: You mean in '58 and '59?

Quintero: No, I mean for the mission, in '60–'61.

Esterline: They reported to us. Miami reported to us. Havana reported to us. Guatemala reported to us and Honduras reported to us as it related to all of these things. One of the things that we struggled with, from start to finish, was what I guess you would call the "Jim Angleton mentality."[19] We were not allowed to advise any group in Cuba, or anybody going to Cuba, of what, when, or where anything was going to happen, until just before we launched the mission. Now, for that reason the groups in the Escambray never got word from us that we wanted to send men to join the brigade. We wanted to send word, but under the terms of the arrangement, we were not allowed to. This problem became even more acute after the embassy was closed down.

Quintero: Why was it that, for example, I will say 95 percent of the infiltration teams who had been trained for months at the Guatemala camps were infiltrated into Cuba *after*—I repeat, *after*—the decision had been made that no infiltration team, no underground, no plan for involving the underground was going to be executed, because there was going to be this invasion. Why still go ahead and infiltrate these teams, that were supposedly to have been the base of the whole organization? Why? I don't get it. What was their basic objective—in being sent into Cuba? They were not even used. And, as long as they were in Cuba, why were they not put together with the invasion group? Why were they sent into Cuba without any real means of support or objective?

Baloyra: And what about their requests for weapons? Okay, okay, it's a Cuban obsession or whatever you want to call it, about getting weapons. But this was a practical issue of life and death. People were there able and willing to fight, but the weapons did not come.

Domínguez: My question really follows the earlier exchange between Tom and Jake. It is a question for Jake. You said, I think quite accurately, that the original plan for sending, say, several hundred guerrillas into Cuba was never tested. Rafael is reminding us that, in spite of this, infiltration groups were going to Cuba regularly. And so a question could be put in two ways: Why were these small—very small—infiltration groups sent to Cuba even *after* the big decision to change the mission was made in late 1960? That is question one—Rafael's question. Question two: How did you evaluate the ethics, the utility, the value of these small infiltration teams compared to your original plan? . . .

Esterline: As best I remember, I think that we just, we wanted to try to determine whether we in fact had the feasibility to get people onto the beach and back. In some cases they did, and in other cases it did not turn out very well. Our photography of the beach turned out not to be as good as we thought it would be. There were coral reefs where there weren't supposed to be any. This was part of a testing program, to see whether some of the elements of the operation would actually work. But I want to . . .

Domínguez: But how did you evaluate—how successful did you, from your perspective, think this was working out? Because if these "tests" didn't work out, then your big idea might not have worked.

Esterline: I don't recall being particularly bothered by that, the reason probably being that I was so totally preoccupied with what was happening in the air, that I just couldn't think of anything else. Let me tell you something. Having fought as a guerrilla for eight long years myself, I did not ever want to put a force into a situation where I couldn't get them out. You've got to build in a way to get them out. That's basic in these kinds of operations. That's why the whole air thing became just a nightmare to me from beginning to end. Without air [cover] over the landing site, and without taking out the Castro air force, our people would be trapped. And that is just what happened.

Smith: It seems to me that your concept of putting several hundred guerrillas into the Escambray was one thing. And a few infiltration teams before the invasion is another. That is an entirely different concept.

Quintero: I am sorry to interrupt. But I was involved in the first concept. Excuse me, but I was involved in the first concept. Many people don't know this, but actually the Bay of Pigs training camps were created based on that first concept. We were going to have fifteen infiltration teams. Somewhere this was changed because that was the basic plan. And nobody knew if it was going to work because we never tried it.

. . . .

Esterline: We would have debates and meetings among ourselves about the merits of this or that plan when, all of a sudden—and this had nothing to do with the White House—but all of a sudden we would get a new order, usually coming from a member of the Special Group, telling us that we "needed" more of this or more of that—always more of something.[20] Very often, it would be generated by some general who was a member of the Special Group. It was often [Chairman of the Joint Chiefs Gen. Lyman] Lemnitzer for example, but others did this too. Those guys just didn't understand anything about guerrilla warfare. They wanted to fight this thing as if it was

World War II in Europe, or something. You know, the whole thing—land a huge invasion force and march forward until you liberate the territory.

. . . .

Smith: I can answer [Rafael Quintero] on the question about coordination. The embassy was in contact with some, but not all, of the many opposition groups. On the so-called coordination between the embassy, Miami, and Washington—there wasn't any, because while the embassy had contact with the resistance forces, we did not direct anything. It is the CIA station that is directing. There wasn't any coordination.

Quintero: But look at the chronology. Why Francisco . . .[21]

Baloyra: Francisco has been to all the provinces, he has beat the bushes there, he has organized people, he has created groups that have leadership, they know how many men they have, they know their task. Twice, he does this. But exactly for what? Because the weapons are not coming.

Smith: Of course not, because the decision had been made that we were not going to support the internal opposition.

Baloyra: But this is later.

Quintero: Based on my experience—later experience—you take a piece of paper that is supposed to be intelligence-related, and you deliver it to where it goes. But in those days, if you get some intelligence paper that is given to you in Cuba by the resistance—the underground—all we know is that it reached the embassy. And somehow we have never been able to find out if it reached Washington or even Miami. I am talking about official channels . . . there was a group of people who had been infiltrated from the Guatemalan camps with a special objective and course of action to follow. And then you find out that—when you are in Cuba—you find out that somebody from Miami sends some other group with the same objective— the *same!* You find a total lack of coordination when you are in the field. And, I still have not been able to get the answer from anyone, who was supposed to be handling this? Was somebody coordinating this from the top? Or were people doing more or less what they wanted to do and nobody was in charge?

Halpern: It should of been you, Jake.

Smith: Rafael, your faith in us is touching. [Laughter.]

Brenner: I am a little concerned because, when we move on to the next session, we are going to leave the Eisenhower administration. Before we do move on, I want to ask a question that relates, in part, to Eisenhower. The question is about the obsession with Castro and the obsession with Cuba. There have been numerous studies indicating that Kennedy was obsessed with overthrowing Castro. But, Arthur has just told us now that part of what was going on was just some naive, inexperienced people who really were not obsessed with Castro, at least in January of 1961. Some scholars believe there is a sense in which Eisenhower's last words of wisdom to Kennedy were: "Get Castro. This is something that you have to do." Can you give us a sense in the agency, and also in the embassy, what the sensibility was, what you thought that President Eisenhower wanted done about Castro? And, did that change in November after the election? Did you have a sense that Kennedy was even more determined to get Castro? Can you give us a sense of how determined Eisenhower was?

Esterline: Let me give you my thoughts on that, having been one of his troops, if you will, during the war. I don't think I ever participated directly in a meeting of Ike's but I had a lot of back and forth with his people. I was *never* concerned that he would fail to do the right thing when it came to moving into whatever the operation might have required at a given point. That's one thing.

I think, however, that I was pushed off my plan before the Kennedys came in. I mean I was knocked off my plan back in August-September of '60. But I don't remember being much concerned about it. You know, plans change all the time; people make suggestions all the time. Now, while this was going on, I didn't know about this back-and-forth briefing with Kennedy, who had just been elected. But when the election went the other way I remember vividly thinking to myself: holy crapola, I don't like this, because this isn't the kind of operation a new administration should be facing unless they know everything there is to know about it. And I assumed that at some point there had been a briefing—a full briefing.

Domínguez: But Jake, still in the Eisenhower administration—what about Phil's point? Why did *you* think the plan changed from a guerrilla operation?

Esterline: Somebody had it in his mind that you needed a lot more than what we were planning for. They looked at the size of the Cuban militia and they said: "Man, you have got to put more troops in there or nothing is going to work." This was a judgment that came, I believe, from the Special Group.

Gleijeses: I don't think it was the Special Group. These things were not discussed by the Special Group. I think it was Bissell and personally, although I am no expert on the internal resistance in Cuba, I think Bissell quite accurately believed that they were not going to overthrow Fidel Castro. I think these were decisions at a level higher than Mr. Esterline. These were decisions of Richard Bissell and Allen Dulles. At that level it was decided. I would like to say one other thing, if I may, and address what Phil Brenner said. I think Kennedy *was* obsessed with Cuba and that obsession led to Operation MONGOOSE—a kind of terrorist operation, but an inefficient one. But I think that the obsession of Kennedy with Cuba came in the wake of the failure of the Bay of Pigs, not before.

I would like also to disagree, if I may, with Arthur Schlesinger's and Phil Brenner's characterization of the Kennedy people when they came to power as a little naive—as a little in awe of the CIA big guys, etc., etc. I think the reason for the failure of orders—one of the reasons that McGeorge Bundy actually suggested, and Richard Goodwin suggested it in his memoir—is that they were a new team who didn't know the president very well, and they didn't want to take a stand unless they were sure of the view of the president. Dr. Schlesinger, of course, was a very honorable exception among these men. The only other person who took a strong stance against the operation was Thomas Mann. . . .[22]

Schlesinger: Tomorrow I will give an explanation as to why Kennedy went along with it, but I think that I will save that for tomorrow.

. . . .

Malcolm Byrne: I was actually going to quote from Piero's article to offer a couple of reasons why the shift was made from a guerrilla operation to an invasion but the author preempted me.[23] But there were two specific reasons that he attributes to Bissell's decision: one was that he felt that "infiltration of guerrilla groups would fall short of the required minimum critical mass." He said, "What was needed was a shock action." This is on page 11 of Piero's article in the red [secondary sources] briefing book. Then Piero quotes Bissell at greater length:

> The real reason for the shift from infiltration to amphibious invasion is that by October we had made a major effort at infiltration and resupply, and those efforts had been unsuccessful. My conviction was that we simply would not be able to organize a secure movement in Cuba. We had made, I think, at least five infiltrations by small boats and in each case the people had been picked up in a day or two. We had also made several airdrops of supplies, but in most cases there was always a delay of several

days between the request for resupply and the actual drop, and several times during that gap of time the people who originally made the request had moved. We had no direct radio communication with the small rebel groups. We may have made one or two infiltrations of men by air, but the majority entered by sea. Therefore we simply had to give up the effort to build a safe underground with communications and command and control.[24]

Quintero: Excuse me, may I say something? I don't know where he got that. I don't know where he got that so-called fact because—well, as a matter of fact, I can tell you for sure that people were not cut—there were no people cut from infiltration teams. The first infiltration was not cut until November of 1960. . . .

Baloyra: For the record, the first infiltrations were done by boats from Cuba coming to Florida to pick up people and bring them back—both new people and crew and everybody. It is in the chronology.[25]

. . . .

Smith: Look, the question was asked as we started into this session: How did we get into this and how did we make this colossal mistake? I mean, this was illogical, as you look at it in retrospect. There is no way this plan could have succeeded. I mean Bissell decides that, you know, a few guerrillas infiltrated isn't going to work. So he decides he is going to overthrow Castro, and he is going to accomplish the objective with 1,200 men against a 60,000-man army with artillery and tanks. It is utterly irrational. And in this case, in this episode, the CIA comes in for a lot of criticism because of the plan, the CIA plan. So the tendency is to lay it all on the doorstep of the CIA.

But let's go forward in time to the Soviet-brigade-in-Cuba episode in 1979, which is handled just as stupidly and just as irrationally.[26] Then we'll go forward to the spring of 1980, and Mariel.[27] Now let's come forward to today with the Helms-Burton Bill.[28] This is perhaps the stupidest piece of legislation I have seen in Washington in the 45 years that I have been there. What is it about Cuba, anyway? We do seem able sometimes to act more or less rationally, with respect to some other countries. We do seem able to formulate an intelligent—sometimes intelligent—policy, and to respond rationally to perceived threats to U.S. interests. So, what is it about Cuba? Is there something funny in the air over the Florida Straits? Something in the water? [Laughter.]

Every agency in the government that deals with Cuba, and administration after administration—it doesn't make any difference who is in the White House—we simply cannot deal with the place in a rational way. So I would just pose that as a question for us to have in mind as we go forward through the conference. This is not an isolated case, by any means. This is typical of the way we deal with Cuba.

Gleijeses: Cuba is an extreme case. But U.S. behavior toward the whole region is not much different than it is toward Cuba.

Smith: I understand, Piero, but—no, I understand. But 37 consecutive years, virtually without letup, of shooting ourselves in the feet—and elsewhere? This is something weird and special, in my view, and I can't explain it.

Schlesinger: One reason is that we regard Cuba as an issue of domestic politics, and the reasons for that go back to the founders of the country. Thomas Jefferson and John Quincy Adams assumed that Cuba would eventually become part of the United States.[29]

. . . .

Gleijeses: Other countries in Central America and the Caribbean did not succeed in defeating the United States. Cuba defeated the United States. Don't you think, Wayne, that this explains a lot?

Smith: Yes, that is part of the explanation. But even before Cuba defeats the United States we have the decision to go *into* the Bay of Pigs, which is utterly irrational to begin with. I have been asking myself this question for three decades: Why can't we deal rationally with Cuba? And yes, there are these partial explanations—I mean [John Quincy] Adams actually said that this is the most important, strategically important, piece of territory, it will fall into the Latin Union, and so forth. Yes, but the world has changed. The Cold War is over, and in some cases we respond to that in a rational way, but when it comes to Cuba, absolutely not.

Gleijeses: Forgive me, but one of the arguments that our Cuban friends were making this afternoon is that the Cubans tended to go with the winner, that in '61 the great majority of the population of Cuba would have gone with the winner. This bothered me when I read it in the CIA documents. I am not so sure. I think perhaps this is the wrong assessment. Maybe the Cubans don't necessarily tend to go with the winners. Maybe this explains why, after all these years, and even now, after the United States has "won" the Cold War, the Cubans still refuse to go with the winner.

Blight: I posed Wayne's question, late one night at the Comodoro Hotel in Havana, to a Cuban Central Committee official. "What is it about you guys?" I asked. And he thought about it a minute, and—this is being done through our student assistant and interpreter, who had a little trouble with this one—his answer was, "Well, I always thought it was that Fidel gave you the finger and got away with it. So now we take turns giving each other the finger." [Laughter.]

Smith: Sure, that's part of it.

Halpern: But, if the Bay of Pigs is irrational, what do you call MONGOOSE? That's irrationality to the nth degree. It's even stupider.

Smith: No, no, exactly, Sam. I rest my case.

Notes

1. The Sierra Maestra Mountains in Oriente province of eastern Cuba were used by Fidel Castro and his fellow members of the 26th of July Movement as their base of operations in the late 1950s in their fight against the government of Fulgencio Batista.

2. The antagonism between the old-line Comintern communists and the group closest to Fidel Castro was deep and pervasive, as would emerge in March 1962 during the so-called microfaction episode. Aníbal Escalante, whose father had been one of the founders of the Cuban Communist Party in the 1920s, was purged, along with his associates, for all sorts of misdemeanors, all of which summed to the accusation that: (1) Escalante was taking his orders from the Soviet Embassy, rather than from Fidel; and (2) that Escalante may have had thoughts of being the Soviet Union's "choice" to replace Fidel, should such a "choice" ever present itself. By March 1962, and thereafter, Castro and the Soviets were at odds about the level of Cuban support for Latin American insurgencies. These and other issues reached a breaking point, again with Aníbal Escalante in the center, in January 1968, when Escalante was expelled from the party and from Cuba, after being accused of spying on the regime at the bidding of the Soviet Embassy. See Jorge I. Domínguez, *To Make a World Safe for Revolution: Cuba's Foreign Policy* (Cambridge: Harvard University Press, 1989), pp. 37, 73–74; and Philip Brenner and James G. Blight, *Reform or Revolution?: Soviet-Cuban Relations from the Missile Crisis to the Invasion of Czechoslovakia* (Savage, Md.: Rowman & Littlefield, forthcoming).

3. Richard Nixon, "Memorandum of Conversation with Fidel Castro," 25 April 1959, p. 5. National Security Archive, Washington, D.C.

4. "A Program of Covert Action Against the Castro Regime," dated 16 March 1960, and approved by President Eisenhower the following day at a meeting in the White House.

5. The statement was released by Senator John F. Kennedy, the Democratic candidate for president, on 21 October 1960, and carried in full in the *New York Times* that day. "We must attempt," said Kennedy, "to strengthen the non-Batista democratic anti-Castro forces in exile, and in Cuba itself, who offer eventual hope of overthrowing Castro."

6. See Russell Baker, "Nixon and Kennedy Debate Cuba," *New York Times,* 22 October 1960. Nixon was forced by Kennedy's aggressive rhetoric to chide Kennedy because his plan, if implemented, would (said Nixon) "cost us all our friends in Latin America."

7. Maxwell Taylor chaired the "Board of Inquiry on Cuban Operations," which first met on 23 April 1961.

8. But this is precisely the claim made by Col. Jack Hawkins in Document 4.3, with regard to the cancellation of the air strikes on Castro's air force, thereby forfeiting control of the air over the Bay of Pigs and Playa Girón that had been anticipated by the planners and by the members of the brigade. Alfredo Durán and Jacob Esterline agree with Hawkins's assessment.

9. Jacobo Arbenz, Guatemalan president, who fled the country during the 1954 CIA-sponsored coup that brought Carlos Castillo Armas to power. See Piero Gleijeses, *The Guatemalan Revolution and the United States, 1944–1954* (Princeton, N.J.: Princeton University Press, 1991).

10. Richard M. Bissell Jr., *Reflections of a Cold Warrior: From Yalta to the Bay of Pigs* (New Haven: Yale University Press, 1996), pp. 152–204.

11. See also Hawkins [Document 4.3] and also Document 3.6. In the latter, Esterline cables Hawkins in Nicaragua to ask whether the brigade should still be sent in, knowing that Kennedy had made a firm decision not to back them up with U.S. Marines. Hawkins's answer, which lauds the fighting prowess of the men in the brigade, is predicated on the assumption (never mentioned in the return cable) that the *brigadistas* will be able to dig in around the Bay of Pigs without fear of air attacks from Castro's planes.

12. Bissell, *Reflections of a Cold Warrior,* p. 156.

13. Frank País was a central figure in the rebellion against Batista in eastern Cuba and Fidel Castro's competitor for leadership of the movement in the mountains. He was killed by Batista's police in Santiago de Cuba at the end of July 1957. José Antonio Echeverría led an attack on the presidential palace on 13 March 1957 in an attempt to assassinate Batista, who narrowly escaped. Echeverría was killed in the gun battle.

14. A general strike was planned for 31 March 1958, but it had to be put off, due to the rebels' lack of ammunition. When it finally got going on 9 April, it fizzled, mostly from disorganization, rather than from repression by the Batista regime. See Thomas G. Paterson, *Contesting Castro: The United States and the Triumph of the Cuban Revolution* (New York: Oxford University Press, 1994), pp. 139–149.

15. See ibid., pp. 206–211.

16. Enrique Baloyra refers to Kennedy's wish to avoid a "noisy" operation in which the involvement of the U.S. government would not be plausibly deniable, on the one hand, and, on the other, the simultaneous desire that, whatever the eventual shape of the operation, that it should succeed, at least to the extent that the members of the invasion force would "melt away into the mountains," or "go guerrilla." The problem was that a "noisy" operation might succeed, but not be plausibly deniable, although the "quiet" operation might be plausibly deniable, but might fail.

17. Something of this view can be seen in McGeorge Bundy's postmortem in the immediate wake of the fiasco [Document 6.2]. See especially pages 3–4: ". . . all concerned managed to forget—or not to learn—the fundamental importance of success in this sort of effort. . . . Success is what succeeds."

18. The Isle of Pines, off the southwest coast of Cuba (now called the Isle of Youth, for its training facilities built there by the Castro government), was where Castro was imprisoned for two years in the mid-1950s by the Batista government, after his attempted insurrection at Moncada, 26 July 1953, near Santiago de Cuba.

19. James Jesus Angleton, head of counterintelligence at the CIA, became well known for his career-long and fruitless search for a high-level "mole," or Soviet agent, at CIA headquarters.

20. The Special Group consisted of the heads and seconds in command of the major security agencies: Defense, CIA, National Security Council (NSC), State, and the military services.

21. "Francisco"—Rogelio González Corzo, coordinator of the MRR.

22. Thomas C. Mann, the assistant secretary of state for Interamerican affairs.

23. Piero Gleijeses, "Ships in the Night: The CIA, the White House, and the Bay of Pigs," *Journal of Latin American Studies* 17, part 1: 1–42. This excellent piece was included in the Musgrove participants' "required reading" prior to the conference.

24. Ibid., p. 11.

25. The "Chronology of Cuban Resistance," Appendix 4.

26. In this episode during the later summer and early fall of 1979, the National Security Council staff, under National Security Adviser Zbigniew Brzezinski, believed it had discovered a Soviet combat brigade in Cuba, in violation of the Kennedy-Khrushchev understanding that terminated the Cuban missile crisis in 1962. However, the brigade had been in Cuba continuously since 1962, although the NSC staff working on the problem at the time apparently did not know this. The episode created major rifts in U.S.–Soviet relations, in U.S.–Cuban relations, and even in Cuban-Soviet relations (the latter because the Soviets capitulated, in a sense, by redefining the combat brigade as a "training unit"). See Raymond L. Garthoff, *Détente and Confrontation: American-Soviet Relations from Nixon to Reagan* (Washington, D.C.: Brookings Institution, 1985), pp. 828–848.

27. In an already highly charged atmosphere in U.S.–Cuban relations, the Mariel affair of April 1980 brought them to one of their lowest points. On 1 April, a group of Cubans crashed through the gates of the Peruvian Embassy in Havana seeking asylum. A Cuban guard was killed in a crossfire. On 4 April, Castro announced that he would no longer protect the Peruvian Embassy. By 6 April, 10,000 Cubans were crowded inside the embassy. Eventually Castro announced that anyone who wanted to leave Cuba could leave, and that the port of Mariel, west of Havana, would be the point of debarkation. Over 100,000 people left, many in small boats sent from Miami. Along with political refugees, Castro also ordered that a large number of hardened criminals and mental patients leave via Mariel. See Wayne S. Smith, *The Closest of Enemies: A Personal and Diplomatic History of the Castro Years* (New York: Norton, 1987), pp. 197–237.

28. Senator Jesse Helms (R-NC) and Congressman Dan Burton (R-IN) are the sponsors of the "Cuban Liberty and Democratic Solidarity (Libertad) Act of 1996," which strengthens sanctions against foreign companies doing business in Cuba and also trading with the United States. President Clinton signed the bill into law following the 24 February 1996 shoot-down by Cuba of two U.S. aircraft over the straits of Florida. The legislation has been repudiated by all U.S. allies, without exception, including Canada and the members of the European Union, which regard it as an unlawful infringement of their right to trade freely as they see fit. See the "Epilogue" for the historical context in which Cubans tend to see the Helms-Burton legislation.

29. See James G. Blight, Bruce J. Allyn, and David A. Welch, *Cuba on the Brink: Castro, the Missile Crisis, and the Soviet Collapse* (New York: Pantheon, 1993), pp. 321–326.

3

Kennedy's Attempts to Topple Castro

My observations of the last few days have increased my confidence in the ability of this force to accomplish not only initial combat missions but also the ultimate objective of Castro's overthrow.

Col. Jack Hawkins, 13 April 1961
[Document 3.6]

I think there was a lot of wishful thinking in Guatemala; wishful thinking not only among the brigade members, but also on the part of the CIA persons who were training us.

Alfredo Durán, 1 June 1996

James G. Hershberg: I want to start by quoting out of context one of these fascinating memos from Arthur Schlesinger, which are included in the briefing book: his memo of February 11, 1961 [Document 3.3]. This is his first tentative argument against the Bay of Pigs operation:

> There is, it seems to me, a plausible argument for this decision if one excludes everything but Cuba itself and looks only at the pace of military consolidation within Cuba and the mounting impatience of the armed exiles. However, as soon as one begins to broaden the focus beyond Cuba to include the hemisphere and the rest of the world, the arguments *against* this decision begin to gain force.

Arthur's advice was directed at President Kennedy. I want to apply his advice—broaden the focus—to our discussion here at Musgrove. I am not a Cuba specialist, and so I see my role as taking the deservedly narrow focus on the Bay of Pigs that is reflected in the excellent questions which are already on your agenda for this session, and looking at the broader context. I hope also to encourage you to discuss these new details directly related to the Bay of Pigs, *and* to explain how they fit into the broader Cold War context. This seems to me important now because we can, for the first time, with access to former East Bloc documents, begin to look at the Cold War as a whole, as a piece of history.

To broaden the focus, I'd like to turn to a document that is not in the briefing book, but which records an event that is: a memorandum of Dwight Eisenhower's farewell meeting with John Kennedy on January 19, 1961.[1] There are about five different versions of that meeting in memos and memoirs. One of the versions of this meeting is good on the atmospherics. In it, Eisenhower concludes the meeting by talking about Laos. He complains that in every Third World conflict in which the United States is engaged, the other side seems to have the better morale. Why is this? he asks. He goes on to complain that the other side also finds it easier to recruit forces. Why is *that?* he asks. Why do the communists seem to be having an easier time of it? he asks in conclusion. I think it is important not to forget this basic psychological fact of that moment of presidential transition. To Dwight Eisenhower, as to his successor John Kennedy, time seemed to be on the side of Soviet Communism. We were fighting an uphill battle.

It is increasingly difficult to put ourselves in that frame of mind, since the end of the Cold War. We see now that time was assuredly on the side of the West. But why did so many people in the American government in the late 1950s and early 1960s seem to feel that history was running against them in the global Cold War? John Lewis Gaddis, probably the leading historian of the Cold War, is about to publish a book that essentially concludes that by 1962 the West, including the United States, had won the Cold War in all of its essential aspects. From 1962 until 1989, says Gaddis, the actors were just playing out their hands. This was anything but obvious in 1959–1961. Back then, there was a severe crisis of confidence. This crisis was obviously a factor in the decision to authorize the Bay of Pigs operation. I would be interested to hear some of the former officials present talk about why that was the case. Why did they feel that it was necessary to take a risky action, one that also raised tough moral questions? In the February 11, 1961, memo from Arthur Schlesinger to the president, Arthur mentions the possibility of taking other measures and so the moral issue will be clouded.[2] The implication, as I understand it, is that the moral issue would be straightforward if the Bay of Pigs operation had stuck with the Trinidad option—the "guerrilla drop," as Jake Esterline described it. That would have been morally okay.

I want now to cite two documents that illustrate how central this issue of historical pessimism was. One is a memo from Arthur Schlesinger on March 15, 1961, referring to Tom Mann, in the State Department. Arthur writes:

> Tom Mann, on further consideration, has backed away from the idea of a demarche on free elections. He argues that the risk is too great that Castro might accept the challenge, stage ostensibly free elections, win by a large majority and thereafter claim popular sanction for his regime [Document 3.5].

Mann points out that for a truly free election, the Cubans would need a longer period of democracy: freedom of the press, etc. Arthur adds: "I agree with this view. It does seem to me that setting up free elections as a test might give Castro an opportunity to put on a show and recover prestige."

This remark is reminiscent of Eisenhower's refusal to sanction elections in Vietnam after the Geneva Conference in 1954. He feared that Ho Chi Minh would win, and win big, with as much as 80 percent of the vote. Was there a fear that even in a free and fair election, Fidel Castro would have won and won big? These issues appear in Senator Fulbright's memo to Kennedy just before the invasion. On page 7, he writes:

> The real question concerning the future of the Castro regime and its effect on the United States is whether Castro can in fact succeed in providing a better life for the Cuban people, in making Cuba a little paradise, a real pearl of the Antilles; and whether he can do a better job in this respect in Cuba than the United States and its friends can do elsewhere in Latin America. In all honesty, one should be wary of dogmatic answers on this point. But if one has faith in the human values of the United States, and if that faith is supported by vigorous and intelligent action, then there is no need to fear competition from an unshaven megalomaniac. To look at the other side of the proposition, it would be a fatal confession of lack of faith in ourselves and our values if we decreed that Castro must go because he might succeed.[3]

To what extent, I wonder, was the Bay of Pigs operation authorized out of fear of losing again, rather than out of—sort of—a feeling of enthusiasm, or a feeling that history is moving in our direction? Tom Mann in his memo also mentions that "possibly the best thing would be to just let Castro run Cuba into the ground and the application of communism will do more to discredit communism in the Western Hemisphere than the operation that was being proposed."[4] Was the operation authorized out of a fear that maybe things wouldn't turn out so bad for Fidel Castro and Cuba, if Fidel ran the country?

The second Cold War contextual issue I wanted to raise has to do with the Soviet reaction. Another way to look at the decisions Kennedy made to constrict the operation, to make less noise, might be this: that the Soviet Union successfully deterred the original plan for the invasion of Cuba. Now, I don't know for a fact that this is true, but it is interesting that as

Cuba is heating up, so is Berlin, so is the nuclear arms race, and so is the fiery rhetoric of Nikita Khrushchev. To what extent was Kennedy fearful of a Soviet reaction elsewhere in the world to a full-fledged American invasion of Cuba?

This is another case where Arthur Schlesinger's memos are very interesting. It appears that there was no serious analysis of how the Soviets would react to a success in overthrowing the Castro government. Arthur, in one of his memos, says that probably they won't do anything, and probably the Soviets are surprised that we haven't done away with Castro already, why we haven't rid ourselves of Castro.[5] I wonder what Oleg's reaction is to that remark. Did the Soviets *expect* the Americans to overthrow Castro? Would the overthrow have been passively accepted by Moscow? Or, would there have been some other reaction elsewhere in the world? It is interesting to note that Arthur, in *A Thousand Days,* reflected on this memo and suspected that he may have been wrong—that perhaps there would have been a Soviet reaction in West Berlin.[6] Would there have been an even more dangerous crisis in East-West relations had the Bay of Pigs operations succeeded?

There is yet another issue deriving from the Cold War context that I want to raise. It has to do with the sort of psychology and ideology of machismo in the Cold War. From the American standpoint, what happened at the Bay of Pigs can be read as deriving mainly from the fear of looking soft on communism. Obviously, for Democrats there was the possibility of this being exacerbated by the fear of attack from the right wing, the fear that they would be accused of not living up to campaign promises—in this case, to unseat Castro. But this fear seems to run deep, psychologically. I am quoting from *A Thousand Days:* "These memoranda look nice on the record, but they represented, of course, the easy way out. . . ."[7] It's hard to imagine a tenured college professor feeling shy about butting in—in any company. [Laughter.] But, Arthur goes on to say that he reproached himself for

> having kept silent during those crucial discussions in the Cabinet Room.
> . . . It is one thing for a Special Assistant to talk frankly in private to a President at his request and another for a college professor, fresh to the government, to interpose his unassisted judgment in open meeting against that of such august figures as the Secretaries of State and Defense and the Joint Chiefs of Staff.[8]

But then he gets into sort of an early form of deconstructionism and gender interpretation of language. [Laughter.] He says:

> Moreover the advocates of the adventure had a rhetorical advantage. They could strike virile poses and talk of tangible things—fire power, air

strikes, landing craft and so on. To oppose the plan, one had to invoke intangibles—the moral position of the United States, the reputation of the President, the response of the United Nations, "world public opinion" and other such odious concepts. These matters were as much the institutional concern of the State Department as military hardware was of Defense. But, just as the members of the White House staff who sat in the Cabinet Room failed in their job of protecting the President, so the representatives of the State Department failed in defending the diplomatic interests of the nation. I could not help feeling that the desire to prove to the CIA and the Joint Chiefs that they were not softheaded idealists but were really tough guys, too, influenced State's representatives at the cabinet table.[9]

This is the kind of issue that would never come up in a formal document. But that does not mean it is insignificant. I'd like to hear to what extent these personal, intangible, psychological factors were motivating you not to say no. Was it the fear of being seen as losing your nerve or being too soft on communism at a critical moment in your relationship to your peers? To what extent did those kind of factors matter?

Blight: Jim has done a terrific job of pointing us in the direction of some of the larger issues—issues that derive from the Cold War context in which all the events under scrutiny occurred. The documents in our briefing notebook are chock-full of the feeling that history was running against the United States and it was running fast. And what about the Soviets? Jim has shown that Cuban barbershops are not the only places in which counterfactuals can be spun off and considered. And the machismo issue, and the way it contributed to the momentum of the operation. I wonder if I could ask Arthur to reflect aloud on some of Jim's comments, to start off.

Schlesinger: On the feeling that history was running against us: there was an overreaction in the Kennedy administration to the Khrushchev speech of January 1961. Khrushchev made a speech a fortnight before Kennedy's inauguration. He predicted the irresistible victory for communism as a result of wars of national liberation in the Third World.[10] In retrospect, I think, that speech can best be understood as an effort to persuade the communist world that the Soviet Union was still the leader of the world revolution and not China. There are also passages in the speech in which Khrushchev talked about the impossibility of nuclear war. And that was designed to impress the United States with the fact that he believed in coexistence between the United States and Soviet Union. Naturally, Peking read that part of the speech which postulates coexistence, while Washington read that part of the speech which salutes wars of national liberation. We didn't understand what appears to me to be the real function of the speech, which was to settle some scores within the communist world.

As I say, there was definitely an overreaction. Kennedy had the speech reproduced and circulated to the members of the cabinet. And that set the tone for the exaggerated, hyperbolic language of the inaugural address.[11] Here, too, the speech can be read from several perspectives. On the one hand, he promises to fight every foe, help every friend, and so on. Then, on the other hand, he came out quite strongly in favor of negotiations: "We must never negotiate out of fear," he said, "but we must never fear to negotiate." That was more or less the state of mind, I suppose, in the background, as Kennedy took office.

Now, on Cuba: I believe Kennedy thought that Castro was the prize exhibit in Khrushchev's threatening vision of wars of national liberation. I think he thought this even though the Soviet Union had not, to any serious extent, committed itself to Castro. But I do not think this accounts for the Bay of Pigs. That kind of feeling was in the background, true. But Kennedy was trapped for other reasons. He inherited this project from Eisenhower. When he talked to Dulles about it, Dulles kept emphasizing what he called the "disposal problem." Dulles was telling Kennedy, between the lines, that if you cancel this venture it means that the 1,200 Cubans we have been training in Guatemala will disperse around Latin America, and they'll spread the word that the U.S. government has changed its policy toward Castro. This, in turn, will be a great stimulus to the *Fidelistas* throughout Latin America. The political impact of cancellation, Dulles implied, will be very serious for the balance of force in the hemisphere.

What Dulles did not add, but what Kennedy fully understood, was that the domestic political implications of Kennedy's cancellation of this expedition would be very considerable. For a lieutenant JG [junior grade] in the Navy in the Second World War to cancel an expedition that had been advocated, sanctioned, and supported by the general who commanded the largest successful amphibious landing in history, would have been hard to explain. I think that this was more important than anything else, that Kennedy felt trapped, having inherited the operation from Eisenhower. Kennedy's basic approach, from the moment he heard about the operation, was to try to do *something,* but as little as possible. He wanted a neat little infiltration that was plausibly deniable, but which had some chance of success.

It is clear in retrospect that Kennedy was seduced by Dick Bissell's smoothly persuasive estimation of how easy it would be to get from the Bay of Pigs up to the Escambray. It is inconceivable to me that Kennedy would have initiated such a project. But he inherited it, he couldn't get rid of it, and he was unhappy about it. Allen Dulles told Tom Wicker years later: "I should have realized that, if he [JFK] had no enthusiasm about the idea in the first place, he would drop it at the first opportunity, rather than do the things necessary to make it succeed."[12]

What would the Soviet Union have done if the United States had seriously tried to overthrow Castro? I'd be interested in what Oleg might have to say about this. I have always assumed that the Soviets expected us to go after Castro and must have thought it bourgeois weakness that prevented the United States from actually doing it. I don't think the Soviets wanted to commit too much to Castro at first, in part because of the fear that they would be exposed and would "lose" Cuba, if the United States really went after Fidel. As Oleg said, the massive aid to Cuba came after the Bay of Pigs.

It is often forgotten that Kennedy was not unsympathetic to Castro. You can easily be misled if you focus too narrowly on that single instance in the campaign that was discussed yesterday. Look in his book on foreign policy, which came out in 1960: *The Strategy of Peace*. He portrays Castro as "part of the legacy of Bolivar" and condemns Batista's "brutal, bloody and despotic dictatorship."[13]

The fear of sounding soft on communism was a very strong one. A liberal Democrat like Kennedy had to be constantly concerned with this issue. For there was massive inexperience in the people who thought they knew it all—and some of them came from Massachusetts. I am sure they *did* know it all at Harvard. [Laughter.] But in Washington, they did not have the institutional support that the people representing agencies or departments had. We did not serve Kennedy at all well. What we needed in that situation was someone like Robert Kennedy, being a less polite man than the president, but having sufficient status in the government to weigh in on questions of foreign policy. The president was not well served, neither did he serve himself well.

All of us—Kennedy and Bundy and the rest—were hypnotized by Dick Bissell to some degree, and assumed that he knew what he was doing. In this, Kennedy made a great mistake. One thing Kennedy learned was never again to take the CIA, or the Joint Chiefs of Staff, very seriously. I believe that saved us in future crises.

One final point. Few believed it—the CIA did not believe it—when Kennedy said that whatever happens, there will be no American military involvement. He meant it. They did not understand that he meant it. And I think the reason why we get all this crap from Bissell—melting into the Escambray and all that rubbish—was that Bissell believed the operation would have to succeed, no matter what. That is because once the invasion started, if it appeared to be faltering, then Kennedy would send in the marines. But Kennedy had no such intention. Kennedy would go to great lengths to avoid escalation of a crisis, especially a military crisis. He refused to escalate at the Bay of Pigs; he refused to escalate in the Berlin crisis; he refused to escalate in the Cuban missile crisis; and I am personally sure he would have refused to escalate in Vietnam, had he lived and been reelected. He was essentially a very cautious foreign-policy president. He used to say, "Never shove your opponent against a closed door." That was his guiding motto. Bissell and Dulles apparently didn't understand this and the country paid a terrible price for their willful misreading of the president. . . .

Blight: I want to call on Alfredo in a moment to talk about the invasion, including some discussion of the "what-ifs." I would also like Oleg to speculate briefly in a counterfactual way—give us any thoughts you might have about what the Soviet response, if any, would have been to an American-sponsored overthrow of Fidel Castro. Finally, I would like to open up a slightly different kind of discussion and ask members of the brigade and resistance what you thought of this new administration and its possibilities. But first, Oleg.

Daroussenkov: [Speaks in Spanish; Alfredo Durán translates into English.] In reality, to rewrite history is impossible. History is made and then it is commented on. It is difficult to speculate on historical processes. But I will try to do as Jim suggests. . . .

When the events of Playa Girón took place, this had an emotional impact on the Soviet Union in two ways. Some even felt that the timing was not a coincidence. Remember that just a few days before Playa Girón, a Soviet man was put into space for the first time.[14] And this was seen as a triumph for the Soviet Union and for the future of communism. But Khrushchev saw the events in Cuba as trying to take away the spotlight from these events. And Khrushchev got the news of the invasion on the day of his birthday, the 17th of April. [Laughter.] The shock was very strong. The Soviet leadership was in reality very concerned now about what was happening in Cuba. . . .

What would the Soviet Union have done if an invasion of Cuba had succeeded? Would the Soviet Union have acted and, if so, in what way? I mean, this question was not dealt with at the time, or afterwards. The missile crisis was a different story, of course. At that time, if the United States had invaded Cuba, I think Khrushchev would have had to order action somewhere, maybe in Berlin or Turkey. This has been discussed at the conferences on the missile crisis. But at the Bay of Pigs? I don't think the Soviet commitment was very strong at that point. In fact, it was the invasion at Playa Girón that most strengthened the Soviet-Cuban relations. This is the only thing I have to say.

Blight: That was useful. I appreciate Jim's stimulus and the responses of Arthur and Oleg. They have helped us to remember that the Bay of Pigs occurred in the context of the global Cold War between the United States and USSR. . . .

Schlesinger: May I say one more thing? Kennedy attached great importance to the possibility of uprisings behind the lines in Cuba. He always saw these as an important part of the package—defections from the militia, and so on. I looked up my notes on Cuba at the time and discovered that on Tuesday Kennedy, having seen a rather critical column by Scotty Reston of the *New York Times,* asked me to call Reston and bring him in for lunch at the White House. He also asked me to come to the lunch. That's three of us. Stewart Alsop, with whom I had had a drink at the Metropolitan Club before lunch, had argued that defeat would cause irreparable harm and that Kennedy had no choice but to intervene if necessary to avert disaster. But the president had already made up his mind on this. At the lunch with Reston, Kennedy said that the test had always been whether the Cuban people would back up a movement against Castro. If they wouldn't, we could not impose a new regime on them. The fact that there was no reaction after the exile landings, suggested—*proved* to Kennedy—that an American military invasion would have been a terrible idea.

. . . .

Esterline: Arthur, we've been going back and forth, and sifting and resifting this, and I want to say that I have learned a tremendous amount here in the last two days. I almost think I'm beginning to understand things a little bit. But there is a vital part missing. It is the memos of conversations between Bissell and JFK. They have to be somewhere, don't you think?

Smith: You think they were kept because Dick Bissell was so concerned . . .

Halpern: *If* anything was written down.

Schlesinger: Kennedy's emphasis on secrecy in this operation was very great. Kennedy said to me after the Bay of Pigs—he said, "I hope you have got notes on all of these meetings." And I said, "Well, I haven't, because I heard that there was not to be anything put on paper." He said, "Well, write it down as best you can. Put down whatever you can remember. In the future we must do that."

Esterline: It never occurred to me before that Dick Bissell might not be relaying what we were saying to Kennedy—what was so desperately vital to the success of this thing. And we—believe me—we didn't spell it out just once, we spelled it out every day as we went along.

. . . .

Baloyra: A question and a comment. The comment is about the business of being on the right or wrong side of history. And also the idea of there being one possible election to make or break the policy. I think that—excuse me—the idea that Castro could win was not scary in itself because committing to an election implied that there would be more elections. So if he were to win the first election, that would not be a problem. You can win one, two, three, but then what? You are going to lose someday. So it would have been a different dynamic, and I think that up to that point you could make an argument that elections did not make much difference in many Latin American countries. But Castro was a different matter, as the last 37 years have shown.

I can remember being in Berlin in 1962 and that was a heroic city. There was not a single American soldier there who ever had any doubt that if the Russians really meant business, and they moved, no one would survive. But I mean morale was just stratospheric. I mean there was no doubt—everyone who was there was there doing something significant. Alfredo said yesterday that there was no doubt on the part of the guys in the brigade that they were going to win. Maybe they believed this because they grew up watching John Wayne beat up on the Indians every time, or the Japanese, or whomever. Maybe there was a cultural thing there. But there was also the idea that we are in the right; I mean we are here to do the right thing and to do it well.

My question is this: Jake, you and Jack Hawkins go up to Bissell and say, "This thing smells, these men are going to be killed, and we want no part of this." In the gesturing and in the conversation that ensued and that at least persuaded you to stay on, or to . . .

Esterline: He solemnly promised us that he would never—he would go down fighting to prevent any further reduction in our air strikes. And the first damn thing that happened is the president said that it couldn't go on, as I understand it. The president said it couldn't go up to the level Bissell asked for. And it was Bissell himself—not Kennedy—who cut that strike in half. Dick said, "Well, we will go with eight. Is that acceptable?" But, my god, this was *not* acceptable to us! We would have, at that point—we would have said, "Listen, we can still stop this . . ."

Baloyra: But you think that, that—wait just a minute. In a sense, I see Kennedy and I see the forces around Kennedy. I see two men, so to speak, and they both look like Kennedy. On the one hand there is the New Frontier Kennedy, all of the promise of a new American foreign policy. On the other hand, there is the fraternity brother Kennedy—the cigar-smoking, tough, Irish war hero. I mean men at State could be looking at one man, men at the Pentagon could be looking at another, and Bissell could be thinking: if I put this guy in a situation where there will be a lot of pressure for him to get involved, he will not be able to resist. Because that side of him will be with us. And he will forget about the liberals like Arthur and the others.

Schlesinger: I agree with you. I think that Dickie Bissell was prepared to accept any reductions, any changes, in the plan so long as it went forward. He was convinced, I believe, that if it failed, military intervention would follow. But Bissell was wrong. Kennedy did not feel the need to prove himself, his manhood, by engaging in unnecessary conflict. He knew what war was like. It is the non–war heroes who feel that they have to prove their virility.[15]

Esterline: Arthur, there is something else that I don't understand. Bissell led me to believe that he had some kind of a special relationship with JFK. Now you say that wasn't so.

Schlesinger: No. They both had a very close friend in Joe Alsop. But Kennedy, though he was fond of Joe—well, I remember one day when there were contrasting columns, one by Joe Alsop and one by Walter Lippmann. Kennedy said to Mac Bundy and me: "Well, Walter's is much better than Joe's." He didn't like it that Joe was taking a very hard line. Then he said to us, "But you must never tell Joe I said this." [Laughter.]

. . . .

Daroussenkov: I think that the Guatemalan experience closes our eyes a little bit in our discussions. Because there was a great difference between Guatemala and Cuba. In Cuba the revolution was very well armed even without the arms that arrived later from the Soviet Union. The support that Fidel had was tremendous.

Esterline: That goes right back to my original plan. That's why I wanted to—to see just exactly whether the resistance, aided by our guerrillas, became viable. I didn't want to get my blood and soul, and my brothers' blood and souls, committed until I knew we had a chance to win, or at least make a go of it.

Daroussenkov: That's why I think that if the moment had arrived where the United States had intervened directly in the island—and here I apply the subjunctive—the United States could have easily found itself in a premature "Vietnam."

Blight: I wonder if we could back up to consider a question on the agenda about the perceptions among brigade members and among Cuban resistance members of this new administration, this group of people coming into office who were going to make the decisions that affected all of your lives. . . . Alfredo, do you recall thinking anything in particular about the new Kennedy administration and the way it might affect your own life as a member of the brigade?

Durán: Yes. Well, I became a lifelong Democrat because I liked Kennedy a lot and I still do. That is in spite of the Bay of Pigs, of course. [Laughter.] I think that to understand our psyche at that moment you have to understand a little bit of the makeup of the people who were involved in the brigade. The Cuban government generally categorizes the members of the brigade as mercenaries. There was not a single mercenary in the Bay of Pigs invasion force. The Bay of Pigs force was a cross section of Cuban society at that time. You had people who were ex–26th of July members. You had some ex-army people. You had some people who were in the anti-Batista opposition, and not necessarily 26th of July members. You had a lot of young people who were mainly coming out of the Catholic universities of Cuba. You had a lot of young professionals—upper-middle-class and middle-class people. It was really a cross section of Cuban society.

There was also a very strong Catholic undertone to the whole brigade. So much so, that our emblem was a cross surrounded by a Cuban flag. The brigade was a crusade. We were strongly anticommunist. We believed that the Cuban government was a communist government, and that it was heading toward a Stalinist-type dictatorship of a very closed society. There was tremendous fear in that group of what would happen to Cuba if the Stalinist leadership took over. Therefore, when Kennedy became president, there seemed to us to be a sort of breath of fresh air blowing at last in U.S. politics. I think it was the first time that most of us who were there were actually looking at what was happening in the United States politically, and what was happening in the context of the Cold War. I think it was the first time that we felt and we analyzed what the Cold War was all about. And the Cold War was all of a sudden focused on Cuba and we were involved in it. And part of our involvement was that we had to rescue Cuba from that Cold War environment. And Kennedy was hoping that could be done. He was Catholic, he was young, he was energetic, he was a leader. And we felt that he would not abandon us. We felt that his fight was our fight.

As I've told some of you, the Cuban government and some others have said that we worked for the CIA—that the CIA used us. I think that the feeling among the people in the brigade was that we were using the CIA, not the CIA using us; that we had a purpose and the purpose was going back to Cuba, to try to change our country and bring about a democratic movement. That was a feeling—a very strong feeling among the people in Cuba who were a part of the Cuban Revolution before being disillusioned, and turning against Fidel Castro. They thought that they had fought well against Batista and they had risked their life against Batista, and the revolution was not turning out the way they thought it was supposed to turn out. So there was a lot of idealistic feeling in the brigade. That is why we felt so strongly that we were going to win—because we thought that we were right, that we had the right on our side, we were morally correct in what we were doing, we were morally right and we were going to win because of that. We were, as I said, on a crusade.

In essence, we felt very good about the Kennedy administration. We thought that the United States was going to be our ally in this fight. And we were, like I said before, a group of young, very idealistic people and we saw in Kennedy and in the Kennedy administration just the same type of guys that we thought we were. And therefore we felt very comfortable with what was going to happen with our whole effort. And we felt, like I said before, that we were going to win.

Blight: Lino, Rafael, Quique: Any thoughts to add to what Alfredo has said about the Kennedy administration? Lino, you are now on the island, you are moving around undercover between the mountains and the cities, and then there is an election in November in the United States, the results of which would affect your life greatly. At the time, what did you think about this change in government?

Fernández: I remember the day of one of Kennedy and Nixon's debates before the election. I met with Manuel Artime for a half hour after the debate, and we talked about it. You know, Artime was a psychiatrist. We had gone through medical school together. And he told me that he had the impression that Kennedy was extremely ambivalent about the Cuban situation. *Ambivalent.* About the whole thing. And he didn't like that. You know this word has a special meaning in psychiatry and psychology. Artime told me that if he is going to be the next president, he will have severe troubles. That's reality. That was what I heard from him. . . .

I want to say something about the attitude of the people in Cuba at this time. Regarding our Russian colleague, Oleg, I respect your opinion. It is your opinion and we are gathered here to share our opinions. But let me tell you, you came to Cuba and you saw Cuba *after* the Bay of Pigs invasion, if

I remember correctly. Let me tell you, being *in* Cuba is different than being in the White House, or in the CIA headquarters, or being in the brigade in Guatemala, being trained in Guatemala, or being at the Russian Embassy in Havana. If you could have talked to the Cuban people freely in our country, you would have found out the truth: that the Cuban people were resisting what the government was doing to them.

. . . .

Gleijeses: I think what Mr. Fernández, Mr. Durán, and Mr. Baloyra are saying is very interesting and I am very glad to hear this. But I also hope we don't lose track of what really happened. The Bay of Pigs operation was not a cooperative arrangement between the United States and the Cuban Resistance. The Cubans who were involved in the Bay of Pigs were U.S. assets just like the Guatemalans who were involved in the covert operation against the government of Guatemala were U.S. assets. And what they thought is not even relevant. The plans were made by the United States. The leadership was selected by the United States. Those who were not happy were sent to prison camps and detained.[16] And the leadership was even put under house arrest, or whatever you want to call it, on the day of the invasion. So when we are talking about the Bay of Pigs, we are talking about U.S. aggression against Cuba, just like we were talking about Guatemala before.

. . . .

Domínguez: Yes, I have a footnote, but before the footnote just a comment on what Piero just said. I agree with your characterization, Piero, but we also should remember why the CIA plan failed. It failed because this was not a cooperative venture.

Gleijeses: It should not offend anyone to say what it was—it was a case of U.S. aggression, just like Guatemala.

Domínguez: But this is one of the reasons why it failed. The other point is a footnote. It came up yesterday and it came up again today. It is about Catholicism. I agree strongly that there was an important Roman Catholic element to the resistance, and to participation in the brigade. In fact, as a personal anecdote, I remember well my first political activity in life in this regard. The time is February of 1959 and I am an eighth-grader, organizing a group of fellow eighth-graders for a street demonstration. This was still legal. You would not get beaten up at that time. We were protesting a bill regulating a variety of aspects of education. It was very much a Roman

Catholic political activity. And there were many other similar activities in that period.

But, just as this was a strong source of commitment and support, it was also a very strong limitation. Yesterday, Lino was talking about a core group and then a support base. It is important to remember that Cuba really was not, in any meaningful sense, a Roman Catholic country. I agree that it is important that Artime was a Catholic. As I said, this was for real as opposed to the more typical Catholic in Cuba. In the late 1950s in Cuba, only between 20 to 25 percent of Cuban adults ever went to church on Sunday. This was not a Roman Catholic country and, to the extent that this was a Roman Catholic movement, that in fact limited its political appeal and its political support. So it was a source of core commitment but it was also a limitation on its broad impact.

. . . .

Baloyra: I agree that the problem is from the people who were sent out to get proficient at certain things—useful skills—and then came back into Cuba, but then were kept totally clueless as to this black hole that the brigade became. But the fact that the brigade was American armed, controlled, etc., does not mean there was no resistance. You ought to remember, Piero, that Mr. Castro is not Cuba. I mean, it was not aggression against Cuba. I had relatives who drowned in 1896 as part of an expedition to run arms against the Spanish colony in Cuba. And the Spaniards could have said this is aggression, and this is a violation of international law, and this is a violation of U.S. neutrality, and we could say—or the old boy could have said before he went under—who the hell cares?

The principle that we are trying to establish here is that up until now, there have been three voices speaking to the events we have been talking about: about the handwriting on the wall in the White House; the high hopes at the camps in Guatemala; and the apprehension in Havana about when the Americans are going to come, or where in Cuba they are going to come. But we say there was a fourth voice, that of the resistance. I for one do not contend that it is the most important and that the other voices are less important. What I am saying is that unless you bring that fourth voice into the conversation you don't understand a hell of a lot of the things that happened.

As we have just heard, the proof of the pudding in the plan from the standpoint of the test of wills between Bissell and Kennedy was: Will there be an uprising in Cuba? The day after the invasion began there were 50,000 people in Havana alone who could not participate in a damn thing because they were under "preventive detention." Okay? The fact that the site of the invasion was isolated prevented anyone who would have wanted to join from going there in the first place. Alfredo and his comrades could blow anything out of the highway that they were covering, trying to protect the beach. Now imagine a bunch of teenagers, you know, in a Chevy, trying to reach that same beach. It wouldn't have been a very likely prospect. So in that sense—in the sense that Alfredo was just discussing—it was *not* an American aggression against Cuba. Sure, it was a violation of international law, and you can get 1,700 priests with their covenants to swear to it.

But it was something else, too, something tragic. And the most tragic aspect of it is that it overwhelmed whatever *Cuban* authenticity you could have claimed for a Cuban opposition that would have been willing to say: okay, we agree with the basic objectives of revolution but we don't think only one guy should be making the decisions. After the Bay of Pigs, it was a moot point. And there were many people whom I admire a great deal who insisted on trying, who kept on trying, to make their point, but after the Bay of Pigs it was futile to try to convince anyone in Cuba that anything other than what the brigade was saying was the right way to go. Fidel said, "They will come," and they came. He was right about that. But he was wrong about who came. He said: "There will be *Batistianos* in the invasion." Of course Alfredo was not a *Batistiano*. The people in the brigade were not. But try telling that to the Cuban people after April 1961, after Fidel had convinced them otherwise.

Durán: I agree. Fidel played that card to the fullest extent. But we were neither *Batistianos* nor mercenaries. That is a fact.

Baloyra: By the way, like Alfredo, I am also a Kennedy Democrat, which is why American politics have always seemed a little bit fishy to me. [Laughter.]

Smith: I hope you vote. [Laughter.]

Halpern: And vote more than once, too.

Blight: This has stimulated a long list of proposed interventions, beginning with Tom [Blanton], here to the left of all you Kennedy Democrats. [Laughter.] But before opening it up, I would like to register a puzzlement that I have. I remember the first time I went to Cuba I learned that the favorite former U.S. president in Cuba is none other than John Kennedy. This didn't make sense to me. I mean: the Bay of Pigs, MONGOOSE, the missile crisis—and they *like* this guy? But I now confess that the Cuban attachment to Kennedy seems positively rational compared to the Kennedy endorsements I have just heard from Alfredo and Quique. I understand even less why you were and are Kennedy Democrats. What a guy. He can invade you and you love him. And he can abandon you and you love him. His approval ratings are airtight, it seems to me. [Laughter.]

Baloyra: Kennedy went back to Miami in December of 1962, to the Orange Bowl, and made a speech in front of 60,000 delirious Cubans. He drove into the stadium—well, I admit it was not an ordinary car, but anyway. I was standing on the corner. I remember that I saluted the car. He was close to me—just from here to where Piero is. . . .

Blanton: John F. Kennedy appears to have been an empty vessel into which people put their own hopes or fears. . . . There has been mention of the 100,000 or so people rounded up when the invasion started. I had a great conversation last night with Rafael, who was one of those rounded up. But one of my colleagues reminded me last night that the United States rounded up something like 100,000 people in 1941, right after the bombs started falling on Pearl Harbor. According to recent historical reassessments, almost none of those Japanese-Americans who were detained were part of any kind of resistance or conspiracy.

I think that one of the factual questions that still remain is how many people actually were rounded up. Because of the tremendous work that Lino has done, bringing out these documents, we know a lot more about the resistance than ever before. But there is, I think, still an issue that we need to take up in Cuba: we need the actual numbers used by the Ministry of the Interior. And what about those 100,000 or so people: How many of them stayed in prison; how many were shot, like friends of Rafael; how many of them, like Rafael, walked away in a few weeks?

. . . .

Skidmore: One thing that strikes me about all of this discussion is that nobody is asking what the nature of the Cuban Revolution was, or the movement that Fidel led. We are talking about how many men, which sites, whether they were guerrillas or whether it is an amphibious invasion, and lots of details like that. But the reason these events constituted a real crisis here in the United States is that we found ourselves dealing with a nationalist movement of the kind that turns out to be a great puzzle to us.

Cuba is a classic case study of this nationalist phenomenon. There is a lot of U.S. property that has been seized in Cuba, and the Americans are not going to get their damn money back. And Fidel's great plans for social reform such as the literacy campaign—whatever you may think of this, it figures into this episode—because in the very area of the Bay of Pigs there had been a very intensive effort to launch the literacy campaign. So that a lot of people in that area were highly politicized. What I'm driving at is that one of the problems in determining whether there is support for overthrowing the government is how to make an assessment of the nature of the government and of the movement that it represents.

To belabor the obvious: Cuba is _not_ like Guatemala! David Atlee Phillips described the Guatemala operation as a comic opera. He just put up a phony radio station and they all danced. And you hire one P-54 to fly over Guatemala City, Arbenz panics, and that's about it. Now, in the case of Cuba, the question is: What is the nature of this creature—this Cuban Revolution—that we are facing, that we say we want to get rid of? I am sure there was real opposition. That is obvious in these documents and from what some of you have said. People could see the authoritarian nature of the regime coming. But the real appeal of this regime is nationalistic.

And so, understanding none of this, the United States sends in a force organized out of Langley to try to get rid of it, rather like they got rid of Arbenz in Guatemala. But because this is fundamentally a nationalist movement, the invasion is a gift of the gods for those like Fidel who are trying to consolidate their power. From all of which I conclude that Richard Bissell was a Cuban agent. [Laughter.]

Halpern: Tom, did you know Jim Angleton? [Laughter.]

Kornbluh: I would like to remind everyone of the encounter in Uruguay at which Ché Guevara introduced himself to Richard Goodwin by saying, "Thank you so much for the Bay of Pigs." And all Goodwin could think of to say in return was, "You're welcome." [Laughter.][17]

Daroussenkov: With respect to Lino's very interesting remarks, I am glad that Tom touched on the nationalistic character of the revolution. I wanted to touch on that aspect, in any event. In the concrete conditions of Cuba at that moment, any movement against Fidel Castro—whether intended or not, for many, I would say for the majority—any resistance to Fidel would have to be tied to the United States and that would mean it would be perceived as antinationalist. This is a psychological and political factor that is very important. Second, it is true that for a foreigner and especially for a diplomat, it is very difficult to fully integrate with the population of the country. It is also true that after the Bay of Pigs, the situation in Cuba changed a great deal. . . .

I used to ride on the buses from one place to the other just to listen to the people. I would not even speak. And I don't have to explain to you that the bus in Cuba is a political club. [Laughter.] I used to travel all over the island: Cuba is not big, and in half a day, or a day, I could travel half the island. I would stop next to a farmer's house to ask for water, to ask for some coconut water. And I would speak with the people. In these conversations, I tried to follow the advice Ché Guevara gave me: that if you wanted to understand what was going on in Cuba, you don't want to be just in Havana, you have to go to the interior. That is where this real Cuba is. Not always would I say that I was Soviet. I preferred not to mention that I was a Soviet, unless they asked me directly.

Skidmore: We say we are Canadian. [Laughter.]

Daroussenkov: And to tell you the truth I . . . I have to tell you that I found that, probably around 95 percent of the population were enchanted with what was happening in Cuba. I know that Lino will disagree with this. But that is what the situation looked like to me.

. . . .

Smith: I want to go back to one of the questions that Jim [Hershberg] posed a while back and see if it helps tie some things together. I think there was a sense by 1961—certainly among a lot of young officers or young people in the U.S. government—that we were placing ourselves on the wrong side of history in the Cold War. That had not been the case initially. During the first years of the Cold War, we courageously faced the Stalinist dictatorship. In so doing, we raised the odds that no country in the world would choose to follow that model voluntarily. The only countries that had become Marxist-Leninist outside of the Soviet Union were in Eastern Europe. And they had no choice. They were, functionally, occupied countries—occupied by the Soviet Union.

Furthermore, we had the moral high ground in Europe, as it were, with the Marshall Plan. Moreover, Stalin had no interest whatsoever in the Third World. He regarded the emerging countries as either colonialist agents or beyond the control of the Soviet Union and so had no interest in them. It is not until Khrushchev—until Stalin is dead—that the Soviet leadership sees real possibilities in the Third World. By the late 1950s, Khrushchev began to speak of these countries as changing the balance of forces in the world in favor of the socialist camp. Why? Because emerging countries tended to be anticolonialist. Most of them had been colonies and they were throwing off the imperialist yoke. And to this we, the United States and the West in general, did not have a very satisfactory answer.

Suddenly we didn't own the moral high ground anymore. I remember at the time, you'd see these films of a spreading black stain of communism—which was supposed to have been red, but we are talking abut a time and place prior to color films. [Laughter.] During the same period, I well remember a speech given by John Foster Dulles before the Senate Foreign Relations Committee in which he described [Venezuelan dictator Marcos]

Pérez Jiménez—this absurd little caricature of a military dictator—as a "democrat." He was indeed the kind of "democratic" leader we liked to see in those days all over Latin America. All any thug had to be was anticommunist and in charge and Washington would call him a great "democrat." Our action in Guatemala in 1954 was a perfect example of this. There was a sense, I think, among American leaders and the American establishment, that if hard questions of governance were put directly to the people to decide, they might make the wrong choice.

Another young foreign service officer said to me at the time, "You know, the most powerful and endearing force in the world since the Western enlightenment has been the egalitarian movement. And we, in reaction to the Cold War challenge, are placing ourselves on the wrong side of history." I've always remembered that. There was disillusionment within the foreign service, I know, because of this. In a sense, we didn't allow ourselves to win, because we didn't practice what we preached, at least not in the Third World. . . .

But then, my god, along came the Kennedy administration. I must say that listening to Kennedy's inauguration speech was a very moving experience. All of a sudden here was an American president who understood that we were putting ourselves on the wrong side of history and we had to change. I felt the same way Alfredo felt and Quique felt about Kennedy.

Because of this, I can understand the frustration on the part of the representatives here of the internal resistance and the brigade to the fact that they were, as Piero said, treated as "assets," rather than partners by the U.S. government. Again, our analysis in the embassy in Havana—and I think it was correct—was that the internal opposition really did not have the capability of overthrowing the Cuban government at that time. But nonetheless, if there was to be a change in Cuba, if it was to be an authentic change, and if it was to have the force of nationalism behind it, then the best thing we could do was to support the internal resistance because it was really our only viable option. And I suspect that had Kennedy been president in 1959 as things developed, that's the way we would have gone and that the plans for the Bay of Pigs never would have been approved—that they would not have gone forward.

I can understand why, as Alfredo has said, he felt that Kennedy was somehow like them. They felt a kinship with Kennedy. So did many in the opposition. And rightly so. Because Kennedy did represent a new force in American politics, a new way of looking at things. Unfortunately, the Kennedy administration came into office just a little too late for it to make rational decisions regarding what became the Bay of Pigs fiasco. Kennedy was trapped, as Arthur said.

Blight: Thank you, Wayne, for what I thought was a very helpful synthesis of many parts of today's discussion. . . . I will . . . turn first to Jorge, and then to Peter for the valedictory.

Domínguez: I want to go back to the exchange between Oleg and Lino a moment ago because I think it is important and because, to some degree, you are also creating a record that will contribute to our understanding of these events. I don't want Oleg to be the only person here to have endorsed the view that Fidel Castro, at that time, was overwhelmingly popular with the majority of Cubans. So I want to add my own judgment: that Fidel Castro's government was very popular at the beginning of 1961; that it would have won an election if an election had been held; and that the degree of support for the government was overwhelming, so that, if an election would have been held, it would have won very big. This is in addition to its capacity to repress and control. It was a very popular government. That's one point.

The second point is that I actually don't think that Lino or Quique or Jake should disagree with this assessment. I think that if we fully absorb what is in these resistance documents, and we listen carefully to why Jake wanted his guerrilla plan, we can see that the fundamental reason is that the Castro government *was* popular, *was* strong. That is why Lino and his colleagues were working for the long term; they knew that in early 1961 they would lose. I don't think there should be any disagreement that this was an enormously popular leader. That's why I began yesterday by quoting Richard Nixon, who also believed that Castro was a spectacular political leader. This point should not be overlooked when we are looking at the reasons why the invasion failed, and I did not want Oleg to be the only person to point this out.

Fernández: I agree with you, totally.

Baloyra: In Guatemala, the CIA won by emphasizing the political side and getting away with minimal military stuff. The Bay of Pigs was the opposite. All the concern was military, military. The operation lacked political sensitivity from beginning to end—I mean in terms of the situation in Cuba.

. . . .

Kornbluh: Arthur, you said just a few minutes ago that in retrospect you felt you needed "a Robert Kennedy" on your side—a vocal, credible, powerful advocate. But in fact wasn't it Robert Kennedy who more or less told you between April 5 and April 10 to "put up or shut up"?[18] And didn't you then change your position on paper? I agree that the new administration found itself in a trap with regard to doing *something* along the lines developed by the Eisenhower administration. But I wonder if we may have given John and Robert Kennedy too much benefit of the doubt here.

Schlesinger: What happened was that Robert Kennedy had nothing to do with the Bay of Pigs. He never came to any of the meetings. In April, he got a briefing from Dick Bissell that I think he was rather skeptical about. He then talked to his brother about it, and he felt that his brother was determined to go ahead.

Basically, he told me: "The president has decided to go ahead and there is no point in upsetting him further by continuing to raise questions about this." It seemed to me a reasonable point. This decision had been made, and there was no further point in pressing arguments against it. From that point on, my negative memos would only be irritating. It was my job simply to accept the president's decision, so that is what I did.

Notes

1. See, for example, the notes of the meeting by Clark Clifford in Leslie H. Gelb, ed., *The Pentagon Papers,* 4 vols., Gravel Edition (Boston: Beacon Press, 1971), vol. II, pp. 635–637.

2. For example, Arthur Schlesinger, in his memorandum to the president of 11 February 1961, asks whether it might not be possible to "lure Castro into sending a few boat loads of men onto a Haitian beach in what could be portrayed as an effort to overthrow the Haitian regime?" See Appendix 5, Document 3.3.

3. J. William Fulbright, "Cuba Policy," Memorandum to the President, 29 March 1961, p. 7.

4. Thomas Mann, "The March 1960 Plan," Memorandum to Secretary of State Dean Rusk, 15 February 1961.

5. See Schlesinger, "Cuba," Memorandum for the President, 5 April 1961: "My guess is that the Soviet Union regards Cuba as in our domain and is rather surprised that we have not taken action before this to rid ourselves of Castro" (p. 2).

6. Arthur Schlesinger Jr., *A Thousand Days: John F. Kennedy in the White House* (New York: Fawcett, 1965), p. 237.

7. Ibid., p. 239.

8. Ibid.

9. Ibid., pp. 239–240.

10. Khrushchev's speech was only one of the better-known versions of Khrushchev's nascent enthusiasm for "wars of national liberation," which he began propounding in late 1960. He stated in the January 1961 speech referred to by Schlesinger:

> Liberation wars will continue to exist as long as imperialism exists, as long as colonialism exists. These are revolutionary wars. Such wars are not only admissible but inevitable, since the colonialists do not grant independence voluntarily. . . .
> What is the attitude of the Marxists toward such uprisings? A most positive one.

Cited in James A. Nathan and James K. Oliver, *United States Foreign Policy and World Order,* 2d ed. (Boston: Little, Brown, 1981), p. 254.

11. Theodore C. Sorensen, who drafted a good deal of Kennedy's inaugural address, says that the president-elect wanted to avoid "any weasel words that Khrushchev might misinterpret." Theodore C. Sorensen, *Kennedy* (New York: Harper & Row, 1965), p. 240. See also p. 634 for a discussion of the way Khrushchev's enthusiasm for "wars of national liberation" played on Kennedy's mind as he came to office in January 1961.

12. Arthur Schlesinger Jr., *Robert Kennedy and His Times* (New York: Ballantine, 1978), p. 488.

13. See Sorensen, *Kennedy,* p. 205, for an authoritative interpretation of Kennedy's views of Castro as he came to office.

14. The Soviet cosmonaut Yuri Gagarin became the first person to circle the Earth on 18 April 1961.

15. Richard Bissell spent World War II in Washington, D.C., working for the Shipping Adjustment Board. His job was to ensure the U.S. Merchant Marine ships were loaded and sent on time to the various theaters of war. As Evan Thomas points out, one virtue of this job, aside from its compatibility with Bissell's high aptitude for quantitative analysis, was that the job was "draftproof." *The Very Best Men: Four Who Dared* (New York: Simon & Schuster, 1995), pp. 94–95.

16. In January 1961, a mutiny broke out and more than 500 brigade members quit. Order was eventually restored. But see Arthur Schlesinger Jr., *A Thousand Days*: "In one of the unhappier passages in this whole unhappy story, the CIA operatives arrested a dozen of the ringleaders and held them prisoner under stark conditions deep in the jungle of northern Guatemala" (p. 222).

17. According to Goodwin: "Guevara began by saying he wished to thank us for the Bay of Pigs. I said he was welcome. Their hold on the country had been a bit shaky, he explained, but the invasion allowed the leadership to consolidate most of the major elements of the country behind Fidel." Richard Goodwin, *Remembering America: A Voice from the Sixties* (Boston: Little, Brown, 1988), p. 199.

18. According to Schlesinger: "Robert Kennedy drew me aside. He said, 'I hear you don't think much of this business.' He asked why and listened without expression as I gave my reasons. Finally he said, 'You may be right or you may be wrong, but the President has made his mind up. Don't push him any further. Now is the time for everyone to help him all they can.'" *A Thousand Days,* p. 243.

4

Assassination and the Use of U.S. Military Force at the Bay of Pigs

I have been a skeptic about Bissell's operation, but now I think we are on the edge of a good answer. I also think that Bissell and Hawkins have done an honorable job of meeting the proper criticisms and cautions of the Department of State.

> *McGeorge Bundy to John F. Kennedy, 15 March 1961 [Document 3.4]*

Bissell's memoir and these discussions make me realize that Dick just wasn't—I don't think he was being honest. I don't think he was being honest up—I mean with Kennedy and maybe with Dulles, too; and I don't think he was being honest down—in dealing with his two principal aides, Esterline and Hawkins. I don't believe he was leveling with any of us.

> *Jacob Esterline, 1 June 1996*

Blight: One of the topics on the docket for the previous session was plots to assassinate Fidel Castro—as an instrument of U.S. foreign policy. But we didn't get to it. So I would like to take a few minutes at the outset in this session to discuss it. Peter has some provocative comments he would like to put to one or two of our participants. Let's take no more than 15 minutes on it. After that, I'll ask Phil Brenner to introduce the next topic on the agenda: this issue of the use of U.S. military forces at the Bay of Pigs.

Kornbluh: In some ways, the most inexpensive way from a paramilitary point of view to overthrow the Cuban government in 1961 would have been to get rid of its charismatic leader, Fidel Castro. Without him, according to many CIA estimates at the time, the revolution would have collapsed and the brigade and resistance forces could have taken over. As early as December of 1959, J. C. King, head of the CIA's Western Hemisphere division, wrote that thorough consideration be given to the *elimination* of Fidel Castro. None of those close to Fidel such as his brother Raúl or his companion Ché Guevara have the same mesmeric appeal to the masses. Many informed people believe that the disappearance of Fidel would greatly accelerate the fall of the present government.[1]

Both Sam Halpern's name and Jake Esterline's name appear on numerous Church Committee notes about the now infamous cockamamie schemes, and a few serious ones, to assassinate Fidel Castro.[2]

The question that I would like to see addressed is whether there was a separate assassination track that was coordinated with, or was supposed to be coordinated with, the invasion at the Bay of Pigs. To be specific: Is it possible that Bissell had something like this in the back of his mind; that the Mafia would kill Fidel just prior to the invasion itself? Therefore, even if he was forced to reduce air cover, and in other ways to reduce the scope of the operation at the landing site, Bissell's plan might still possibly succeed.

We do know that there were two Mafia-linked assassination efforts prior to the Bay of Pigs. We've also come across a recently released document in the Kennedy assassination archives.[3] And a good deal had been summarized previously in the 1975 Church Committee report. In the report, we discover that the CIA—that Jake—received cables from Cuba two weeks before the invasion discussing a specific assassination effort against Fidel. Fidel was to make a speech at the Sports Palace on April 9. You had an agent—whose code name was NOTLOX—in Cuba who was sending messages back to you, through an agent presumably in Florida, named Bell. These messages were mainly requests for machine guns, Springfield rifles with telescopic sights, and things of that nature.

On March 27 this agent in Cuba, agent NOTLOX, wrote a message that was passed on to the CIA. It said: "We are going to sabotage the electrical company in order to leave Havana ten days without power. We can coordinate with an attempt against Fidel in public appearance at the Sports Palace. Suggest attempt against Fidel in accordance with general plan." Another cable came two days later, also from agent NOTLOX: "Fidel will talk at the Palace. Assassination attempt at said place followed by general shutting off of main electrical plants in Havana, Vedado, etc. We have sufficient men and courage, state of mind desperate, impossible to endure this longer, we can blow up any electrical company at any time. Consider what this represents for us after the action." These messages all arrived within a week of another cable on April 5 from agent NOTLOX, and in a similar vein.

I wonder, Jake, if you have any information about this sequence of cables and, in general, about any thought that may have been given to the coordination of assassination attempts, sabotage of the power plants around

Havana, and the invasion at the Bay of Pigs. I would also like to ask Rafael Quintero what he can tell us about the efforts focused on Agent NOTLOX.

Esterline: I don't have any clear recollection. But we were getting messages from an agent in Cuba. My recollection is that we thought the guy must have been captured and turned and he was being played back into us to get us to do something that would put things like arms in their hands.[4] That is the only thing I can think of in that context.

Let me explain what—what I knew of the development of this whole thing. I had a huge budget in those years starting in 1958, '59, and '60. But over all the years I ran things, I always had my own auditors, my own staff, and I never once challenged how that money was being spent. And I had a strict limit on the amount of money that could be spent, without my personal approval. Then, maybe in '59–'60, I suddenly started getting big requests—one was for $75,000 and that other was for a big amount of money—it was blank. And I wouldn't sign, and then I called King and he said I had to sign. I said: "J. C., I am not going to sign those unless I know what I am signing." He said: "Well, you are not cleared for it." I said: "Well, then, I guess maybe you had better get somebody else to head the project because I am not going to sign it."

So to my consternation I got myself briefed on what you are talking about now. I looked at J. C. and I said: "J. C., I really can't believe what I am hearing." He said: "Well, this is for real and this is going, and you're briefed and I have to have that money." And that was the beginning and the end of my knowledge. One of our journalistic colleagues who came to interview me a couple of years ago said to me: "You were never in that loop, were you Jake? They didn't trust you." And Christ, I guess that's right, I wasn't in the loop. But I knew it existed and I knew who the basic characters were. That was the beginning and end. I did have to sign and I passed maybe a couple hundred thousand dollars. I don't remember exactly how much now. But beyond that, I never knew what they were up to and I didn't even tell Hawkins, because the thing that bothered me about it is that if you are a soldier, you don't like to think in those terms, and I was a soldier, and so was Jack. I didn't even know that Bissell had been briefed on it. And, apparently he was more than briefed. Apparently he was one of the driving forces behind it.[5] But I didn't know that.

I'll tell you what really bothers me about this. This stupid cockamamie idea may well have compromised serious support and backing of the brigade operation that was the main event, or should have been. I mean: Who knows what Bissell was thinking, after all we have read in this notebook, and all we have heard here? Maybe he didn't even care much whether my people made it or not. Anyway, that one briefing—that was the beginning and ending for me. I was never briefed again beyond that. . . .

Kornbluh: This is important. As head of the task force of the Bay of Pigs operation, part of your budget was being diverted to an assassination track?

Esterline: That's correct. That's correct. I don't think it exceeded $200,000, but I am really not sure at this point. J. C. King and I were in the trenches together for many, many years and that was really the only falling out we had. And this is what bothers me. I didn't know what the hell the $200,000 was being used for, but I could be pretty sure that it was doing the main plan no good. It would diminish—it would diminish attention from the invasion plan.

. . . .

Schlesinger: It should be pointed out that the assassination project was initially an integral part of the invasion scheme.

Kornbluh: How so?

Schlesinger: Howard Hunt, who was billed as political coordinator at this early point of the operation, in recommendations to Bissell in May 1960 listed, "first, assassinate Castro before or coincident with the invasion. . . . Without Castro to inspire, the Rebel Army and the *milicia* would collapse in leaderless confusion."[6] And Bissell himself told Michael Beschloss that assassination was intended to reinforce the plan.[7] There was the thought that Castro would be dead before the landing. Later, the Mafia became associated with the plan when [Robert] Maheu brought in [Sam] Giancana and [Johnny] Rosselli. . . .[8]

Kornbluh: But you were not aware of this?

Schlesinger: No.

. . . .

Kornbluh: Rafael, can you talk about this NOTLOX plot?

Quintero: Yeah, I was part of that plot, that specific plan, and the plan was a casualty of the political fighting in Miami. There was going to be a big fight, a big boxing match, and we knew Castro was going to be present. And we planned it to have him hit with a bazooka. There were two organizations that had been fighting at that time in the CIA and in Miami for the backing—the right to go ahead with the plan. The MRP was supposed to be a more progressive organization than the MRR. Both sides wanted to do it;

both wanted to claim the success of this operation. They both were selling the same plan to the United States.

We were trying to make radio contact with the CIA, both MRR and MRP. But at a given moment, one of the radios—our radio—the MRR radio—*my* radio to be more specific—received a different order that was not in accordance with the overall plan to go ahead. We were told not to do it. And they allowed the MRP to go ahead with the plan. That is why they were asking for weapons. We already had our own weapon for this operation. It was a bazooka. The MRP was asking for all kinds of weapons to do it. But the MRP not only didn't have the weapons, they also didn't have the capability or the people to do it. The CIA needed to understand that the MRP really didn't have an organization capable of mounting anything big in the underground in Cuba. They couldn't do it. We were told not to do it; and they *couldn't* do it! That was the reason that the operation was not ever done.

Esterline: Rafael, do you remember: Was Howard Hunt in place in Miami at that time?

Quintero: Yes. Yes, he was. He was probably the one who decided not to let us go ahead with it, and to let the MRP do it. I don't know for sure. I don't know who answered . . .

Esterline: We were in and around at that time. As far as I remember, we knew that you-all were running the radios. So we had—we were very careful about what we—how we reacted to these things one way or the other. But there we are. . . .

Blight: The agenda for this session also deals with the subject that is probably the number one Bay of Pigs counterfactual among all the people I have talked to in Miami: What if the United States had backed up the brigade with military force? There are many views, some incompatible with one another, about what the United States was or was not prepared to do, what it had pledged to do, could have done or should have done at the Bay of Pigs with regard to air power and backup invasion forces. This is a big subject, and an important one, because of the feeling shared by some that a small U.S. intervention here or there would have, or might have, made the difference between the humiliation that was suffered, and the victory that was expected—as Alfredo mentioned earlier this morning. Phil, would you start us off?

Brenner: Well, as you said Jim, the military aspect of the history of the Bay of Pigs has probably gotten the most attention. So I will start with the military issues. But several other questions also arise, and I will try to be provocative about those, too.

Probably the aspect that has gotten the most attention is the question of air strikes. There is general agreement that the lack of a second air strike, and cutting back the first air strike, was decisive. The Taylor Commission says that, Bissell says that—the piece we got from Hawkins says that quite succinctly—"air power was the key," said Hawkins.[9] It was the key and it wasn't there when it was needed.

There were other military problems as well. For example, the boats didn't have any antiaircraft capability because it was assumed that, with air power, the Cuban air force would be knocked out, and therefore there was no need for antiaircraft on the boats. That was a mistake. Had the *Houston* had some antiaircraft, it might have been able to shoot down the Sea Fury that hit it. . . .[10]

A second element of the military question is the question of Cuba. It is striking that there has been so little discussion until near the end of the last session about Cuba itself. It is a little bit like keeping Cuba out of the Cuban missile crisis. What were the preparations like in Cuba? Colonel Hawkins says: "These activities were conducted with all possible secrecy, but I did not doubt that Castro knew what was going on from his agents in Miami and in the countries of Central America."[11]

Just to confirm Hawkins's intuitions, let me read to you a brief excerpt from Fidel Castro's speech at the time of the buildup toward the invasion. He makes it clear that he knew something was going on. This is from a speech on April 8, 1961. It's to a group of people who are preparing for the May Day demonstrations.

> We believe that the Central Intelligence Agency has absolutely no intelligence at all, because if it were intelligent it would not have sent us as many weapons as it has lately. If it were intelligent it would have realized that most of the times those who were waiting for the arms to be dropped were our militiamen. If it were so intelligent, it would not have had so many illusions. Really none of them, the Central Intelligence Agents, are intelligent. They should be called the Central Agency of Yankee Cretins. [Laughter.] For months the Central Agency of Yankee Cretins has been preparing on the soil of Guatemala and the soil of other countries ruled by puppets of imperialism, military bases and armies of mercenaries to attack our country.[12]

He concludes by saying: "When they place a foot here—something Miró Cardona will not do, for he knows what he is doing—they will learn the fury of the people who will fall upon them."[13]

This simple point is Colonel Hawkins's point: there was knowledge about the preparations for an invasion. So since the United States was aware that Castro knew of these preparations, how was that taken into account in the military planning that then went forward? Fidel Castro told Tad Szulc that the Cuban military was divided into three tactical regional units, and that the eastern unit, the one in Oriente, was headed by Raúl Castro.[14] My own sense is that Fidel would have put as the head of the most important unit, Raúl Castro. The others were headed by Ché Guevara and Juan Almeida. Did this mean that the Cubans believed that the invasion was coming from the east, not in the south central region?

Esterline: That's possible.

Brenner: Why might the Cubans have believed this? It raises questions, for example, about [the U.S. naval base at] Guantánamo. There are indications here that there was a unit preparing to land there as a diversion.[15] But nothing has been said here about the use to which the U.S. naval base in Guantánamo would be put. What was to be its role in helping to ensure the success of the invasion?

That leads to a third kind of question. There has been very little written and very little discussion about what is sometimes called Phase 2 and Phase 3. That is to say, what happens after the actual invasion? Bissell's writing and the Taylor Commission report's views on Phase 2 and Phase 3 paint a scenario of very dubious likelihood. They read like fantasies or fairy tales. Let me read to you from Bissell. He says: "Well, Hawkins' view was that Phase 2 would involve the defensive ground action, gain a firm hold on the beachhead and simultaneous air operations and psychological warfare. In Phase 3 as perceived by Hawkins, the brigade was to break out from the secure beachhead after a number of weeks and march on Havana, picking up local volunteers."[16]

This is stunningly unreal—a Timothy Leary kind of thing.[17] [Laughter.] Did these men actually believe that the brigade would march to Havana? "My own speculation," Bissell says, "differed somewhat from Hawkins' scheme. I believed that securing the beachhead and operating aircraft from its landing strip would have served to confuse and disorganize the Castro regime."[18] Not to belabor the point, but—I mean—this sounds like they are confusing Guatemala with Cuba and Arbenz with Castro. Isn't it kind of hard to imagine that Castro would get confused and disorganized by this?

Not for Richard Bissell. He goes on: "A few days of this might have caused it to lose touch with what was going on at the other end of the island and impair its ability to move troops at will." Mysteries are added to mysteries: With the Bay of Pigs in the south central area of Cuba where, exactly, *is* "the other end of the island"? But Bissell is not quite finished:

> Either Castro's nerve would have broken under these circumstances or important elements of the armed forces . . . would have defected. . . . If the beachhead had been held and Castro had proved incapable of driving the invaders out, at the very least a stalemate would have been achieved that would have allowed a provisional government to be flown in. . . .[19]

These rosy scenarios seem to be completely out of touch with the reality on the ground.

And yet, Bissell was a very intelligent guy and his agency was staffed with some highly intelligent, informed people. The CIA, Fidel notwithstanding, was not really an agency of "cretins." Does the key to this puzzle lay with Bissell's expectations for Phase 2 and Phase 3?

These unanswered questions return us to the issue of possible U.S. military support. We have Arthur's memo of his conversation with Miró Cardona. It very explicitly says there will be no U.S. military support. Got it? None. No military support.[20] And yet, Miró—and not only Miró—seems convinced that there *will* be U.S. military backup, to the tune of something like 16,000–30,000 troops. So what is this about? Where does this feeling—these numbers—come from? And when was the Cuban Revolutionary Council supposed to arrive? Early on, wasn't there some discussion of U.S. military support arriving simultaneously with the [Cuban] Revolutionary Council?

Finally, there are two memos from Arthur Schlesinger that raise very interesting questions about the use of U.S. military force. On April 10, he says let's suppose that there is this invasion. What is going to be the likely consequence of this? There is a real possibility that there is going to be a civil war. And what is the model for this? "The model for this operation, of course, will be the Spanish Civil War. But the added dimension of imperialism versus nationalism will mean that the whole thing is even more made to order for Soviet exploitation."[21]

What *if* this invasion had succeeded, in the sense that the brigade held out and some resistance forces were operating as well? I think this needs to be discussed from the State Department and White House perspective, as well as CIA. Arthur, this is a very shrewd analysis. Were people thinking about this: that maybe the worst possible outcome would be a sort of partial "success," leading . . . to a "premature Vietnam," only in Cuba?

. . . .

Gleijeses: I would like to address the issue of Phase 2—just one aspect of Phase 2. There is an interesting memo of January 4, 1961—Memorandum for Chief WH/4 written, probably, by Hawkins. Now, this memo says they will establish the beachhead, the lodgment, and perhaps the Castro government would collapse, etc., etc. Now I come to what to me is the key part of it:

> If matters do not eventuate as predicted above [i.e., the Castro government does not collapse] the lodgment established by our force can be used as the site for establishment of a provisional government which can be recognized by the United States, and hopefully by other American states, and given overt military assistance. The way will then be paved for United States military intervention aimed at pacification of Cuba, and this will result in the prompt overthrow of the Castro government.[22]

This was a memo for Bissell. Bissell endorsed it. I would argue that the whole plan of the CIA—I am not talking of the agent in the field, I am talking of the top leadership—was Phase 2, the U.S. invasion of Cuba. This is the rationale of the Bay of Pigs on the part of the CIA leaders. And Allen Dulles says as much in an unpublished paper that he wrote.[23] At least I think so. They believed that any option required for success would be authorized, rather than permit the enterprise to fail. So this, to me, is the rationale of Phase 2 for Richard Bissell, for Allen Dulles, and I think at the time was endorsed by Mr. Esterline and Colonel Hawkins. . . .

Esterline: Jack [Hawkins] and Bissell worked it out, really. In my own thinking I never got beyond Phase 1.[24] My position was—and Bissell knew it—we are in this thing now, and we are not walking away from it, away from these men; we are going to stay with the program. I was hung up on the point—I admit it—that the beachhead must be established, it must be secured, and we must get that *Frente* [*Front*—the leadership of the Cuban Revolutionary Council] into that beachhead. And, not in three days, either. They must be there within 48 hours.

There is another gray area for me, Arthur. It has to do with Miró.[25] Believe me, in terms of our task group, we never led anyone to believe that there would be any support coming in from U.S. armed forces. We just never did. I was one of those who ended up surprised that we didn't get what we thought that we *were* getting. I am a little bit confused now in terms of Bissell and Kennedy. You know: what was happening to the information we were developing. I never really knew. But I kept hearing that Miró Cardona had talked to somebody in the Kennedy administration and he, for some reason, had got some ideas from that person. Was it Adolf Berle, Arthur?

Schlesinger: Berle and I had lunch in New York with Miró. The figure of 10,000 came up. We made it very clear to Miró that there would be no American invasion. Miró said that once the invasion began, 10,000 Cubans would come to its support. Berle and I talked about this later. That is the only way that the figure 10,000 came in.

Esterline: Well it was never within our—I don't think the brigade expected that the marines would back them up. So, how did so many Cubans arrive at the conclusion—the wrong conclusion—that the marines were going to land?

Baloyra: Knowing a little bit of the mentality of the Cuban politicians at that time, I think probably what Miró thought was that this is a set piece. You know, there is a tape recorder going somewhere and the American government is getting it on record that it did not promise us anything. But we know that you have to do this, and I know that you have to do this, and that's all there is to it. That is the way I read it. . . .

Schlesinger: Here's what happened exactly, at the lunch with Berle and Miró on April 13, 1961 [reading]:

> Miró, Berle, and I had lunch at the Century Club in New York. Everyone knew, Miró said, that the United States was behind the invasion. Berle said it could not succeed without an internal uprising, that if one came, we would provide the democratic Cubans with the things necessary to make it successful. Once the provisional government was established on the beachhead we would offer all aid short of U.S. troops. Miró said that 10,000 Cubans would immediately align themselves with the invasion forces. Berle replied there would be plenty of arms. The kind of help we were prepared to give he didn't feel would be enough, if in fact the revolutionary situation existed within Cuba.[26]

I reproduce this part of the conversation with Miró from notes made at the time, because he wrote to all of his colleagues and later claimed publicly that Berle had promised the support of 10,000 U.S. troops. Either Miró's knowledge of the language or the translation was sadly at fault. Miró, a liberal man, probably heard what he desperately needed to hear.

. . . .

Esterline: I had a long talk with Hawkins on the phone the day before I came down here. We were going over what he wrote in the letter to Jim Blight [Document 4.3]. And he said to me: "You know," he said, "I sometimes wonder if Frank," as he was called, "Frank or Rip, in talking to the Cubans," they were the trainers, "I sometimes wonder if they said things that they didn't have any right to say—that were false."[27] That's the only time I've heard that maybe Frank and Rip were, well, leading the Cubans on, maybe—I don't know—maybe to keep the morale high and so on. But it seems to me that something like that must have taken place. Miró was a lawyer; he was a very sensible man. He visited the camps in Guatemala. Maybe that's where he got this idea. . . .

Blanton: I see almost a classic disjuncture of perceptions on all different levels. To take one small example, in the small world category: John White, who is over here, is a research assistant at the [National Security] Archive. His father was one of the marines waiting offshore in the amphibious force of men who understood that their mission was to provide the follow-on wave. At least, that was their assumption. Why else would you be sitting offshore—off the Bay of Pigs, off Cuba?[28]

At another level, if you go through Piero's article, you'll see the Bissell-level decisionmaking in really stellar terms, it seems clear to me. Piero demonstrates very clearly that Bissell's assumption was that all he had to do was establish the beachhead long enough to force Kennedy's hand. And then the marines were to be brought in. And the marines themselves apparently thought they were going in. At Bissell's level, he thought they were going to go in according to a predictable sequence of events.[29] But at the level of the people in the brigade—and this is a question for Alfredo—did *you* think the marines would come in if you got into trouble? And so, at multiple levels of this whole operation, people were proceeding on the same assumption—a *false* assumption—the marines, the military commanders, the brigade people, and Bissell, that Phase 2 or Phase 3 was going to be authorized, and this meant the marines.

Esterline: I guess it must have been four or five days after—after the fiasco—I had a personal meeting with Burke.[30] I'm sorry, but I'm afraid I am going to get emotional. . . . Anyway . . . Burke broke down and cried about these mistakes that had been made. And I cried with him, I'll tell you that. We just could not understand it. We gave them the hours clearly, they were supposed to give us the air support. We were supposed to have that support not at 20,000 feet in the air, but down on the deck to protect—to protect our ships and supplies and men for that critical hour to let them get ashore. And what happened? The goddamn planes were 20,000 feet in the air and totally useless, because those were their orders. And somebody mixed up the times, even the times were screwed up! That is when I lost my American pilots, because they and we had . . .[31]

Durán: Three or four days before the invasion, we moved from Guatemala to Nicaragua—I mean the invasion force, the brigade. We were under the impression that we were going to land in Trinidad. And once in Trinidad, we would from there organize the expansion of the invasion. We were under the impression that there were people in the Escambray who would be blocking off highway accesses to Trinidad and that a percentage of the population of Trinidad would support us and join with us in the invasion. The night before we left Nicaragua on the boat, the leaders of the brigade were called and when they came back they advised us of a new plan. The new plan was the landing at the Bay of Pigs. Of course to me and in fact to many of us, this did not make any sense unless the explanation that was given to us at that time—why the plan was changed—was in fact true.

The explanation was as follows. We were to land at the Bay of Pigs, which had Playa Girón in the center. You had Playa Larga toward the west and you had San Blas toward the north, which were major highway junctures. If you held those junctures you could establish a beachhead in Playa Girón, assuming that we were going to have air cover and that we would therefore not be attacked by air. This made sense because, in fact, while we had ammunition, nobody could get past San Blas, which is where I was. I can speak only to that point. But also the other highways: the highway to Trinidad, the other highway to the sugar mills, and the one to San Blas up north to Covadonga. And so the interpretation—or not the interpretation, but what we were told—was that after we held the beachhead for three days, Miró Cardona and the council would land with the support of, and a resolution of, the Organization of American States, and that we would be supported by the United States Marines. That is more or less what we were told.

Looking back on it now, I can see that the individuals from the CIA who were helping train us, and the people from the National Guard, identified themselves very much with the members of the brigade. They were really into this project. They really wanted this project to succeed, and I believe that in their own minds they really and truly believed that there was going to be a marine landing at some point, if we got into trouble. All the way over to the Bay of Pigs we were more or less escorted—that was the perception—by the aircraft carrier *Essex,* and a couple of destroyers.

On one of the days, I think it was the second day of the fighting, a couple of jets from the *Essex* flew overhead, over the Bay of Pigs, and that to us appeared to be the guarantee. We had suspected, because we saw some planes going north, that those two jets were taking care of Castro's air force at that point. Also, the communications of San Román with the *Essex* gave the impression that it was about time that the promised help arrived.[32] But it never did arrive. So that was the plan, that we believed while we were coming in. Our mission was to hold the beachhead for three or four days. After that, there would be a second plan that was a little more hazy, but nevertheless it involved the landing of Miró Cardona with the cabinet, and some additional support for the invasion process.

The question of the air power was absolutely crucial, as Jake stated before. It was absolutely crucial. I don't know—I don't think we could have moved out of the Bay of Pigs because, in the same way that they could not get at us, we probably could not have broken out of there either. But I think that had we had air power, and had Castro not had an air force, we might still be there fighting, if we had ammunition. It was a very difficult place to get into; it was a very difficult place to get out of—in San Blas. As long as we had the 4.2 mortar shells, there was no way that anybody could cross that highway. They crossed it only after we ran out of ammunition.

The air power was crucial. The only way that the Bay of Pigs landing site made any sense was if we had control of the air. It made no sense just to establish a beachhead, without backup from the marines, because we probably would never have been able to get out of there. So that was our impression. We were there to establish a beachhead, which we did, as long as we could. And we thought that there was more coming. . . .

I think there was a lot of wishful thinking in Guatemala; wishful thinking not only among the brigade members, but also on the part of the CIA persons who were training us. As I said before, the Americans who were in Guatemala really got taken by that whole effort. Also a very strong relationship grew up between the trainers and the brigade personnel. I guess it is the type of bonding that occurs in this type of event. When you are on the top of a mountain, in a very inhospitable place, and a whole bunch of people have a dream, well, you become close. There was no way that the people who were training us believed that this event was going to be allowed to fail. And I guess that was transmitted to us. And again, the Bay of Pigs landing site made sense militarily only if it was just for the limited purpose of establishing that beachhead. Otherwise there was no way we could get out, and no way anybody could join us.

. . . .

Hopmann: All of this discussion about the importance of establishing a provisional government sounds like something that would have come in response to criticism from the State Department, OAS, the UN, and elsewhere, who might be expected to oppose this invasion, but who might change their view if the nature of the conflict could be changed: from a U.S. invasion against Castro's Cuba to supporting one side in a civil war and a government that has been legally "recognized." I'd ask Arthur, in particular: Was there discussion at any point with Rusk, or others—Stevenson comes to mind—who might have raised this criticism?[33] Could they have developed a new, different justification for the use of U.S. military forces had they had a provisional government on a beachhead, which the United States might then have formally "recognized" as the legitimate government?

Schlesinger: There was certainly an effort to put a kind of quasi-legal facade on the CIA operation. And an important part of that, once mentioned, but never explored or considered in any serious way, would be an OAS resolution, recognizing a government or at least giving some kind of sanction to the effort. But there was never any serious constitutional or legal analysis. Abe Chayes, who was the legal officer in the State Department, was never consulted, as he was later in the Cuban missile crisis.[34] And there was this ridiculous assumption that the U.S. hand would be so well concealed that this would be regarded as an internal Cuban affair, which was supposed to be sanctioned later, after the provisional government arrived.

Hopmann: But somebody must have thought differently. Otherwise why is it so important to have that provisional government there? Why does that become the key to saving this operation, once you have moved away from Trinidad to another location? . . .

Smith: Tom Mann also pointed out that this violated international law. He then withdrew from that position. He knew well that it wasn't going to do any good anyway.

Schlesinger: Bill Fulbright brought that up in his intervention with Kennedy. He made a powerful case against it, talking about things like treaties and international law. Needless to say, Fulbright was a lone wolf speaking in that final meeting to decide to go ahead. He can't have been too popular with Bissell. [Laughter.]

Smith: I just want to say that the disconnections here are simply incredible. It's like a Greek tragedy. I have this image of forces moving towards a tragic conclusion—everyone, everyone involved—just tragic. Each element of the force had a totally different conception of what they were about and what they were going to do. . . .

Kennedy . . . tells Bissell that he will not use U.S. forces. Bissell does not believe it and thinks that if he puts the brigade ashore and it starts to fail—or even that there is a possibility of failure—that Kennedy will have to change his mind. He thinks Kennedy will not let it fail. And then there are those 2,000 marines standing off the beach. Who orders those marines there? The president has said no U.S. forces are going to be used. So who gives the order for 2,000 marines to be standing offshore, ready to go in?

Esterline: Well Arleigh Burke, I think, issued that order.

Halpern: He did that on his own authority.

Esterline: I agree. He did that on his own authority. He didn't have any authority from the president, did he, Sam?

Halpern: It's the same as during the missile crisis, when General Power of SAC put out DEFCON 2 on his own, without authority from anybody. Washington didn't find out about it until hours later.[35]

Smith: My God! It's *Burke* who issues orders to the *Essex?* There was the president saying we don't want any indication of U.S. involvement; then there is the *Essex* standing offshore from Playa Girón. . . .

Schlesinger: This is one reason why, during the missile crisis, Kennedy was so insistent on maintaining very tight command and control over all the units of the American forces. That is why McNamara and Admiral Anderson got into their famous fight and nearly went to fisticuffs because of it. McNamara was laying down specifications as to how the quarantine should operate. Sometimes, this concern over details has been wrongly attributed solely to McNamara's penchant for control. But it was Kennedy who insisted on it. Kennedy was very concerned that something might get out of control down the line. That is one of the lessons he learned from the Bay of Pigs.[36]

. . . .

Kornbluh: I wonder if we might take this opportunity to get Arthur to tell us the state of mind in the White House as the invasion went forward. For example, there was a dramatic meeting after a state dinner the night of the 19th. What happened there? We don't really know much about how Kennedy was beseeched by the CIA personnel to actually send in the marines. We know he was asked to send air cover. But did anyone push for an invasion at that point? Did Dulles or Bissell or the chiefs ever go to him and say: now you *have* to send in the marines? . . .

Schlesinger: Well, I was summoned to the White House about midnight. This says 1:00 AM in the morning, Wednesday the 19th. I'd gone to bed, before being awakened by a call from the White House. It was Mac Bundy. He said, "I'm in the president's office; he would like to have you come down here as soon as possible." And I got there . . . at 1:00 AM, early on the morning of the 19th.

Blanton: Is this your journal entry from that time?

Schlesinger: Yes.

> [Reading from journal.] It is interesting that Mac Bundy said that he personally did not feel that the cancellation of the air strike had fundamentally changed the situation. Mac believes air power does not alter the immense Castro advantage on the ground. His conclusion is that Castro is far better organized and more formidable than we had supposed. For example, the insurgents appeared to have run out of pilots despite the months of training. As for Bissell, Mac said that he personally would not be able to accept Dick's estimate of the situation. . . . The next day, everything is going wrong, and the Cuban Revolutionary Council is under house arrest. They don't believe it and are getting more and more restless. Kennedy asked Berle and me to come to the White House at this hour.
>
> The strike was argued back and forth, but this was discussed in a desultory, rather distraught way. Finally Berle arrived. The president described the scene of the matter of the Revolutionary Council; one member is threatening suicide, others want to be put on the beachhead. All of us fear that they do not know how dismal things are. We must go down and talk to them. Berle said, "I can think of happier missions." [Laughter.] The meeting broke up about 2:00 AM and the president said to me: "You ought to go with Berle."[37]

So, I mean, we went down there about three in the morning.

Blanton: When you say desultory and distraught—can you describe that?

Schlesinger: Well, people were milling around and there was a general sense of gloom. It was one in the morning, and half the people present were in white tie after the annual congressional reception. Everyone was in a state of denial or shock.

Smith: And there was a long line from the State Department over to Kitty and Alice's bar after midnight. [Laughter.]

. . . .

Baloyra: I have just been thinking about what Wayne and Arthur and the others have been saying about the situation in Washington. Your government, if I may say so, was very mixed up. There were unclear objectives and, at the operational level, a kind of deadly coincidence between too many assumptions and too little redundancy. I mean things were just strung together. And when something failed there was no backup; whether for aircraft or pull-back or resupply. No backup for anything.

And, in terms of larger lessons—well, I will leave the big lessons to the people who were born here as to what the United States should learn from this. But the lesson for the smaller countries is that when you get involved with bigger powers, your interests just go to hell. I mean, can you imagine the leaders of the Allies in Europe "being under lock and key," at an old airplane hangar in England, or somewhere. It is inconceivable. But these were your allies and they were putting you under house arrest. I repeat: your *allies!* . . .

The word "tragedy" has been repeated so often, for so many years, about these events, and abused a lot by people who are feeling sorry for themselves, that it has sort of lost its meaning. But, I mean, what else can you call it, really? It was the wrong thing to do, at the wrong time, done in the wrong way. And people suffered because of it. I mean, nobody tried to do all these things wrong. Not Jake, not anybody, not even Bissell, probably. So it is a tragedy.

I keep coming back again to this point: that the political conditions were not right in April 1961. Okay? The U.S. government was divided about what to do, or whether to do anything. Internally, we in the resistance had not advanced enough. In private, the Latin American countries were saying to the United States: What are you going to do about Castro? But they also said don't expect us to support some more or less traditional American invasion. In Washington, it all comes down to Dick Bissell and John Kennedy, it seems to me. Kennedy was saying to Bissell: if you are not bullshitting me and this thing has a chance, even though it is "quiet," then I might then consider recognition, and then we might send that out and get a resolution, etc. But if not, you don't get anything. Nothing. And Kennedy is thinking, probably, I have done enough so that he will not succeed anyway.

And then we are caught in the middle. And we are here, and we can tell the story. People who were at Retalhulcu—they don't have that advantage.[38] I don't want to get dramatic because that is not my style, but I have to reflect that, you know . . . it's . . . this is the tragic part of the story, so full of things that cannot be retrieved: reputations, dreams, our country, to say nothing of those who died or were imprisoned—and not just the guys in the brigade, but people who were just caught in the middle.

I think this explains a little bit the bitterness of the people in our community. Their side of the story always gets told as if they had been mercenaries or simple CIA employees, stooges of imperialism. This hurts. Because, as Lino's documents say, it was not like that . . . it just was not like that. You know, some of us took some political risks—okay, maybe not huge ones, but some risks—to come here to this conference. I am feeling that this was worthwhile—you know, to bring, our perspective here, to this group. We were naive. But we were young—a lot younger than Richard Bissell, who, despite his famous intelligence and experience, believed that

the Cuban militia was not going to fight, that there were going to be uprisings all over the island and that this could be done, you know, even though
the air power had been withheld.

Schlesinger: I agree with Quique. The men in the brigade were mostly idealists. I have no trouble at all understanding why, as many of you have said,
you were attracted to John Kennedy. But the CIA's treatment of the people
in the brigade was reprehensible. And the treatment of the Cuban
Revolutionary Council was just as bad. Lem Jones, the public relations man
from New York, treated the leadership as if they were. . . . It was a shame-
ful moment in American history.[39]
    In 1963 John Nolan of the Justice Department went over to Cuba with
Jim Donovan to negotiate release of the prisoners, and he talked with
Castro about the air strike. Castro said that air cover for the brigade would
not have been decisive because his antiaircraft was so strong that it would
have been able to knock off even much stronger air support. And indeed, at
least one B-26 was shot down, perhaps more.

Esterline: We had our daily overflight photographs. We knew where all of
Castro's planes were. Every last one. We had lined them up for that second
strike. If we had been able to use the total number of planes that we had—
Arthur, I mean those T-33s of the Cubans would have been completely
destroyed. But Bissell—I guess you would say that he rolled over and
played dead and settled for half the number of planes we needed to hit
those targets.

Smith: On this particular subject: it seems to me that the cancellation of the
air strikes would have been vital, only if the objective was other than what
it was. I mean, if the objective was simply to go in and establish a beachhead and hold it for two or three days, before a provisional government
comes in, supported by U.S. forces, then it is of course vital to have the air
coverage to establish the beachhead. But that was not, in fact, the plan.
Bissell was telling the president there was going to be an internal uprising;
you are going to put the brigade ashore and there will be an internal uprising. The cancellation of the air strikes, therefore, is almost irrelevant.

Esterline: No indeed. Wayne, that's dead wrong!

Smith: They are irrelevant because . . .

Esterline: No indeed! No *way* are they irrelevant!

Smith: Well Jake . . .

Esterline: When you put men on shore you protect them if you are any kind of a man.

Smith: Well sure, but in . . .

Esterline: Don't use that word "irrelevant"!

Smith: I think the cancellation of the air strikes *was* irrelevant, in the following sense: the objective, according to Bissell, is to spark an internal uprising. But there isn't going to be any uprising. But look, Jake, I take your point. No, when you order forces to occupy a beachhead, you have got to protect them.

Baloyra: Wayne, could Bissell have believed that himself? I mean, he said that the resistance didn't exist. So how the hell could he say—you know—that there was going to be an uprising from this nonexistent internal resistance? Isn't that contradictory?

Smith: I think Piero is right. He talked to Bissell. It is quite clear from Piero's work that Bissell went ahead with the plan, cancellation of the air strike and all, because he thought that if he could just put the guys ashore, no matter what else happens, the president will not let it fail—he will order in U.S. forces. So that is what Bissell is saying. Well, no, that is what Bissell is *planning,* that is not what he is saying. No, what he is saying *is* totally contradictory. Absolutely. He is saying to the president, even if they don't succeed they can fade away into the mountains. That's the face that he showed to the president.

Esterline: Dick never got that from me. You don't just fade into the mountains from Bahía de Cochinos, believe me.

Smith: I am sure that he didn't, Jake. But that is what he is telling the president. We know that. But his thinking and planning is completely based on the assumption that the president will, at a given moment, order the use of U.S. forces. When I said the air strike is irrelevant, I meant it not in terms of protecting your troops. You shouldn't, in all good conscience, put people on a beach and then not protect them. Absolutely. I couldn't agree more. But in terms of the overall objective, I am not sure that the cancellation of the air strike was the element that led to the failure, because there wasn't going to be any internal uprising and the whole thing would have failed for that reason anyway. . . .

Kornbluh: Let me read to the group what Bissell has to say about this in his recently published memoirs. In 1961, he agreed with Jake Esterline's position. In his rebuttal to the Kirkpatrick Report, he stated that the cancellation of the air strikes was critical. But many years later, stimulated by a letter from John McCone, Bissell posed the air strike question to himself, again:

> Would we have succeeded if the air strikes had not been cut back and supply ships had not been sunk in the attack? I believe that, even if the supply ships had been able to continue to resupply the brigade, the brigade might not necessarily have established and held the beachhead. Even in the best scenario, the air arm would have been stretched to the limits of its capabilities, and while there would have been no problem in purchasing more B-26 bombers to increase its strength, there were no additional qualified Cuban pilots to recruit. In the latter weeks of the operation [right before the invasion], it became clear that the only way to bolster the air force was to use U.S. volunteers, but doing so meant violating Kennedy's mandate against involving U.S. military personnel. Given the constraints on the number of air crews that could be recruited and the limited training time, I am not sure that a different and better plan could have been produced with more safety margins built into it. I hold myself responsible for not having better judgment on some of these features of the plan and for not voicing warnings to Dulles and the president that would have made these risks clearer.[40]

Let me now raise an issue that, it seems to me, has not gotten the attention it deserves: the *first* air strike! It seems to me that this too was a fiasco, and not just because its strength was cut in half. In addition, the story of the "defecting plane" that Hawkins devised was revealed to be false by U.S. reporters within 15 minutes of the plane's landing in Florida. What is the origin of that idea and why was it thought to be necessary? I ask this not just to haul another screw-up out of the closet, but because this really upset Rusk, and also seems to have put Kennedy on edge about having a second air strike. Jake, can you speak to that?

Esterline: I can. Dick Bissell forced us to come up with a plan of that sort, allegedly to create a better cover for the operation. Now Jack was really good, and he did the best he could in coming up with something. He thought it would work, but it didn't.

Bissell's memoir and these discussions make me realize that Dick just wasn't—I don't think he was being honest. I don't think he was being honest up—I mean with Kennedy and maybe with Dulles too; and I don't think he was being honest down—in dealing with his two principal aides, Esterline and Hawkins. I don't believe he was leveling with any of us. How can I believe anything different? I was struck by what Wayne said—that Dick was giving different faces to different people. I think that may be right. But something still doesn't quite click for me. If, as Arthur says—and I believe Arthur on this—if the president never, on any occasion, gave anyone cause for believing that he would send in the marines, then why would a guy as smart as Dick believe otherwise, and in fact would wager the whole ball of wax, the whole operation, on the belief that the president *wasn't* shooting straight with him? I don't get it. . . .

The thing I can't understand—I have thought about this, and I've thought about this—the president would have been available that last evening, wouldn't he, Arthur? If Bissell had insisted. . . . I couldn't understand it when Cabell and I had that explosive meeting that night. I never spoke to Bissell again afterward. I just couldn't believe it—because we laid it out in spades for him, for Dick—believe me, I never mince words when I lay things out, particularly when I was younger. I am an old man now, and my wife says I'm more polite. [Laughter.] But I just couldn't accept, couldn't believe, that he—or Cabell, a four-star air force general—that neither one of them elected to talk to the president of the United States and tell him what the almost certain outcome would be. I couldn't believe one of them didn't lay it out for the president in spades. He deserved to know what was going to happen if he pulled back on the air.

Schlesinger: As I said before, I think the reason is that Bissell felt that Kennedy had his mind made up and he saw no point in an argument with the president.

Halpern: That is what Bissell says in his memoirs, Arthur. The same thing. He says there is no point in arguing about it again.

Notes

1. Memorandum from J. C. King, CIA deputy director for plans, to Allen Dulles, director of the CIA, 12 December 1959, "Cuba Problems," pp. 2–3.

2. For example, Esterline is cited as the source on cigars that were supposed to produce temporary dementia in Castro (Church Committee Notes, TOP SECRET [IG Report, 1967: Contaminated Cigars], 3 July 1975); Halpern is the source for the report on Desmond FitzGerald's idea for an exploding seashell that was to kill Castro while he was skin diving (Church Committee Notes, TOP SECRET [Testimony of Samuel Halpern, 18 June 1975: Castro], 1 July 1975).

3. The "NOTLOX" material cited by Peter Kornbluh derives from a file memorandum of R. Mason Cargill, dated 21 May 1975, on "Documents from DPD Files Related to Cuban Operations During the Period 1959–1961." In addition to the various communications back and forth to Havana regarding attempts to kill Castro, there is mention of a scheme to knock out the main power station in Havana, dated 1 April 1961.

See also "Report on Plots to Assassinate Fidel Castro," 23 May 1967 (the CIA's in-house report on the history of its attempts to kill Castro, including recollections of its key people of the various contacts that were made with the Mafia along the way). Interestingly, Esterline is reported at least twice to have tried to terminate the assassination program, once the Bay of Pigs operation got underway. But the report concludes: "Whatever the intention in this respect, if the decision to terminate was actually made, the decision was not communicated effectively. It is clear that this plan to assassinate Castro continued in train until sometime after the Bay of Pigs" (pp. 33–34).

4. "Captured and turned": that a U.S. agent had agreed to act as a double agent for Cuba, in return, perhaps, for not being tortured, imprisoned, and/or killed.

5. In his memoirs, Bissell says this: "No doubt as I moved forward with my plans for the brigade, I hoped the Mafia would achieve success. My philosophy during the last two or three years in the agency was very definitely that the end justified the means, and I was not going to be held back." Richard M. Bissell Jr., *Reflections of a Cold Warrior: From Yalta to the Bay of Pigs* (New Haven: Yale University Press, 1996), p. 157.

6. Arthur Schlesinger Jr., *Robert Kennedy and His Times* (New York: Ballantine, 1978), pp. 488–489.

7. See Michael R. Beschloss, *The Crisis Years: Kennedy and Khrushchev, 1960–1963* (New York: HarperCollins, 1993), pp. 134–135.

8. Robert Maheu, a former FBI agent, at the time an operative working for a U.S. attorney at the CIA, was a key link to Sam Giancana and Johnny Rosselli, the two Mafia figures most closely involved with attempts to kill Castro. See Evan Thomas, *The Very Best Men: Four Who Dared* (New York: Simon & Schuster, 1995), pp. 226–228.

9. Hawkins, "Covert Actions Against the Castro Government of Cuba," p. 5. National Security Archive, Washington, D.C.

10. At 6:30 AM on 17 April 1961 the *Houston,* carrying among other things all the medical supplies for the brigade, was hit by a torpedo from a Cuban government Sea Fury and sank 700 yards off shore. See Peter Wyden, *Bay of Pigs: The Untold Story* (New York: Simon & Schuster, 1979), pp. 228–229.

11. Hawkins, "Covert Operations Against the Castro Government of Cuba," p. 4.

12. Fidel Castro, speech in Havana on 8 April 1961, at 0155 hours, at a meeting of workers arranging for observance of May Day, pp. 3–4. Foreign Broadcast Information Service (FBIS), 10 April 1961, "Castro Lecture on Education and Revolution."

13. Ibid., p. 6.

14. See Tad Szulc, *Fidel: A Critical Portrait* (New York: Morrow, 1986), p. 544.

15. A boat led by Nino Díaz left South Florida intending to land its party in Oriente province, in eastern Cuba, not far from Guantánamo, more or less simultaneous with the main landing at the Bay of Pigs. But after being told en route that there were to be other landings, and that theirs was not the most important, the group decided not to land. See Wyden, *Bay of Pigs,* pp. 171–172.

16. This is a paraphrase from Bissell, *Reflections of a Cold Warrior,* p. 195.

17. The reference is to Dr. Timothy Leary, the late Harvard psychologist who achieved notoriety in the early 1960s for his work with, and advocacy of, psychedelic drugs, especially LSD. His motto was: "Tune in, turn on, drop out." Phillip Brenner's implication is that in order for Bissell to believe what he says he believed is the equivalent to being in a Leary-like "altered state of consciousness."

18. Bissell, *Reflections of a Cold Warrior,* p. 195.

19. Ibid.

20. Arthur Schlesinger Jr., "Conversation with Dr. Miró Cardona," Memorandum from the President's Special Assistant (Schlesinger) to the President, 14 April 1961. The conversation with Miró took place on the 13th, in New York.

21. Arthur Schlesinger Jr., "Cuba: Political, Diplomatic, and Economic Problems," Memorandum for the President, 10 April 1961, p. 2.

22. CIA Memorandum, "Policy Decisions Required for Conduct of Strike Operations Against Government of Cuba," 4 January 1961, p. 2.

23. Allen Dulles, "My Answer on the Bay of Pigs," unpublished ms., in the Allen Dulles Papers, Mudd Library, Princeton University. See also Piero Gleijeses, "Ships in the Night: The CIA, the White House, and the Bay of Pigs," *Journal of Latin American Studies* 17, part 1.

24. See Documents 4.1 and 4.2 for the sequence in which the so-called noisiness of the CIA plan was reduced. On 11 March, McGeorge Bundy issues an action memorandum on behalf of the president explaining that the CIA is to come up with a new plan. Then on 15 March the plan is presented and accepted: "a small-scale World War II–type of amphibious landing" [Document 4.2], p. 1. As Esterline indicates, Hawkins became central at this time due to his specialization in amphibious landings.

25. José Miró Cardona, head of the Cuban Revolutionary Council, which would, according to the plan, be flown into the Bay of Pigs to proclaim the presence of the "legitimate" government of Cuba.

26. See also Arthur Schlesinger Jr., *A Thousand Days: John F. Kennedy in the White House* (New York: Fawcett, 1965), pp. 247–248, for the previously published account of the meeting with Miró.

27. "Col. Frank," as he was known to the members of Brigade 2506, was Frank Egan, the CIA's director of operations at the Guatemala training camp. "Rip" was William ("Rip") Robertson, a former marine pilot in World War II who was at various times on the CIA payroll and had a reputation for unconventional tactics. See Wyden, *Bay of Pigs,* pp. 56–58 (on "Frank"), and pp. 84–85 (on "Rip"). Egan's identity is revealed in Bissell, *Reflections of a Cold Warrior,* p. 158.

28. John White Sr. was a marine on board the *Essex,* which had moved into position just outside the Bay of Pigs, in case President Kennedy chose to order the 2,000 marines on board to land. In a recollection conveyed by his son (who spoke with him during a break at the Musgrove Conference), the marines fully expected to be sent in, had been issued live ammunition, and were in every respect ready for battle.

29. Gleijeses, "Ships in the Night."

30. Adm. Arleigh Burke, chief of naval operations.

31. Esterline makes reference to the four American pilots from the Alabama Air National Guard who were pressed into service to fly the B-26s that were supposed to provide air cover for the members of the brigade. They were downed by T-33s from Castro's air force. See Wyden, *Bay of Pigs,* pp. 240–241.

32. José San Román, the military commander of Brigade 2506.

33. Dean Rusk, secretary of state; and Adlai Stevenson, U.S. ambassador to the United Nations.

34. See the amended Schlesinger statement in "Epilogue," p. 146.

35. Halpern refers to a view first put forward publicly by Raymond L. Garthoff at a conference on the Cuban missile crisis in March 1987: "The Commander-in-Chief of the Strategic Air Command, Gen. [Thomas] Power, sent out the DEFCON [Defense Condition] 2 alert instructions *in the clear,* without

authorization, just so the Soviets could pick it up." James G. Blight and David A. Welch, *On the Brink: Americans and Soviets Reexamine the Cuban Missile Crisis,* 2d ed. (New York: Noonday Press, 1990), p. 75. Garthoff's point was basically that Power took advantage of the vast U.S. nuclear superiority to try to intimidate the Soviets into capitulating. However, Gen. William Y. Smith, who was at the time of the missile crisis a special assistant to Chairman of the Joint Chiefs of Staff Gen. Maxwell D. Taylor, has stated more recently that Power's instructions were done according to standard procedures, on 24 October 1962, "with the approval of the president." See Anatoli I. Gribkov and William Y. Smith, *Operation Anadyr: U.S. and Soviet Generals Recount the Cuban Missile Crisis* (Chicago: Edition Q, 1994), p. 138.

36. See Blight and Welch, *On the Brink,* pp. 63–64.

37. See also Schlesinger, *A Thousand Days,* pp. 259–261.

38. Retalhuleu, the location of the Brigade 2506 training camp in Guatemala.

39. Lem Jones ran a public relations firm in New York and was hired to improve the image of the Cuban Revolutionary Council, led by José Miró Cardona.

40. Bissell, *Reflections of a Cold Warrior,* p. 194.

5

Operation MONGOOSE and the Fate of the Resistance

The course of action set forth herein is realistic within present operational estimates and intelligence. *Actually, it represents the maximum target timing which the operational people jointly considered feasible.* It aims for a revolt which can take place in Cuba by October 1962.

> Gen. Edward Lansdale, 20 February 1962
> [Document 5.5]

When you . . . cannot find a safe house, you go a little bit crazy. So one night, being very desperate, I went to my grandfather's to sleep, to spend one night, to sleep one night. But he told me, you can't be here. My own grandfather—he told me: you can be here for one night only. You've got to be out of here in the early morning because if you get caught here, I will receive the same sentence that you will receive. You are a spy for the CIA and you are going to be executed. I am not going to be executed. I don't want it. Out!

It came to that kind of situation. I am talking here about the summer of 1961.

> Rafael Quintero, 1 June 1996

Blight: We now come to a set of items that get less attention from scholars than things like air cover, and its lack, or why the strategy and site of the invasion changed. We will now turn our attention to what happened after these events. I would like us to look first at what happened on the island in the aftermath: What happened to the brigade members who were captured, during their imprisonment and after their eventual return to the States? Our second large topic is one of the key policy outcomes in the Kennedy administration deriving from the Bay of Pigs events: Operation MONGOOSE. In retrospect, this attempt to hurt the Castro government via covert action seems strained and unfortunate. What we'd like to know is a little more about how the situation appeared at the time, a situation in which MONGOOSE seemed like the thing to do. I have asked Malcolm Byrne to start us off. Malcolm?

107

Byrne: Thank you. . . . I'd like to start by drawing your attention to what is, to me, one of the most striking documents in this briefing book: Chester Bowles's notes of the NSC meeting in the immediate aftermath of the Bay of Pigs [Document 5.1]. It starts out by saying, "There were some thirty-five people at the NSC meeting on Cuba. Again Bob Kennedy was present, and took the lead as at the previous meeting, slamming into anyone who suggested that we go slowly and try to move calmly and not repeat previous mistakes." Bowles notes that "on two or three occasions" he had tried to suggest that some mistakes had been made, etc., and then notes that "these comments were brushed aside brutally and abruptly by the various fire eaters who were present." [Laughter.] "I did think, however, that the faces of a few people around the table reflected some understanding of the views I was trying to present, notably Dick Goodwin, Ted Sorensen (which is surprising)," he says in parenthesis, "Arthur Schlesinger, and above all Jerry Weisner [sic]." He closes by saying, "I left the meeting with a feeling of intense alarm. . . ."

This highlights an interesting point about the aftermath of the Bay of Pigs, particularly the transition to MONGOOSE, and that is how the Kennedy brothers reacted. Much probably derives from the general mood in the corridors of power in Washington. But this seems also to have been a devastating episode to the Kennedys personally, as unused as they were to this kind of humiliating failure. Their reaction was not to walk away from it, and assume that things would get back to normal on their own. They chose instead to, as they saw it, fight back. John and Robert Kennedy seemed to consider this round one of a match, and they immediately set about preparing themselves for round two.

The concrete result of their feistiness was pressure by the White House, from May to November, for the creation of what Richard Goodwin called the "command operation" run by Bobby Kennedy. This is referred to in the November 1, 1961, document from Goodwin to the president [Document 5.3]. Goodwin says, "I believe that a concept of a 'command operation' for Cuba, as discussed with you by the Attorney General, is the only effective way to handle an all-out attack on the Cuban problem." Part of this memo is addressed to the question of whether, or to what extent, lessons were learned from the previous fiasco. Goodwin says: "The beauty of such an operation over the next few months is that we cannot lose." This is reminiscent of a passage from Arthur's *A Thousand Days,* where he describes the period immediately before the president's decision on the Bay of Pigs. He says: "By this time we were offered a sort of all-purpose operation guaranteed to work, win or lose."[1]

Goodwin's memo of November 1 also deals with the problem of plausible denial [Document 5.3]. He says:

> Everyone knowledgeable in these affairs—in and out of government—is
> aware that the United States is helping the underground. . . . The precise
> manner of aid may be unknown but the fact of aid is common knowledge.
> We will be blamed for not winning Cuba back whether or not we have a
> "command operation" and whether or not the Attorney General heads it.

This raises the question of how the president understood plausible deniability and how realistic he was in thinking about it.

Alright. By January 1962, things have moved briskly along toward a unit devoted to attacking the Cuba problem. On the 19th of January, Bobby Kennedy is discussing what he would like to see happen with Gen. Edward Lansdale and other officials from several agencies. According to Richard Helms's notes of the sessions, RFK says: "Accordingly, a solution to the Cuban problem today carries 'the top priority in the United States Government—all else is secondary—no time, money, effort, or manpower is to be spared'" [Document 5.4]. Considering some of the other problems facing the administration in early 1962, both foreign and domestic, this is a remarkable statement. It is a statement of ultimate goals, but is unclear as to means. Since this was supposed to be the top priority of the government, but since overt U.S. force was not to be used, thereby ensuring deniability, how exactly was Castro to be brought down? I wonder if we could get those of you who worked on the Cuban problem in those days to comment on your reaction at the time to this strange philosophy of "damn the torpedoes, and half-speed ahead." [Laughter.]

Specifically, with regard to the CIA: How did the CIA react to all this, to the transition to an intense focus on Cuba, but with the huge caveat of plausible deniability? It looks to me that the CIA really took a beating from the White House following the Bay of Pigs affair. Is this accurate? *Did* leadership in the attack on the Cuba problem slip quickly over to the White House? In reading the documents on this, you can almost hear a "giant sucking sound" coming from the White House that resulted in Cuba policy being placed in the not-so-velvet gloves of RFK. But why was CIA hammered in this way? By this time, John McCone was the DCI [director of central intelligence], he was an acknowledged hawk on Cuba, and from that perspective the stated goals of the Cuba project should not have been the problem. Was there a difference in philosophy between the CIA and the White House? Was there bitterness among the professionals over having been preempted by the politicians?

While this was a devastating episode for the Kennedys, it was also devastating for the people who actually participated in the planning and the execution of the Bay of Pigs operation. I would like to ask Rafael Quintero if he could talk about his experiences inside and outside of Cuba in 1960, '61, and '62. What was the training like? And was the training relevant to the tasks to be done on the island? What kind of lessons did you learn from that? Thank you.

Blight: Thank you, Malcolm. I love the way these guys are rubbing our noses in the documents. I just noticed that when Malcolm began, most of the people at the table cleared off space for their briefing notebooks. . . .

The chair has no particular bias here toward the chronological approach, necessarily. But, I am wondering if it would make sense at this time to ask Alfredo to say a few words about the immediate aftermath, from your point of view as a captured prisoner; the atmosphere, what you may have been subjected to, your impressions then of what was happening, and your impressions later, upon reflection. We are talking now about the first few weeks or so after the invasion.

Durán: I think that to gather those impressions I would have to go back to the moment at the Bay of Pigs when we realized that we had lost. And I think that the moment for me when I realized that we had a good chance of losing was when I was being shot at by a Sea Fury that was not supposed to be there.[2] There was another occasion, after the third day, on the beach. All of a sudden we all were trying to direct our attention towards the place where our headquarters was set up and I saw [José] San Román, who was the chief of the brigade, take his pistol out and shoot the radio. I really thought that . . . uh-oh . . . we are in trouble. [Laughter.]

So we tried to decide what to do. The order came down: let's see if we can reach the famous Escambray Mountains. After walking I suddenly realized, well, I looked at a map and I said that there is no way that we are going to make it to the Sierra de Escambray. Everybody realized it. Some of us took to the boats that were there at the Bay of Pigs, at Playa Girón, and tried to sail out. Some went into the swamp, and some continued to walk toward Trinidad. There were some who were caught behind the offensive. Several of the Cubans of the Bay of Pigs brigade were even able to make it to Havana and escape, by getting into embassies and so forth. Those were the ones who were left behind when the Castro offensive came in. They were left behind Castro's line. And since all the Castro people were moving this way, our guys were able to move and get to Havana in a couple of days. And they generally made it to embassies or got out in other ways.

In my particular case I took the wrong side. Well, I don't know if it was the wrong side. I guess both sides were the wrong side of the Zapata Swamp. The swamp is divided by a highway that goes to San Blas. And on one side, there is no water. On the other side it is full of water. I took the side without the water. I started walking north trying to see if I could somehow get behind the Castro forces and try to make my way into Havana, or the north coast, and try to hijack a boat or something and get out. The fact of the matter is that I wandered through that swamp for 30-some days. My main objective was not to be captured, because I felt that they were going to shoot us. I thought that we were dead once captured. And during those 30 days, we were constantly being searched for by helicopters and by patrols up and down the—there were something like rural highways or rural roads within the Zapata Swamp that were used by people who make vegetable coal from the mangroves there. And there were constant patrols of Castro's militia down those roads.

Finally, to make a long story short, after evading them for 30 days, they captured me and two other persons who were trying to cross through a sugar mill. We were captured by dogs. At that time we had spent about three or four days without water. My mouth was completely full of sores. As we were captured and I remember telling the militia, I said, "Give me some water and then shoot me." I am still trying to figure out why I didn't want to die thirsty. [Laughter.]

But the guy told us that there had been an order that nobody was going to be shot. We were taken—I was taken—to a small hut in the sugar mill. Later on, I was transported in a bus to Havana. Along the way, in every town where we stopped, they stopped the bus for a little while so that people could yell at us. And they did. Finally, I was taken together with the rest of the brigade to what was at that time the Naval Hospital, and I was outfitted as a prisoner. We were kept there in the Naval Hospital. At the very beginning, we received humane treatment. We were not abused, except on that bus trip through the towns. We were not mistreated; we were not tortured; we were not beaten. We were fed and those who needed medical treatment were given medical treatment. That continued to be the case for the time that we spent in the Naval Hospital, which was about four or five months.

We really didn't get much to eat. In the morning, we got a piece of bread. After several months, the bread stopped. Usually there was some coffee. Then we had something that is called *pansa*. We used to call it *patria o muerte* because if you ate it, you have to be brave as hell.[3] [Laughter.] But anyway it was the intestines of cows, I guess. And we got that once a week and then most of the rest of the week we got lentil soup once a day. And then in the evening we got a piece of bread. Other than that, we were pretty much left alone inside what we called the galleys, which were overcrowded. Some had to sleep on the floor. The sanitary facilities were pretty bad. But there was no physical mistreatment. In other words, it was not comfortable quarters but we were pretty much left alone.

Sometimes, when for some reason or other there seemed to be tension arising between Cuba and the United States, they would harass us. They would take us out, take us out naked into the patio, search and throw everything that we had into the galleys, yell at us, and sometimes poke us with bayonets. That happened four or five times. One time we started complaining and a mini-riot broke out. We were complaining because of the lack of medicine. We had some very sick people and they were not being treated. And some of the guards got nervous and shot into the galley and three persons were wounded. All in all, I would say that I expected worse treatment than I received. . . .

So all those things made our tenure as prisoners of war—which is the classification that we ultimately received—more acceptable, in the sense that it was a livable experience. Generally, in my personal case, I expected worse treatment than I received. And so therefore I can say that I was pleasantly surprised that we were really not beaten up, or worse. So that was more or less the experience that we had as prisoners of war.

Blight: Arthur, I wonder if you would enlighten us a little bit about the aftermath in the White House. Alfredo has described the reality of some Bay of Pigs participants in Cuba. But what was the feeling like in the Kennedy administration when the dust had settled and you all got back to work? What was the general feeling about what should be done? In particular, how did the president and the attorney general feel about it? And what was going on in your mind? . . .

Schlesinger: The passion for counterinsurgency that was a big thing in 1962, was beginning to wear off by 1963. And though there were a few lingering remnants of the kind of harassment typical of Operation MONGOOSE, it was tapering off.

I think the real concern about Cuba in the last months of the Kennedy administration was the possibility of normalizing U.S.–Cuban relations. Bill Attwood, who had been editor of *Look* magazine, had gone to Cuba in 1959 and interviewed Castro. He had been appointed ambassador to Guinea and had gotten along well with [President] Sekou Touré. Attwood then heard from Sekou Touré that Castro was restless to break away from the grip of the Soviet Union. Bill Attwood got a mild case of polio and was sent back to the United States in 1963 for recuperation. While recuperating, he was assigned to work with Stevenson at the UN.

While at the UN, Attwood heard from the Cuban ambassador to the UN, Carlos Lechuga, that maybe an improvement of relations was worth exploring. So he sent a memorandum, which is in my book on Robert Kennedy, to the State Department—to Averell Harriman—asking for his views.[4] Harriman said, in effect, "Well it's a fine idea as far as I am concerned. But you had better check with Robert Kennedy, because of its political implications." Nineteen-sixty-four was an election year, of course. Robert Kennedy said that he thought it was well worth pursuing, and that

Attwood should talk to Mac Bundy. Mac endorsed it, and took it up to Kennedy. Bundy reported back to Attwood that he should pursue it.

So Attwood had a series of conversations in the autumn with Carlos Lechuga. I understand that Lechuga has written a book describing his side of these talks.[5] Attwood was scheduled to go to Cuba in December of 1963 but Dulles cut off that. Later, Lyndon Johnson told Mac Bundy: "Let's put this on ice for awhile," and it has remained on ice ever since, or at least until Bill Rogers, with the backing of Henry Kissinger, tried to thaw it in '74.[6]

So, I think the direction of the movement is very clear in the Kennedy administration: from the Operation MONGOOSE approach to exploration of the possibility of normalization. By the way, in Kennedy's view, normalization required two things, and only two things: (1) the end of the use of Cuba as a Soviet base; and (2), the end of Cuban attempts to foment revolution in the Western Hemisphere. . . .

Blight: Sam, the first time we talked about this you told me you were in the Far East enjoying yourself, when you were called back to Washington after which, as I remember, your life was somewhat more complicated. And several of the reasons you gave for the recall and the complications were associated in various ways with the attorney general.

Halpern: Very true. Very true. . . . Now, about MONGOOSE. You've got to divide MONGOOSE into at least three periods. The first period is from the end of '61 to the missile crisis, and through the missile crisis. . . .

I came back from Saigon where I was sent to do another one of those stupid Lansdale programs in Vietnam. [Laughter.] I had known Ed Lansdale many years before, when he did a fine job in the Philippines with Magsaysay.[7] As a result of that success, Ed had this aura around him. Some people believed Ed was a kind of magician. But I'll tell you what he was. He was basically a con man. A Madison Avenue "Man in the Grey Flannel Suit" con man. You take a look at his proposed plan for getting rid of Castro and the Castro regime; it's utter nonsense [Document 5.5].[8] It's unrealistic, it's stupid. He's got people being recruited by each day. You are going to recruit three here, four here, eight here, ten here. And he is building whole organizations by rote. But life doesn't work that way. If he had had any sense at all, he would have talked to somebody about how difficult it is to recruit people to do a whole variety of jobs.

So, now it is after the Bay of Pigs. Dick Helms was not the DDP [deputy director of CIA for plans], he was still the COPs—the Chief of operations—I think it was called. Dick was still trying to stay away from this whole Cuba thing even after John McCone came in.[9] And Dick Bissell was the guy who assigned me to the Cuba desk. I was deputy branch chief of Branch 4, which had been started sometime before. And we were responsible in Branch 4; this meant not only for Cuba, but all the islands in the Caribbean. . . .

These were papers for the Special Group. There wasn't a Special Group–Augmented at that point. By the way, the "augmented" was simply two "augmentees." One was Robert Kennedy, who chaired the Special Group–Augmented, and [Chairman of the Joint Chiefs] General [Maxwell] Taylor, who sat in at Robert Kennedy's insistence. That became the augmented part of the Special Group. The special group was simply number one and number two of each of the key agencies in town, sitting together once or twice a week, or once a month depending on what the business was. Anyway, we were supposed to write papers that promised the moon and six pence, all by mirrors.

There was a basic contradiction in everything the Special Group–Augmented did, or tried to do, or considered doing. Number one, things were supposed to be quiet. Not a lot of publicity, just a lot of damage inflicted on the Cuban regime. However—and this is the contradiction—they also wanted "boom and bang," that was the phrase they used. "Boom and bang, boom and bang, boom and bang." Let me give you an example of "boom and bang" and the Kennedys. We had—after Bill Harvey took over, and I will get to that in a minute—we did have a very small success with some "boom and bang." I don't know whether it was a small sugar mill or some little bridge of some kind, or maybe it was a tobacco factory where they were making cigars or something.

But it hit the media: the press, and the radio and television. And of course it got picked up in Havana, and the first thing that Bill Harvey knows is he is getting chewed out on the phone by Robert Kennedy for this particular piece of sabotage that we were doing, we thought, at his orders.[10] Says Kennedy, "I thought you did things secretly. How come it's all over the papers?" And Bill Harvey had to explain to the gentleman with one-syllable words that when you are going to blow something up, boss, it's going to make a noise, and it's going to be talked about, and it's going to be talked about in all kinds of media. You can't have "boom and bang" without somebody knowing about it. Well that kind of sunk in over a period of time, but it took a little while.

Let me come back to the end of December 1961. McCone is now in charge and Helms is still trying to keep away from anything to do with Cuba.

Smith: December of '61, Sam?

Halpern: December '61. We are still in '61 and Harvey doesn't come into this thing until January-February '62. Helms is still COPs. . . . I say to

Helms: "We can't do this. We can use all the words in the English dictionary, and we can write all kinds of fancy papers, but it will be far worse if we say we are going to produce something and we are not able to do it. We are going to be in worse shape than we are today. We have got to be honest with everybody and tell them what our limitations are."

And as I said to Helms, over and over again, "We don't have a pot to piss in—in Cuba. We don't know what's going on. We don't know who is doing what to whom. We haven't got any idea of their order of battle in terms of political organization and structure. Who's got what jobs? Who hates whom? Who loves whom? We have nothing." We had to start from scratch.

So then what happens? We get [Gen. Edward G.] Lansdale's stupid and unrealistic paper with everybody marching down the streets of Havana in the last week of October 1962 [Document 5.5]. I mean, it was unbelievable, even by Ed's standards. You take a look at a calendar and you see that the very next week—the first week of November 1962—there happens to be a congressional election in this country. Lansdale wanted to be sure that the Kennedys got whatever kudos were there for the taking by marching in Havana the week before. That's how unrealistic the whole thing was.

As a matter of fact, if you want to take a look at Bill Harvey's notes as to why that's unrealistic, look at his August 7 and August 8 memos in this nice big blue book [Document 5.6].[11] Bill worked real hard on this problem. Bill was trying to show in those two memos how unrealistic Ed Lansdale's stuff was. . . .

So what we ended up with was me talking to Helms, arguing with him over and over again, until we got a draft produced over the Christmas and New Year's holidays. We were in that office night and day trying to make some sense out of what was coming from Lansdale. Ed finally came over to where we were located, in WH/4. We were still located in Quarters Eye. . . .

To me, as far as I am concerned, MONGOOSE was a totally unnecessary, as well as a stupid operation. It wasn't necessary for the security of the United States of America. And take a look: we have been living for 35 years or more with the man down there and we still happen to be a country, and we are still in good shape. This was totally unnecessary.

When I started to talk to Dick Helms about it, I said: "Look, this is a political operation in the city of Washington, D.C., and has nothing to do with the security of the United States." . . . And then Dick says: "All right, let's see what we get from Ed in terms of what we have to do."

Well, you've got Ed's January '62 paper in here [Document 5.5]. It's a mess. It's basically a textbook of things that ought to work, ought to be done, but nobody expects anybody ever to do it. It is like a war plan. I used to say: "You don't have war plans on the shelf to tell you how to meet the situation that you are going to be facing. It never does. Things change.

Nobody can predict. The only reason for war plans is to have gone through the exercise so that you know exactly what to do on a checklist." It helps, sometimes, if you have been through all of the options and stuff like that before, and you've made adjustments as you go. And that's the only conceivable use for Ed Lansdale's plan as to how they were to going to get to Havana by the last week of October 1962.

In early 1962, we had a lot of senior officers come over to help us draft proper language for the Special Group–Augmented. None of it really passed muster. But none of us—senior, or junior, or just guys fresh from the field—were willing to guarantee on a piece of paper that we could accomplish Ed's tasks, when we knew damn well that we didn't have anything to go on inside Cuba. And I start to scream and yell and fight and holler and chew the rug. I said that the first thing we've got to do is to get an intelligence operation going. We've got to find out what's happening there. And bit by bit that kind of sunk in. Finally, Bill Harvey comes over and takes a look. He agreed with me totally on that, and then I said to Bill, "Okay. Bill, this is all yours now. I'm leaving." He says, "No way. You are staying as my executive assistant and I am going to get Mr. X from overseas to be my deputy." Mr. X was called because he was a colonel in the U.S. Marine Corps reserve and therefore would have had some kind of clout when he was talking to the Pentagon people in the military.

So Mr. X gets pulled out from wherever he was and comes back in about two weeks. Harvey takes over and so we are now a task force, and all task forces have to have a name. So Bill Harvey picks one: "W," Task Force W. I won't go into why he picked "W." Somebody is going to be writing about that and it will come out then. But anyway, he picks "W" and it's Task Force W. I then send the book message around the world to all CIA stations and bases that says: "Bill Harvey is now in charge of Cuba. By presidential directive, Cuba is the number one priority." Vietnam goes down the list to almost nothing. Everybody has to concentrate on things having to do with Cuba. That will give you some idea of the atmosphere in our shop after the Bay of Pigs. Cuba was the be-all and end-all. And of course, "Cuba" was a code word for "get rid of Castro." That was the number-one priority of the agency. Number one. . . .

Now, on the main characters in this soap opera: Ed Lansdale and Bill Harvey never saw eye-to-eye.[12] But then nobody I know ever saw eye-to-eye with Ed Lansdale on anything. Ed realizes right away that, in Bill Harvey, he has a tough guy to work with. No love is lost between the two. They somehow work together, though, and as the documents show, we did produce what Ed asked for—in terms of the paperwork at least. We have a document in here [in the conference briefing notebook] in which Bill writes to the DCI, after responding to Ed's silly orders, as to why we can't go along with this nonsense.[13] Bill tells McCone that it's just not going to work. McCone doesn't like what Lansdale is doing, or asking for, either. Neither does Dick Helms. We all figure that we've got to be honest at least among our own people as to what we can and can't do.

Bill Harvey then took the bull by the horns and began to attack the Cuban problem in a way that made sense, by getting moving on what we really needed most of all, which was intelligence. And the Special Group–Augmented agreed. So Bill assigns Ted Shackley as chief of the Miami station. Ted Shackley was a middle-level officer—I guess he was a GS-13 or GS-14. Bill sends him down to Miami to take over and help reorganize the whole place. Ted had a lot of good middle-level and senior officers who had a lot of experience, at least against the Soviets and the Eastern European bloc, as his officers. And they started to organize, thank the Lord, an intelligence collection operation, basically. . . . Yes, once in awhile we had to try some sabotage operations but they were few and far between, and as you see from the record none of the big ones really succeeded. We tried three times at the Matahambre copper mine, but nothing succeeded there. And every time we didn't succeed we got blasted by Robert Kennedy—usually on everything under the sun.

One thing that I am still kind of confused about—and I've tried for a long time to figure out the answer—is what made these two gentlemen—both the president and the attorney general—so full of hysteria, paranoia, and obsession about Cuba. Lino, you're the psychiatrist; you're the doctor. What the hell was going on with those two guys? I am not a doctor, but it seems to me that there has got to be something more to this, other than the fact that they got bloody noses at the Bay of Pigs. Maybe their father convinced them to, you know—don't get mad, get even. I mean: to make Cuba the number-one priority of the agency, at the expense of everything else; then to put Bobby in charge of the operation and this—well, this boy, really, this hot-tempered boy—to try to run it and do the personal bidding of his brother. Unbelievable.

A lot of people got bloody noses at the Bay of Pigs, but not very many went off the deep end like the Kennedys did. And it continued, as I said before, after the Cuban missile crisis into '63, and even into '64. We finally got sabotage stopped completely in April of 1964, when we were able to convince President Johnson that we were wasting time and effort and money, and we were taking losses, and the other side was taking losses and it wasn't doing a damn bit of good. . . .

Blight: Sam. . . . This has been one of the few times during a conference when I have almost felt literally transported back to the time and place under discussion. Sam, you are a human time machine! [Laughter. Applause.]. . . .

What I would like to do now is to ask Rafael for his view of what was going on. After Rafael is finished, I'd like to come back and ask Arthur and Wayne, too, about this issue of Cuba and the Kennedys. Because, as I understand one of your main points, Sam, MONGOOSE, and in fact everything relating to Cuba in those days, was coordinated by, and motivated from, the White House—from the Kennedys.

. . . . .

Halpern: Excuse me, let me just add one thing. As Dick Helms was fond of saying: "If anybody wants to see the whiplashes across my back inflicted by Bobby Kennedy, I will take my shirt off in public." That's how he felt about this stuff. It was unbelievable. I have never been in anything like that before or since and I don't ever want to go through it again.

Quintero: In the summer of 1961, after the invasion, the reaction of the underground was—total shock! This is the main fact you have got to realize. When I say "shock" I don't mean "disappointed" or something like that. I mean: shock, like they were in a state of shock, almost paralyzed. You could identify members of the underground in the streets by the way they would walk, and by the emptiness in their eyes. Because losing—losing totally, with the Americans on our side at the Bay of Pigs—was something that nobody ever thought could happen. And then you have to face the future. What now? What is next? What is going to be next? Sam was saying that Castro's people got a lot of help from the Russians and East Germans in setting up their counterintelligence. That was true. Those became very tough moments for the underground.

One of the most important developments was starting up the Committees for the Defense of the Revolution—the CDRs. The CDRs were everywhere, all over the place. Everybody was watching everybody. The CDRs became very strong. In fact, they totally destroyed the underground. Second, recruitment was very difficult for two different reasons. The main reason for the hard-core anti-Castro people was—well, I mean people would say: If there is no chance to win this war, then why do you want me to risk my life to conspire against the government? To do what? What is at the end of this? If I send intelligence to the gringos, I am going to be executed. Do you think I am this stupid?—people would say and think this. Send intelligence to the Americans? You've got to be kidding me. I mean I am going to set you up. I mean don't bring that to me; don't even talk to me about the gringos, because I am going to just set you up.

That is what people would say. And could we convince them that sending information to the Americans would do any good, anyway, even if they weren't scared of the CDRs? No. It was impossible.

There was also a second reaction—the reaction of the people who were not hard-core conspirators, the undecided, the people who were cooperating but not very active in working with us. They acted in a very funny way. They went with the system. They went with the winner, always with the winner. And who was the winner? Castro. So this "undecided vote" went, I would say, almost 95 percent for him. They saw the situation as basically leaving one choice: either you leave the country or you join the system. That is how many people decided: well, if we cannot live right in Cuba, we are going to live right in Miami. If we cannot have Cuba, we are going to Miami and take it away from the Americans. And that's what we did. [Laughter.]

Some people stayed and worked for the underground. But it was very difficult because the whole infrastructure of the underground was totally destroyed. You didn't have any safe houses. You didn't have transportation. You didn't have any, any . . . well, I am going to give you an example, one example. When you go to a country, the first thing that you are taught is: don't ever get close to your family, to your real family, that is a no-no. Right, Sam?

Halpern: Absolutely.

Quintero: But when you are sleeping in the back of a bus station for three or four nights and you cannot find a safe house, you go a little bit crazy. So one night, being very desperate, I went to my grandfather's to sleep, to spend one night, to sleep one night. But he told me, you can't be here. My own grandfather—he told me: "You can be here for one night, and then one night only. You've got to be out of here in the early morning because if you get caught here, I will receive the same sentence that you will receive. You are a spy for the CIA and you are going to be executed. I am not going to be executed. I don't want it. Out." It came to that kind of situation. I am talking here about the summer of 1961.

I came back to the States in September of '61 to find out what the future was. I had to know what we were going to do. In December 1961 I was convinced to go back to Cuba to organize a resistance. I remember the first time I went back, when I was infiltrated, they gave me a .22-caliber, with a silencer. This time I went in with a .38 short-nose revolver. I thought to myself: we are losing it here. I mean, instead of gaining time we are losing it. The only thing better was the radio equipment. We had radio equipment where you could record while you were sending and you didn't have to spend too much time on it.

Okay, so we have some good equipment, but basically we have the same problem. The problem was that you didn't have an assignment. There was no such thing as an assignment—I mean, about what you are going to do in Cuba. People in the States say: don't worry. You go there, you start recruiting people, start getting people together again, reorganize the underground. You do that and we will see what we can do. That is what we were told: "We will see what we can do." They should have said: We will see what we are *not* going to do—that's it! [Laughter.] Not only that, but we begin losing people very fast. This time we are losing. I mean we are losing people every day.

And the commitment and the makeup of the people working with you is totally different. We are coming here to a second level of motivation. You know the saying: "Highly motivated people you find the first time around." Now, you cannot talk to people about going to the mountains. Actually, I went to the mountains to see a black guy who was a guerrilla. I went to offer him a radio, so he could stand there and receive weapons drops from the Americans. When I mentioned the word "Americans" he turned around and said: "Kill this son-of-a-bitch." Because now we were the enemy. Before we were comrades, now we were the enemy. That fast, it happened that fast. I had to run for my life. The militia surrounded one of our people in a sugar field. They just didn't even try to take him alive. They just burned the sugar field, and they burned him up inside there.

So, we are talking here about two different things. The government becomes very, very good—very, I would say, competent. And the underground becomes worse, much worse. I agree with what Sam was saying about trying to recruit people for gathering intelligence. I think I was one of the guys with the idea of working with Ted Shackley. I said that there is not a chance that you can get a person who has been in Miami for six months or a year, and then send him back in, because he cannot survive. From one month to the other, things change so much. People notice very small things that you do wrong. This is a very serious thing. I was away for one month and when I came back, I didn't know how to ask for a pack of cigarettes. They had changed the cigarettes. And that was enough for you to get identified. Or you might ask for a ticket, or something like that, which they don't have any more.

So, because things like that were happening, I came up with the idea that the only way we can do this is to recruit people inside who could be sent outside. I thought we could give them ten days—ten days of a crash course in training and send them back in. A week or ten days and send them back. I thought maybe we could create another underground. The idea was to get people who, for example, were from Santiago de Cuba and they could say, I am going on vacation to Havana for a week to ten days. Then we would bring them out for that amount of time and send them in again. They could go back to their houses, to their families, to their regular flight, and they could report to the people up here. But you couldn't get any hardcore people this way.

Finally, I came out and they tried to convince me to go back. I said: "I am not going back. We are not going to survive another three months. Another guy went back in May. He went back on May 2 and he was caught May 20. He was executed August 1.

I was thinking about this—I mean, actually, the Bay of Pigs invasion did really accomplish something. In only three days in April 1961, the invasion was successful in totally destroying the underground and giving Castro everything that he didn't already have before. Actually, the Cuban Revolution didn't start the 1st of January 1959. The revolution—it started with the Bay of Pigs, because that's when Castro consolidated his power; that's when he was able to eliminate the underground resistance; that's when the Soviets starting arriving all over Cuba.

Blight: Thank you very much, Rafael.

Quintero: May I mention one thing more here? Sam was talking about the Kennedys. I had the luck—I don't know why, exactly—to become a good friend of Bob Kennedy. I first started seeing him when I was working on the release the prisoners from the Bay of Pigs brigade. I worked on that for a long time.

Anyway, I was involved in an operation with Artime in Central America. I was Artime's adjutant there. I had many chances to talk with Bob Kennedy. And I agree with Sam: Bob Kennedy was obsessed— obsessed with the idea that they had been beaten by Castro, that the Kennedy family had lost a big battle against a guy like Castro. He had to get even with him. He really wanted to get even with him. He mentioned this to me often and was very clear about it: he was not going to try to eliminate Castro because he was an ideological guy who wanted to do right in Cuba. He was going to do it because the Kennedy name had been humiliated.

Halpern: That's what I've been saying. . . .

Quintero: That was very clear. There is no mystery in that. He mentioned it to me very clearly one day—we went to the circus together and he mentioned it to me. That was before the Bay of Pigs people were released.

Brenner: Rafael, not all of us are familiar with what you did with Artime in Central America, starting in 1963. I wonder if you could elaborate a little on this. For example, Félix Rodríguez describes in his memoir why he felt you had come to him in 1963. He had just been commissioned into the U.S. military, and you asked him if he would join you. And, according to Rodríguez, you say that this time, "We are going to overthrow Castro. This time we're really going to do it."[14] So Rodríguez asks himself: Why should I join with Quintero and Artime? Why should I trust these guys? He says:

> I'd met Chi Chi Quintero in 1956. There were three good-looking sisters from Camaguey who were spending the summer at Varadero Beach that year. I dated the eldest, Chi Chi the youngest, and his brother dated the middle sister. I hadn't seen him since then, until just before the Bay of Pigs, although I knew from mutual friends that he had become close to the political leadership of the Cuban resistance movement. After Francisco's death, Chi Chi was one of the resistance leaders I infiltrated back inside Cuba—there is a picture taken of us together on one of those missions. . . . Now he was Artime's deputy.[15]

And so Rodríguez joined your group, under the auspices of the CIA. Can you tell us a little bit about how that worked?

Quintero: Sure. This operation was what Bill Casey or Oliver North later on called a "self-standing operation." We were supposedly—I emphasize supposedly, Phil—we were supposedly to be the only part of the CIA that was totally independent to develop our plans for doing anything that we want. That was supposed to be the rule of the game.

Halpern: We supplied money and told them where to buy arms. It wasn't our arms. They bought them on the open market. We told them where the sellers were, what they could get, what they had to pay for it. It was decided to let the Cubans do this on their own. They needed money, and we gave them the money; and we gave them intelligence support, too.

Quintero: We had all the intelligence we wanted and asked for, and the money.

Halpern: Yeah. We gave them everything.

Quintero: Just anything we wanted. That was supposed to be the rule of the game. And we were happy, of course. Then we started recruiting people for this operation, and we thought, this is going to be great.

But when we started running the operation, we found out that was not the way that it was, because the CIA didn't want it that way. They were totally against an operation with the Cubans running it. Really, it was almost the same old CIA. And Bob Kennedy, it seems, was the person who was pushing them and making them do it—I mean, put the Cubans in charge of their own operation—but they definitely didn't want to do it. . . .

We were just really getting started with our operation when President Kennedy got assassinated. After that, there were big problems—you know about these—between Bob Kennedy and Lyndon Johnson. And at last, we had an accident. We had an accident: we blew up a boat that was the wrong boat. We thought it was the *Sierra Maestra*. Instead of a Cuban boat it was a Spanish boat and we blew the hell out of it. We made a mistake, and so that was good enough for them to terminate the whole operation. It was a political decision. . . .

Blight: Arthur, would you like to comment on this?

Schlesinger: Yes. I have several comments. First on the assessment of Operation MONGOOSE: I totally agree with Sam. It was total nonsense. Mac Bundy thought so. Dick Goodwin thought so, too.

Halpern: Why did they continue?

Schlesinger: Well, Dick was transferred to the State Department. Dick always said it was nonsense. We used to discuss it. But we didn't know that we had allies in the CIA.

Halpern: Well, you had a lot of them.

Schlesinger: We assumed that this was your project—the CIA's project.

Halpern: No way. This was a Lansdale project.

Schlesinger: There seemed to us to be a significant difference between Lansdale and Harvey. Lansdale was filled with lots of ideas, most of which were terrible. But he did have one basic purpose, if I understood it, and that was that you could only build your operation by creating a strong force inside Cuba. Harvey, on the other hand, operated in terms of agents sent in from the outside under CIA discipline. And there was that difference in teamwork, too. Lansdale was better than Harvey.

Halpern: Except we weren't trying to build a resistance, Arthur. We were trying to get intelligence first, and then decide what kind of a resistance you could have.

Schlesinger: Okay. On this question—a minor point that Sam brought up— there must have been some misunderstanding. Robert Kennedy said in 1964 [reads from book]:

> "We had a terrible experience.". . . CIA's Task Force W was "going to send some 60 people into Cuba right during the missile crisis." One of

them sent word to the Attorney General that they did not mind going but wanted to make sure he thought it worthwhile. Robert Kennedy said, "I checked into it, and nobody knew about it. . . . The CIA didn't and the top officials didn't." . . . Kennedy [then] called a meeting at the Pentagon. As Harvey later put it, the Attorney General "took a great deal of exception." "I was furious," Kennedy remembered, "because I said, you were dealing with people's lives . . . and then you're going to go off on a half-assed operation such as this. I've never seen [Harvey] since."[16]

Now, on the obsession—the events Rafael mentioned—what brought the Kennedys to this alleged obsession? As I said, I think Robert Kennedy—if anyone was obsessed—Robert Kennedy was a good deal more obsessed about Cuba than John was. But if Robert Kennedy was so obsessed with vengeance and the desire to redeem the Kennedy family name after this humiliation, why did he not seize the chance provided by Fidel Castro himself with the acceptance of Soviet nuclear missiles? Why did he not seize the chance to invade Cuba? Why did he not recommend that the United States attack, when Castro had given him the perfect pretext?

Hershberg: Well, wait a minute. I mean, there was a risk of nuclear war. That was a U.S.–Soviet crisis. I mean a lot of different considerations would have entered into it, other than how much he did or did not want to get rid of Castro. If getting rid of Castro was going to cost you Atlanta or Miami, then I'd say it's pretty much out of the question.

Skidmore: On the contrary, Bobby Kennedy led the fight against people who did have this obsession.

Schlesinger: Yes—people like the Joint Chiefs of Staff; John McCone, Douglas Dillon.[17]

Gleijeses: I think the evidence is unequivocal: both Kennedys were obsessed with Cuba. Maybe there is a genetic explanation. [Laughter.]

Smith: But Piero, seriously, if he were obsessed, if you are obsessed with something . . .

Schlesinger: But Piero, think of the decisions that Robert Kennedy was making. An obsessed man doesn't make rational judgments. Also, if he were that obsessed, why the next year did he back the exploration of normalizing relations with Cuba?

Skidmore: But there is still the evidence—you have to deal with—of his behavior. . . .

Schlesinger: Well his behavior—the evidence are his words and his behavior. I see evidence of intelligence and balance on both counts.

Skidmore: But Arthur, what about these instructions that he gave to Helms, the ones that—as Sam was saying—put all the "scars" on his back?

Schlesinger: These were not instructions, they were exhortations. He never gave specific instructions. He didn't know what the hell should be done. He knew even less than the CIA people knew about what to do about it. He wanted something done but he didn't know what.

Halpern: The instructions came from him to Ed Lansdale. From Ed Lansdale, they went to State and Defense and so on.

Schlesinger: Look, he just wanted to do something about it. Those aren't instructions, they are exhortations.

Okay, I will tell you what I think was driving the Kennedys. It's what drives American policy toward Cuba to this day. It was domestic politics. Barry Goldwater had come out in 1962 with a book called *Why Not Victory?*, calling for the total elimination of communism from the Western Hemisphere.[18] The supposedly enlightened Republican senator from New York, Ken Keating, was making a big thing of Cuba. It was a constant nag in domestic political circles for the Kennedys. Concern for the domestic political implications of Castro and Cuba was driving both Kennedys. Of course, Robert Kennedy had a fighting Irish side. But as I say, there is plenty of evidence that Bobby Kennedy made rational judgments about the Cuba issue that should preclude the accusation that he was obsessed.

Kornbluh: Let's look at the documents. Please turn to the last document in Tab 6 [Document 5.7]. When I first saw this I thought: Is it possible that RFK could have done this—take the most irrational position during the most extraordinary crisis in the history of U.S. foreign policy? This is the October 16, 1962, memo for the record by Richard Helms. Remember at 11:00 or so on the morning of the 16th the first executive committee (EXCOMM) meeting is held on the missile crisis. At that meeting, all the members of the EXCOMM are informed that there are Soviet nuclear missile installations going up in Cuba. Directly—it seems as if it may have been directly—after the EXCOMM meeting, RFK convenes a meeting of the Operation MONGOOSE team. Helms says:

> The Attorney General opened the meeting by expressing the "general dissatisfaction of the President" with Operation MONGOOSE. He pointed out that the operation had been under way for a year that the results were

discouraging; there had been no acts of sabotage; and that even the one which had been attempted had failed twice [Document 5.7].

Halpern: At the Matahambre mine.[19]

Kornbluh: Right. Helms goes on:

> The Attorney General then stated that in view of this lack of progress, he was going to give Operation MONGOOSE more personal attention. In order to do this, he will hold a meeting every morning at 0930 with the MONGOOSE operational representatives from the various agencies [Document 5.7].

Looking back on this I would think that Robert Kennedy might have called the team together and said, you know, I can't tell you exactly what is going on but we are going to stand down for a little while—things are a little dicey with regard to Cuba. Instead, he convenes the MONGOOSE team and says, more or less, that both my brother and I are incredibly pissed off at you guys for doing nothing. This is a rerun of the "get off your ass" statement to Bissell.[20] Now, he says, I am going to oversee this more closely.

If Sam's boss, William K. Harvey, was spurred to start sending in sabotage teams at that point, it is easy to understand why. But what I personally can't understand is the lack of caution, the disregard for the ominous news the EXCOMM had received just that morning. I'd like to ask Arthur, who knew RFK well, to help us understand what might seem to be the behavior of someone obsessed with Cuba.

Blight: Excuse me, Arthur. Peter, I just want make sure our group understands your point. Your reflection here is that the EXCOMM has now accepted the fact that nuclear missile sites are being constructed on the island of Cuba. That's fact number one. But that these MONGOOSE operations that are supposed to blow up bridges and that sort of thing somehow do not seem to jibe with—with what?

Kornbluh: With the tremendous tension and danger associated with the crisis over the missiles.

Brenner: The crisis with the Soviet Union is over Cuba. Should the United States be trying to destabilize the island, to blow things up—knowing, or believing, or suspecting, at this point—that nuclear weapons are on the island as well?

Kornbluh: Not to belabor the obvious, but for chrissake, a nuclear crisis is happening and Bobby wants to start blowing things up—or he wants Sam and his crews to blow things up.

Skidmore: And Bobby is saying why aren't you sabotaging more effectively inside Cuba?

Blanton: Yeah. Get on with this plan aggressively. Get with the new action program. Get on with the acts of . . .

Kornbluh: Can you explain this, Arthur, based on your knowledge of RFK?

Schlesinger: No, I can't explain that. But I do know that the position he did take when the EXCOMM was trying to think about these matters was very rational. In fact, at several points during the 13 days, Robert Kennedy seems to be the sanest man in the room, and the most courageous at facing down the hawks.

Kornbluh: Well, that's true. But doesn't this just make his behavior with Helms and the others on the afternoon of the 16th of October all the more strange?

Domínguez: I find it interesting that, following a morning of solemn discussion about Soviet nuclear missiles, Khrushchev's intentions and all that, Robert Kennedy can still focus his mind on the Cuba problem—on the Castro problem—the problem, Sam, that you guys were not, according to the attorney general, doing anything about.

Halpern: We were trying but we were lousy at it. We didn't succeed in lots of things. And with the pressure to keep on doing it, more teams were sent. And they didn't do any good either, to speak of.

Quintero: Let me make something clear. If you do something at that time, if you do any sabotage in Cuba at that time, you were going to lose all your ability to collect intelligence. For us inside Cuba, making even the smallest act of sabotage was very costly. And with a limited number of people left inside, we had come to a decision that unless it was a worthy sabotage action—namely killing Fidel Castro, or making a huge economic mess for Castro—it was not worth it. Planting a stupid bomb in a car in the middle of nowhere—it wasn't going to pay off. It was just stupid because it alerted Castro's security people and did not hurt the government even a little bit.

Domínguez: So, MONGOOSE had a lot of bark but no bite.

Halpern: It never had any bite. . . .
   We collected a lot of intelligence by the time the missile crisis had hit. We had a pretty good rundown on what was going on inside of Cuba. We were successful because of people like Rafael, here. It worked from an intelligence point of view. Sabotage never worked very well.

Brenner: But setting fields on fire, destroying factories, and so on. Isn't that what you were trying to do—and doing?

Halpern: Let me explain. CIA and the U.S. Army and military forces and Department of Commerce, and Immigration, Treasury, God knows who else—*everybody* was in MONGOOSE. It was a government-wide operation run out of Bobby Kennedy's office with Ed Lansdale as the mastermind. One of the problems is that people get confused about groups like Alfa-66, for example, and other organizations of similar type, operating out of South Florida and the Florida Keys. These were often attributed to the CIA or the U.S. government. But we had nothing to do with them.
   In early 1963, when Des FitzGerald moved in, one of the first things he had to do—on Bobby Kennedy's orders—was to go down to Miami, and call a big meeting of every single U.S. government installation in the area.[21] Even the Florida State Police were involved. Bobby Kennedy's idea—it was strictly his idea—was to coordinate and keep up on what the heck all other elements such as Alfa-66 were doing. He didn't want anybody else doing it—no one except the U.S. government. In other words, he wanted to control all of the action against Castro—against Cuba. Just to take an example, Alfa-66—I am only using them as an example, there were other groups in the area—we didn't want their boats to run across our boats. There were lots of coordination problems like this.
   And so Bobby Kennedy told Des to go down and organize this as a U.S. government action. This is why you would find in the local Florida papers that a Cuban exile group complained that they were being hampered by the Coast Guard, by Immigration, by the local police; they couldn't get their boats out of harbor and things like that. This was deliberate on Bobby Kennedy's part and I think it was a good idea to control this thing so that you wouldn't have a half a dozen different groups all going after the same target. And that's one of the problems in terms of what you did, and what you didn't do. All of this had to be coordinated somehow. And it was a bloody awful mess. We antagonized an awful lot of Cuban people who were in the Miami area, and around the Keys.

. . . .

Blanton: At my peril, I want to take issue with Arthur's characterization of Bobby Kennedy's reaction to the missile crisis—your answer to Peter. I have just been consulting with Jim Hershberg about Bobby's interventions in the EXCOMM on the 16th of October. It was summed up in a phrase: "Sink the Maine."[22] In other words, let's create a pretext and invade. It wasn't until the 17th and 18th when, maybe because he's picking up his brother's caution, he challenges his colleagues to compare a U.S. attack on Cuba with the Japanese attack on Pearl Harbor. Bobby was a hawk on the 16th. He changed later in the week.[23]

Schlesinger: He was more emotional than his brother. John Kennedy was preeminently a man of reason. But while Robert Kennedy was a man of strong emotions, he was also an intelligent and reflective man. For example, Robert thought it preposterous to prosecute American students who wanted to inspect the Castro revolution. "What's wrong with that," he said to me one day. "If I were 22 years old that is certainly the place that I would want to do something. I think our people should go anywhere they want." I would say there was a broad mixture of emotions about the man. When one says that he had an "obsession," it implies that he was locked into one emotion to the exclusion of all others. He wasn't like that.

Blanton: Thanks.

Blight: Let the record show that the subject of the Cuban missile crisis was not raised at this table by the chairman. [Laughter.] But as the subject is on the table, let me inject something that Janet [Lang] just mentioned to me.

At the end of the first meeting, on the first day, October 16, the president and, if I am not mistaken, *all* his advisers, concluded that the missiles would have to come out.[24] As I read the transcript of that meeting, this meant an air attack was coming, though probably not an invasion of the island, though that would be an open question. But after that meeting, the group began to evolve and the evolution, as Arthur pointed out, was led by Bobby Kennedy, along with Bob McNamara. They began discussing what they believed the Soviets would do in response to the attack on Cuba that they initially all thought would be necessary. This meant they had also to discuss questions like Berlin and Turkey, and at least some of the members were pretty horrified by their conclusions.

So, yes, Bobby Kennedy was a kind of hawk, the same kind of hawk the others were, including his brother, before they had a chance to examine the possible consequences of their hawkishness. On the 16th, he was just beginning to think about what to do. It is possible that he hadn't yet connected in his own mind the goings-on in Cuba regarding MONGOOSE, and the crisis over the Soviet missiles. Let he who is without historical blindness cast the first stone. It took some of us—it took me—many years before I made that connection.

. . . .

Baloyra: Rafael referred to people who have been outside and in and out of Cuba. The brigade guys were in jail. Many of our senior leaders were in their late 20s or early 30s. Most of the underground were in jail on account of trying to organize guerrillas. In the case of the directorate [DRE], many of our people were able to get to embassies to get out. The average age of the seven national secretaries was about 22. Okay? We were young. We were basically kids, and in 1961 we were trying to reconstitute the net in which we might still be able to operate.

The Cuban government issued a decree at that time whereby they changed the currency. I remember that I had, by Cuban standards, a hefty sum of money to get rid of, and no citizen was able to exchange more than, I believe, $1,000. I'm sorry, I mean pesos. Or maybe it was 500 pesos. I had to get a hell a lot of people together in a hurry and I was able to produce enough people to exchange a few thousand pesos of old into new currency. So there were some things you could still do. They were still not that great operationally, in the sense of keeping tabs on you. They could lose you and you could still dodge them. But the vise was tightening and the vise was the Committees for the Defense of the Revolution, the CDRs, as Rafael said. Eventually you had to go and sleep somewhere, and they had on every damn block in Havana an organization that knew who was supposed to sleep where. As you can see, they had anthropologists doing this, not political scientists. [Laughter.] They would nab you there.

We lost some people in a very bad incident in December of '61. One of our more beloved people got killed. Beginning then, we were in a similar situation to MRR or to what MRR would be in '63, in the sense that there was a "payroll." And each person on the payroll was supposed to be getting x number of dollars per month. But what happened is that we would be paid half of that, and the other half would be used to buy weapons and organize things on our own. This is how in August of 1962—the 24th to be exact—that the directorate was able to shell Havana from the harbor. There was a big brouhaha in the station in Miami because, obviously, somebody got on the phone and asked what the hell was going on. And the poor bastard who was on the Miami side of the line had no idea. And the organic matter hit the fan. [Laughter.] And there was much confusion about that.

There is a certain psychology involved in all this business, a psychology shared by groups like Alfa-66, and, later on, Omega-7.[25] The basic assumption these people make is that you cannot trust the Yankees, so you have to operate in the shadows and totally disconnect yourselves from any

American agency. Their philosophy was: we are not going to follow what you tell us to do. What is sensible for you is not necessarily sensible for us.

Notes

1. Arthur Schlesinger Jr., *A Thousand Days: John F. Kennedy in the White House* (New York: Fawcett, 1965), p. 240.

2. Alfredo Durán refers to the failed attempt to destroy the Cuban government's air force on the ground prior to the landing of Brigade 2506 at the Bay of Pigs.

3. The reference is to *patria o muerte* ("fatherland or death"), which is the traditional salutation with which Fidel Castro has ended his speeches in Cuba since the very early days after he and his colleagues came to power.

4. William Attwood, "Memorandum on Cuba," 18 September 1963, in Arthur Schlesinger Jr., *Robert Kennedy and His Times* (New York: Ballantine, 1978), pp. 594–595.

5. Carlos Lechuga, *In the Eye of the Storm: Castro, Khrushchev, Kennedy, and the Missile Crisis* (New York: Ocean Press, 1995).

6. See Peter Kornbluh and James G. Blight, "Dialogue with Castro: A Hidden History," *New York Review of Books* (6 October 1994): 45–49, on the evolution and eventual collapse of the probe to Cuba initiated by Kissinger.

7. Ramón Magsaysay, defense minister of the Philippines. Gen. Edward Lansdale, the U.S. military adviser to the Philippine army, assisted Magsaysay in putting down a communist insurgency in the early 1950s.

8. Edward Lansdale, "Guidelines for Operation Mongoose," 14 March 1962.

9. John McCone succeeded Allen Dulles as director of central intelligence on 27 September 1961.

10. William K. Harvey, chief of Western Hemisphere (WH) operations in the CIA's Directorate of Plans.

11. William K. Harvey, "Operation MONGOOSE—Future Course of Action," 8 August 1962.

12. Gen. Edward Lansdale is perhaps best known via the two fictionalized accounts of his exploits in Asia in the 1950s: Graham Greene, *The Quiet American* (New York: Bantam, 1957); and William J. Lederer and Eugene Burdick, *The Ugly American* (New York: Fawcett, 1960).

13. Harvey, "Operation MONGOOSE," 8 August 1962.

14. Félix I. Rodríguez, with John Weisman, *Shadow Warrior* (New York: Pocket Books, 1989), p. 135.

15. Ibid., p. 136.

16. Schlesinger, *Robert Kennedy and His Times,* p. 574.

17. See David A. Welch and James G. Blight, "The Eleventh Hour of the Cuban Missile Crisis: An Introduction to the EXCOMM Transcripts," *International Security* 12, no. 3 (winter 1987/88): 5–29, esp. 11 and 19; and McGeorge Bundy and James G. Blight, eds., "October 27, 1962: Transcripts of the Meetings of EXCOMM," *International Security* 12, no. 3 (winter 1987/88): 30–92, esp. 43–44 and 61–62.

18. Barry Goldwater, *Why Not Victory?* (New York: MacFadden, 1963).

19. A copper mine in western Cuba that CIA-trained infiltration teams tried unsuccessfully (on at least three occasions) to sabotage.

20. See Richard M. Bissell Jr., *Reflections of a Cold Warrior: From Yalta to the Bay of Pigs* (New Haven: Yale University Press, 1996), p. 201.

21. Desmond FitzGerald, a long-time Asia ("FE," or Far East) hand at the CIA, was Sam Halpern's boss during several assignments in Asia in the 1950s. Later, FitzGerald took over "WH" (Western Hemisphere) operations and was again Halpern's boss during the MONGOOSE operation.

22. See the Transcript of the Second Executive Committee Meeting: "Off the Record Meeting on Cuba, 16 October 1962, 6:30 PM–7:55 PM." In Laurence Chang and Peter Kornbluh, eds., *The Cuban Missile Crisis, 1962* (New York: New Press, 1992), pp. 97–113, esp. 107.

23. But see Robert Kennedy's remarks at the conclusion of the first EXCOMM meeting. With Defense Secretary Robert McNamara, Kennedy already had begun to see the danger of escalation deriving from a U.S. attack on Cuba, something the others in the group do not seem to grasp until later. "Off the Record Meeting on Cuba, 16 October 1962, 11:50 AM–12:57 PM: Transcript of the First Executive Committee Meeting." In Chang and Kornbluh, eds., *Cuban Missile Crisis,* pp. 85–96, esp. 95–96.

24. Chang and Kornbluh, *Cuban Missile Crisis.* John F. Kennedy concluded the meeting: "We're certainly going to do number one; we're going to take out these, uh, missiles. . . . At least we're going to do number one, so it seems to me we don't have to wait very long. We ought to be making *those* preparations" (p. 96).

25. Membership in these groups involves paramilitary training in the Florida Everglades, or elsewhere, for infiltration of Cuba and the use of firearms, explosives, and the like.

6

Aftermath of the
Bay of Pigs Invasion

Our orders to execute the strikes were so different from what we had been told that we would do, that when I saw the orders that we were calling off the war, I really thought we were trying to lose it intentionally, though I didn't say anything aloud in regard to this.

> *Speaker's identity classified, testimony to the Taylor Committee, 24 April 1961 [Document 6.1]*

Esterline: I have been looking at this guy Arthur Schlesinger over the last two days, and wondering if he is the same Arthur Schlesinger I have had some pretty terrible thoughts about over the years. Well, based on what I have learned here, I am going to have to amend my views. He's been just terrific. Except on this one thing. I think he taught most of these guys, so he must be the one who taught them not to take notes. [Laughter.]

Schlesinger: Not me. They all went to Yale. [Laughter.]

> *Exchange between Jacob Esterline and Arthur Schlesinger Jr., 1 June 1996*

Blight: In this session we want to step back from our detailed analysis of events and ask some questions about the meaning, implications, and some of the consequences of the events of April 1961. I can't think of a better person than Tom Skidmore to lead us in that direction. . . . Tom, a few thoughts? What should we conclude from what we now know or believe about the Bay of Pigs?

Skidmore: Well, after a careful study of the documents, I have concluded that it didn't work. [Laughter.]

Blight: Thank you, Tom. I hope you all wrote that down. Tom is obviously a morning person . . .

133

Skidmore: Well under that general rubric: I read carefully the "Aftermath" documents, which were many fewer than the documents for the previous sessions. But of course the aftermath is still with us. I want to start with some quotations from documents and then make a few cosmic comments, as requested by our chairman. And then leave. [Laughter.] That will enable you to not have to be accountable for my statements, which I think is in the spirit of the Bay of Pigs. [Laughter.]

Lyman Kirkpatrick Jr., who was at one time a professor at Brown, produced this document. The report—the Kirkpatrick Report—has never been released. But he has one section in his *Naval War College Review* article that I think is a good place to start.[1] He notes that the United States was very shocked

> that the United States was not going to be able to do business with Fidel. This I might say was a very great shock to Americans. Cuba was a country that we regarded as our protégé. We had helped liberate it from Spain; we had assisted it.

I like that "we had assisted it." He goes on: "We had helped it achieve independence." Remember the Platt Amendment? More: "We had looked at it as one of our offspring"—now we are getting into the nice muddy area— "but perhaps we were guilty of having looked after it too closely and in too patronizing manner."[2] Well, there is a psychiatrist among us and I leave it to him to plumb the depths of this emotional relationship. But I think in the end it is not going to be bureaucratic politics that explains what's going on between the United States and Cuba. It's got to be some other level of emotional involvement.

As we know, the CIA got blamed, and the general impression in the public, as I well remember at the time, was that poor JFK was badly served by his advisers, and he is going to look into all this to make sure it won't happen again. Now as a naive liberal from Ohio, I thought this meant that we would stop invading countries. That of course was not the point. [Laughter.] The point was that it wasn't done correctly. The Taylor Commission hearings produced an interesting document in which just about everybody other than the president and the White House get blamed. We also encounter some inadvertently incriminating remarks, like this one from Bobby Kennedy, which doesn't jibe with most of what we heard earlier. Bobby says, "One thing sticks in my mind with regard to this meeting. I remember at that time we were told it would be impossible to successfully overthrow Castro because of his control over his armed forces and over the country in general, unless you had the invading force backed up by intervention by U.S. forces."[3] Well, that is quite a different description of the options we heard in most of the documents.

Arthur Schlesinger went to Europe and obviously had a very good time and saw a lot of interesting people [Document 6.3].[4] [Laughter.] Including the most reactionary English Lord of all, Lord Lambton, who wishes us to go to fisticuffs with just about everyone.[5] At any rate, in reporting to the president following his trip, Arthur said:

> As the Algerian affair showed, CIA is going to be blamed for everything, especially so long as it continues to operate under its present management. People are eager to believe that the President was mislead by bad advice in the matter of Cuba. But they are also eager to be assured that he will not get the same bad advice in the future.[6]

So, the picture was set that the CIA would take the fall, Allen Dulles would take a walk, and that now Maxwell Taylor would come in and find out what went wrong. As a matter of fact, in the postmortem, we don't learn anything very new.

That said, some interesting points arise. One is that there are now some doubts about our Cuban "protégés." Indeed, there are a couple of rather ugly comments in the report about how the Cuban pilots wouldn't fly, about how the ammunition was used up too fast on the beachhead, and so on. It turns out that our surrogates did not carry out their assignments very effectively. I think these are important comments to notice, because they reveal a good deal about the U.S. attitude toward the Cubans—comments like: "Cubans wasted their ammunition in excessive firing," and so on. So, there is some recrimination toward the surrogates who were supposed to have carried out what was, as we have been discussing here this weekend, truly a "mission impossible" [Document 6.1].[7]

The second point that I find interesting in the deliberations of the Taylor Commission is its conclusion that the one thing we must do is move ahead with the development of a counterinsurgency capability. Now, this is of course completely inappropriate in the case of Cuba, since it's a country already controlled by another power. You are not trying to fight an insurgency in Cuba; you are fighting an insurgency that's already won. Never mind, we will get back to that later. But the commission concludes enthusiastically that counterinsurgency must be improved, as a counter to the feeling that the other side—you know, the communists—is winning the hearts and minds of the Third World. They also say that the U.S. government should increase its assistance to Latin American countries, which we did, through the training missions of the U.S. Army and through the Office of Public Safety. All sorts of activities were accelerated.[8]

Now, finally, within this discussion of what went wrong, my favorite explanation is "not enough coordination." Now anybody who has worked in a bureaucracy knows that in the end, anything that goes wrong is caused by insufficient interdepartmental coordination. So the executive branch of the government—this is in one of the conclusions of the study—was not organizationally prepared to cope with this type of paramilitary operation. Conclusion? We need a new intragovernmental committee. No such mechanism exists today. It should be "created to plan, coordinate and further a national Cold War strategy capable of including paramilitary operations."9 So, the implication is that if something went wrong it was in the bureaucratic design of the operation, and that is a very understandable reaction in the midst of all of this confusion about the plan. . . .

One thing that is very clear from all of this is that the CIA was not a rogue elephant. This was a favorite concept of the press, especially in those days. You know, that the good-hearted president has had something perfectly awful done behind his back. Had he known about it, he would of course have strongly disapproved. Our colleagues here from the CIA react vigorously against this and I am totally sympathetic to them. These operations, as far as we can see from the documentation, are absolutely approved from the top down. I think we can go further than this, in light of these documents. Some people at the top of the government were, it seems, among the *most* anxious to overthrow Castro, and toward that end were prepared to use virtually all weapons that the CIA would provide.

What is so interesting about this is that in the case of Cuba, the legacy is still alive and well. The Cold War is over. And yet, Jesse Helms can whip up just as much animus toward Cuba as was possible in the early 1960s.10 So the question arises—it's been raised here many times, with special pungency by Wayne: What *is* there that makes this relationship between the United States and Cuba so weirdly impervious to changes in, so to speak, the outside world? I think that if I were a psychiatrist—forgive me, Lino— and had Fidel on the couch, I might say that Fidel Castro is simply a genius at knowing how to push the buttons of the United States. He knows intuitively exactly what will most irritate the Americans about their self-image. And he has been able to irritate us through the administrations of nine presidents—and we are still counting.

Alright, then, what is the "cosmic" sense to be made from these events and this supremely dysfunctional relationship? I see this as a kind of dialectic between the two countries that now has survived the Cold War and has its own rationale. An important question is how all of this has affected U.S. policy toward Latin America, which interests me. . . .

What has impressed me very much about this case of the Bay of Pigs, and subsequent Latin American–U.S. relations, is the way in which they were sustained by the power of domestic anticommunism in the United States. And that of course is one of the reasons why the Kennedy brothers were so anxious to have a follow-up action in Cuba. It's why the number of Cuban voters in the United States seems to grow daily. Why Dade County alone must have millions of voters by now who are going to be attracted by a new tough measure toward Cuba. . . .

As to conclusions. This operation—the Bay of Pigs, and the post-mortems in the "Aftermath" documents—represent, to me, an excellent expression of U.S. arrogance. Of course, the Cold War didn't help. In some ways, it increased the capacity of the United States to try to manipulate the region. Everything was seen in the 1960s in a bipolar context. The misestimate of what was going on in Cuba in the early 1960s has a great deal to do, I think, with the misestimate of the entire Latin American situation in the 1960s. It was very convenient, but not very helpful, to believe that everything going on in Latin America that we didn't like was due to a kind of virus arriving from the east that had few, if any, domestic origins.

. . . .

Schlesinger: On the impact of the Bay of Pigs on Kennedy and the administration: the first thing to keep in mind is that thereafter he never paid much attention, or gave much value, to policy proposals from the Joint Chiefs of Staff or from the CIA. And that was a very important development in the education of the president. From that point forward, Kennedy was skeptical about any policy thoughts emanating from the Joint Chiefs of Staff and the CIA.

There was no administrative overhaul. Kennedy did not think in terms of administrative mechanisms. Kennedy, like Roosevelt, thought much more in terms of personnel than process. He did think that people made a difference. This is demonstrated, for example, in Kennedy's reaction to the Taylor Commission Report. He had no use for the veritable library of organizational proposals in the report. But Kennedy liked Taylor and made him chairman of the Joint Chiefs of Staff in order to inject some discipline into the chiefs. He did this even after he had rejected Taylor's administrative ideas.

What Kennedy did in foreign policy questions was to bring in two people he trusted, and both made a big difference thereafter: Bobby Kennedy and Ted Sorensen. Neither Bobby nor Ted had been involved in the Bay of Pigs. Robert Kennedy in particular had a key role in the missile crisis. As I said, JFK brought in Taylor, in due course, as chairman of the Joint Chiefs of Staff. He also brought in John McCone, a conservative Republican, as head of the CIA. I opposed his appointment, but I think that was a mistake. I think McCone did a pretty good job. Kennedy greatly strengthened the president's Board of Oversight for the CIA. He gave Clark Clifford considerable responsibility in this area to try to bring some sense and order into the agency. So, in these various ways, by bringing people he knew and thought he could trust into the administration, he tried to guard against the kind of messiness that seemed to him to be the dominant feature of the Bay of Pigs.

As far as Latin America was concerned: the Alliance for Progress was the project that was close to his heart, and which he pursued and promoted vigorously. I agree with Tom that the CIA made something of a comeback in the Johnson years, and thereafter. Those operations, however, always carried risks. As we know, they almost landed one Republican president in jail later on. I do think that there was undue emphasis on counterinsurgency training, and it persisted throughout the Kennedy years. But after the Bay of Pigs, there were no covert actions of any significance that I can recall.

On the question of whether the CIA was a rogue elephant, I would dissent from what Tom just said. I believe that all intelligence agencies become rogue elephants, in whatever country, whether it is the United States, France, Israel, the Soviet Union, or elsewhere. After a time, people in intelligence agencies come to feel that they know the requirements of national security better than transient elected officials who, in the view of many intelligence professionals, are in office too short a time to know what the game is all about. They also tend to take advantage of the lack of oversight.

I say this not simply from my own experience. But people with much more experience than I had thought the same thing—people like Bob Lovett and David Bruce, who were members of the Board of Foreign Intelligence Advisors under Eisenhower and criticized the CIA's freewheeling covert action habits as early as 1956.[11] Recently I got a call from the CIA saying that they couldn't find the Bruce-Lovett report. They then asked me if *I* could provide them with a copy. So I gave them my notes but was curious as to where the original documents could be. The file of the president's Board of Foreign Intelligence Advisors must be somewhere. They said: "Well, they are at the NSC." I said: "Well, can't you see if I can get them from the NSC?" They said: "Well, we have had problems doing that." I said: "Why don't you send one of your clandestine teams over?" [Laughter.]

The assassination project began under Eisenhower, and continued through the Kennedy administration and into the Johnson administration. I doubt if any of those three presidents knew about or authorized the assassination project. I think it is inherent in the nature of intelligence agencies to turn their techniques of disinformation and dissembling—which they are taught to use against the enemy—to turn them against colleagues or agencies that might disagree with their favored course of action. I have had many dear friends in the agency who do none of this. I consider Jake Esterline and Sam Halpern here to be examples of agency officials who are responsible and serious. But there are also plenty of operators who get excited by the lack of accountability, the money they are given, and by the sense of adventure. Many of the players in the Bay of Pigs from inside the agency seem to me to have fallen prey to one or more of these temptations.

I think I would disagree with Tom on the question of how popular Jesse Helms's Cuban policy is in America in general. Remember that the China lobby for a generation paralyzed American policy towards China. Presidents regarded the question of the admission of Red China to the UN as a forbidden possibility, because of the supposed power of the China lobby. Of course, we all know that Nixon and Kissinger went to China. It turned out to be a very popular act. The China lobby disappeared like the one-horse shay. Today, the Cuba lobby is in the same position relative to normalizing relations with Cuba. It is my impression that if a president were to move decisively to end the embargo, it would probably be a very popular act. Even the *Wall Street Journal* endorses this now. If we think about it, it is easy to see how the embargo protects Castro. The Helms-Burton Act gives him new weapons in playing his last card, which is the card of nationalism. I believe the quickest way to get rid of the Castro revolution is to drown it in a torrent of American tourists, American investors, and American consumers. I feel that would be a popular action too. . . .

Blight: Thanks very much, Arthur. Jake? Sam? We know that after the Bay of Pigs, Bissell was gone, and Dulles was gone. But how was life different in the CIA as a function of having gone through this awful experience?

Esterline: I never lived it down. . . . Every time my name came up in discussion, it was always in the context of having been the goat at the Bay of Pigs. Everybody always had their fun with me about it. . . .

Halpern: I notice that one of the questions on the agenda for this session is: How did President Kennedy's and Robert Kennedy's views change toward the CIA following the failed invasion? Well, that's easy. Following the failed invasion, they wanted to destroy the CIA! Maybe they should have destroyed it at that time. But Bobby took a real close look at CIA, even before the Taylor Commission got to work. He became sort of an amateur expert on its facilities and its manpower. And I don't mean just in the clandestine service but also in the important part of the CIA, which is the analytical part. And of course the technical end. He decided that the best way to handle the CIA was not to destroy it, but for him to take it over and run it and use it as his own facility. And this is what actually happened.

The CIA was put back into covert action—paramilitary covert action—in a place called Laos in 1962 when the United States found out that the Soviets were violating the Geneva Accords. There were pictures in the *New York Times* of Soviet planes dropping supplies into northern Laos. The agency was put into Laos again, in a big way, to run what became known as the covert war, or the silent war, or the secret war. That was a lot of non-sense. . . .

Bobby also went bonkers on counterinsurgency. We went up to our bloody eyeballs in counterinsurgency. Everybody had to go to a special counterinsurgency school down at Fort Benning. A special force was given green berets and God knows what else. It was a nightmare because it had no real relation to what actually went on in the field, either by the military or by us, or by the Office of Public Safety in AID [Agency for International Development], which was really a combined operation of AID, CIA, and the military, all working together under AID's Office of Public Safety to train police organizations, both internal and external, in all of the countries of Latin America. And not just Latin America, but also Africa, South Asia, Southeast Asia—we were all over the place. I think we wasted a lot of time, effort, and money. . . .

But as I think everybody knows, CIA did not go out of business after 1961, or even '62 after the missile crisis. We were put back in action both on Cuba and everywhere else in the world. You know, it was almost as if nothing really had happened. I won't get into a big argument with Arthur on whether or not the CIA was a rogue elephant or not. But those of us at the "troop" level did not like what was going on. We objected. We had lots of discussions. But what can you do if you're working in the boiler room of a steamship? Make the ship go the other way? You can't. You're not near the helm. And unless you're at the helm—well, the ship goes where the helmsman wants it to go. All you do is keep on pumping the coal into the engine or putting the oil in the engine to try to keep it going. And that's what we did.

Blight: Thanks, Sam. I want to turn to Wayne, but I couldn't help noticing Rafael's expressions while Sam was speaking. I have a good view of Rafael's profile here and I saw something like this [makes nodding gesture, as if in agreement]. [Laughter.] So before Rafael forgets what he was reacting to, I wonder if you'd like to offer us some reflections on the feeling inside Cuba, among what was left of the resistance, after the Bay of Pigs?

Quintero: I was feeling what Sam was saying. I didn't know what was happening after the Bay of Pigs. I did not have any chance to get close to what was happening. I mean, I talked sometimes with Bob Kennedy, but we talked about the prisoners—stuff like that—not about the organization of the government.

From the point of view from inside Cuba, the basic feeling was that there was indecision—that there was great indecision on everything. It was a very difficult period on the few radios that we had working at the time. And the few reports we were sending—it was dropping things into a big black hole. I mean they would absorb everything—we thought they did—but there was no noise from the other side. Like there was *nothing* coming. But like nobody was saying anything. It was a very scary feeling. I mean, are there people still there, eh? Knock, knock, is somebody there? Are the gringos still there?

When I came back, I tried to find out what was happening. I asked some people whether we are going to continue this or are we finished? And I remember coming to Washington for my first time—coming to Washington, D.C., more or less directly from Cuba—and I had my first meeting with the CIA guy. He was with me and another guy, a guy who was later executed. We went to a hotel. He looked at us, and you knew that he didn't have anything to say. But he didn't know how to say to us: hey guys, you are going to go back. In four days, you are going to go back. How are you going to say that? Because he knew then that we were going to be harassed in Cuba. What for would we be going back? And he didn't have an answer to that question.

So finally this guy started talking about the way that we were dressed. The way that we were dressed is the same way that we have come from Cuba. We didn't have any other clothes. None. We are sitting there in the middle of the hotel, and you could tell he was ashamed because people were looking at us—like, who the hell are these two guys here? So he turned around, to his second in command, and says, "How much money, what can we give these guys? They need some new clothes before we can start a serious conversation. The second in command said: "Well, we can give them $999." Then the boss says: " Okay, we'll send them to buy some clothes so we can start talking the day after tomorrow."

Basically, they had nothing to say. They didn't have any plan. We had more plans in Cuba than the CIA had in Washington.

. . . .

Durán: When we began talking about the Bay of Pigs and the brigade, the question kept coming up of the "disposal" of the brigade. It seems that in the aftermath there was also a question of disposal. When the brigade was let out of jail in Cuba, some of those who were officers in the brigade, and had college degrees, were given the opportunity to go to officer candidate school and eventually become officers in the U.S. Army. I mention this because there was the strong presumption, and even insinuation, that such training would be in preparation for another attempt to overthrow the Castro government.

Blight: Alfredo, was that ever explicitly laid out for brigade members—that they would be trained for service in the army so that they could lead another invasion of Cuba, or something of that sort?

Durán: I didn't hear it personally, but that is not too surprising, since everyone knew I hated the army. I went to military school and hated marching up and down. [Laughter.] So I didn't participate in any. I immediately put it aside.

Esterline: Is that how Erneido Oliva got to be a general?[12]

Durán: Yes, that is exactly how Oliva got to be a general. In fact, Oliva was the one who more or less recruited or gave the message to the brigade about the possibility of an army position. I don't know if he was told this specifically by his superiors, but he told the people who were recruited that the purpose was to continue the training, and to ultimately be prepared to go back to Cuba. So you can see in the aftermath of the Bay of Pigs, the U.S. government was trying to deal with this so-called disposal problem. But really, there was no need for the "disposal" of anything. It was really a nonissue. But obviously, the U.S. government was very concerned—there was this continuous worry about "disposal."

Blight: Thank you. Quique, on this "disposal" issue?

Baloyra: Yes. Shortly before the missile crisis, there was a program launched to recruit able-bodied young Cubans out of Miami. We thought that we were being trained to be used in some future action against Cuba. In reality, this was, I think, a program of Americanization. It was a square deal. I got a GI Bill out of it, and it put me through school, and I bought my first house with that. It ran from shortly before the missile crisis through the late summer of 1963. We were on standby for service for six years, but we were never sent anywhere. . . .

The main thing for us was that these guys like Lino had been left behind in Cuban jails. I stayed with it until '64. I thought that just in case anything broke one way or another, there had to be a critical mass there to do something. We all felt that way—or most of us felt that way. We had a sense of obligation to the thousands who were now in jail and who would be in jail for the next 18 years or so. We were the only group who went on record—the DRE went on record—opposing the prisoner exchange in 1962. It was our contention that though the *brigadistas* were certainly worthy of consideration, they were no different or better than the rest of the political prisoners who were in Cuba. And we saw this as a very proper way for the administration to, you know, to get that off its chest and then be able to sleep a little better at night. In a sense, we saw an intimate connection between or among all of these different activities. So that is when there were all of these episodes of diversion of CIA-provided monies to buy things, and do things, and get some of you guys into trouble.

Halpern: We didn't get into trouble. We just gave you money.

Baloyra: There was a progressive estrangement. There were some people who stayed in as guerrillas. And incidentally there was a little bit of pique between the people who had taken up the offer of going into the U.S. Armed Forces and those who did not. So there was a gradual scaling back. We saw no purpose in terrorism for terrorism's sake. We thought we had had a couple of chances to nail the big enchilada, but it didn't work out. So we got on with our lives.

Blight: Thanks. Just before asking our scholarly colleagues for their thoughts, I'd like to ask Wayne to give us an idea of his own state of mind, and maybe a little of the State Department's with regard to Cuba. . . .

Smith: We broke relations and sailed out of Havana harbor the next day, or most of us did anyway. I went back to the department and, as I think I mentioned yesterday, I was one of those coming out of the embassy who were being held in Washington, for reasons I couldn't understand. We continued to be paid by the Embassy Havana pay clerk. There was a little sign on the door downstairs: "Embassy Havana Pay Room." [Laughter.] We were assigned to the "Embassy" and it soon became apparent why: somebody thought we were going right back in. I asked Tom Mann in a meeting: "Do you have some sort of an expedition? Do you think you are going to send us back in?" And of course Tom said, "We don't discuss these things at all." So I said to myself, obviously we *are* going back in. [Laughter.] So we were held to make ready to accompany the triumphant forces marching to Havana to, as they put it, reopen the embassy.

Well, the Bay of Pigs failed and the Embassy Havana Pay Room closed. I was then sent to work for Adolf Berle and, in that capacity, became the executive secretary of the president's Latin American Task Force. It is the grandest-sounding title I ever had in the foreign service. Of course, what it really meant was that I was Mr. Berle's spear carrier. [Laughter.] But I did get to sit in on all the meetings of the Latin American Task Force. There were a few discussions of the Bay of Pigs and why it failed. But very little, really. Attention was instead concentrated on the Alliance for Progress, and a good thing too . . . [because] that was the positive side of the Kennedy policy toward the hemisphere. We had a two-track policy: one track was to contain Castroism by supporting military forces, giving assistance, combating insurgencies, and so forth; the other side was the Alliance for Progress. And I thought that reflected the best side of our country and was what we should have been doing all along.

But although we were concentrating on the Alliance for Progress, it didn't seem to me that we learned anything at all from the Bay of Pigs. The assumption was that we had to get rid of Castro. This was absolutely vital and necessary to protect U.S. interests. Now it is one thing to say that we don't like the guy, and that we would like to be rid of him. It is another to say that we *must* get rid of him to defend vital U.S. interests. And I saw no second thinking at all on that score.

Schlesinger: I think what Wayne says is basically correct. Kennedy saw the competition in the hemisphere as a contest for the future of Latin America—a contest between the Castro way and the Betancourt way, after Rómulo Betancourt, the president of Venezuela.

Smith: I would still say that there was no second thinking regarding the assumption that we had to get rid of Castro, somehow. And with respect to Cuba also, there came to be a two-track policy. On the one hand there was MONGOOSE. And this is of course after the missile crisis. On the other hand, there was this second track that Arthur was talking about yesterday: the negotiating track.

You would think that in the wake of the missile crisis, with tensions at an all-time high on either side, that times would not have been good for an exploration of rapprochement. But if you look at it from Castro's view, the Soviets had just double-crossed him in the missile crisis; they were not helping him in his quest to start revolutions in Latin America—certainly to nowhere near the extent he wanted. Castro must have asked himself: What have I really bought with this relationship? Some economic assistance, to be sure, but perhaps I should put out some feelers to the Americans. . . .

Castro, I think, would have been willing to meet us halfway. In fact, Castro continued to pursue it. He told a reporter in 1964 that he was willing to draw back on extending the revolution, and that he would respect international conventions and so forth, *if* the United States would call off the dogs, and begin to move toward an accommodation or modus vivendi with Cuba. That didn't go anywhere at all. And so we were then locked into the Cold War policy.

I go to some lengths on this because I think the second track was serious—that the Kennedys were serious about it. I suspect that had Kennedy lived, relations with Cuba would have turned out very differently. . . . We have never had an intelligent policy toward Cuba. Perhaps we never will. I would agree with Arthur. I don't think Jesse Helms is a popular figure in U.S. politics, nor do I think that his Cuba policy is necessarily popular. It's a policy that is put forward by a very a small group of people who were able to take advantage of the shoot-down on February 24, to push it through Congress, and have the president sign it.[13]

I left the foreign service in 1982 because of my disagreements with the Reagan administration's policies, not just in Cuba, but in Central America. But I would have to say that the Reagan administration's policy was logical and enlightened, compared to Helms-Burton. This policy is irrational and totally illogical. I think we have reached, with Helms-Burton, a degree of irrationality greater than that which we demonstrated at the Bay of Pigs.

. . . .

Kornbluh: I will try to leave the fantasy world for a moment. Arthur, I wonder if you would recount your visit to Europe right after the Bay of Pigs and what you were told at that time? We have your memo to the president, which is comprehensive. One thing that is striking about it is how it resonates today. European leaders, then as now, have trouble appreciating our peculiar obsessions with Cuba, obsessions that they thought were self-destructive for the Kennedy administration.

I would also like to get your views on the Kirkpatrick Report. We couldn't get the report declassified. We have instead Kirkpatrick's article.[14] He lays out three or four conclusions from the Bay of Pigs that we have reason to believe are stated far more pungently in his final report. One is that the Bay of Pigs failed because of inaccurate intelligence about the reality of Castro's popularity inside Cuba—his control of the Cubans—and the whole issue of the militia defecting. Second, he says that organizationally, a large part of the CIA was out of the loop of the operation. Talented people were excluded and the opinions and analysis of the intelligence side were never requested. He raised the question of whether the same agency that is gathering intelligence should be permitted to conduct covert operations. Finally, he pointed out that keeping massive U.S. involvement covert was impossible. He said that trying to mount this operation was about as covert as trying to walk nude across Times Square without being noticed. As he put it in his article, "I must say that the latter is becoming more of a possibility every day." Could you speak about the European trip and the Kirkpatrick Report?

Brenner: Wyden says: "It's about as secret as Christmas Day."

Schlesinger: The European reaction was: Why in the world would you be so troubled about the presence of a communist regime on a small island in the Caribbean? They lived in much closer contact with communist regimes. They thought that we were overreacting. They were not aware of the fragility of many of the Latin American governments. We told them about the necessity we felt to defend the social democratic model against the communist threat. They generally didn't take that point. But the main issue was not that we had failed in the attempt but that we had ever made the attempt at all. That was when the Cold War was raging. So now, with the end of the Cold War, they of course feel that it makes no sense at all.

Smith: And it's not just Europe. The vote last year in the UN General Assembly to end the embargo of Cuba was 117 to 3.

Schlesinger: Yes, the naysayers were an interesting group: the United States, Israel, and Uzbekistan. [Laughter.]. . . .
      I would like to make a correction about something that I said yesterday. The question arose as to whether any effort was made to find out the conditions for the recognition of a provisional government. And I said, pontifically, that no effort had been made to find that out. Looking through the documents last night, I discovered a memorandum from me to the president. [Laughter.] It appears that I had a discussion with the legal adviser to the State Department, Abe Chayes, and we pinned down the conditions under which a provisional government might be recognized.[15] [Laughter.]

Esterline: I have been looking at this guy Arthur Schlesinger over the last two days, and wondering if he is the same Arthur Schlesinger I have had some pretty terrible thoughts about over the years. Well, based on what I have learned here, I am going to have to amend my views. He's been just terrific. Except on this one thing. I think he taught most of these guys, so he must be the one who taught them not to take notes. [Laughter.]

Schlesinger: Not me. They all went to Yale. [Laughter.]

Blight: Jake, you know there is an old baseball expression that seems an appropriate way to conclude this session, and this very long day of discussion. At the conclusion of batting practice, you always want to end on a line drive. If and when you do this, you are entitled to say: "Boy, that is a good one to quit on." [Laughter.] In a conference on the Bay of Pigs, that "perfect failure," I can think of no better occasion to conclude than with a double mea culpa: one from the White House and one from the CIA.

. . . .

Blight: Here at the end, I'd like to use the chairman's prerogative to say a word of appreciation to those of you on my right, the participants in the events we have been reexamining this weekend. All of you, each in your own individual way, has made a difference to this conversation—has raised the odds that in a year or two or three, these events will be discussed in ways that would have been impossible to imagine, had not you agreed to come forward and speak with us in the honest and forthright way that has characterized all these sessions. We scholars, those of us who have something to learn from you, appreciate it very much.

But while we scholars appreciate this, I sometimes think that we don't really understand just how much courage it sometimes takes to re-live events, particularly events that are something other than great victories or great successes. I once asked a senior member of the Kennedy administration this question: "If we had gone through Kennedy's foreign policy crises in chronological order, rather than starting with the Cuban missile crisis, do you think we would have ever gotten to the missile crisis?" And he said, "I doubt it. In fact, I doubt that I would today even know your name." [Laughter.] Something like that. Why? Because these events—the Bay of Pigs and related events—are so painful to recall. That pain has been manifest in various ways throughout our discussions. None of you who came here as participants in the events are happy with the way things turned out. It cannot have been an easy decision for some of you—to come to Musgrove and re-live what must be one of the worst nightmares of your lives.

But that didn't keep you away from Musgrove this weekend—away from that huge notebook of homework, and from all these nosy, rude, insistent scholars over here on this side of the table. [Laughter.] Because you came to Musgrove, we have succeeded. So I would like to lead the charge from the chair in expressing deep gratitude to all of you. Thank you very, very much. [Applause.]

Thanks to all of you for an illuminating weekend, that was also a lot of fun. [Applause.]

Notes

1. Lyman B. Kirkpatrick Jr., "Paramilitary Case Study: The Bay of Pigs," *Naval War College Review* 25, no. 2 (November/December 1972): 32–42.
2. Ibid., pp. 33–34.
3. Memorandum for Record of the "Taylor Committee Report," 24 April 1961, p. 8.
4. Arthur Schlesinger Jr., "Reactions of Cuba in Western Europe," Memorandum from the President's Special Assistant (Schlesinger) to President Kennedy, 3 May 1961.
5. Ibid., p. 3.
6. Ibid., p. 5.
7. See, for example, page 24 of Document 6.1 where General C. P. Cabell says: ". . . when the going was easy and morale was high, they did a good job, but

that by the end of the operation, when things were very difficult, it has been almost impossible to get them [the Cuban pilots] into the air at all."

8. Memorandum from the Cuban Study Group to the President, "Conclusions of the Cuban Study Group," the Taylor Committee Report, 13 June 1961.

9. Ibid., p. 3.

10. Theodore C. Sorensen, *Kennedy* (New York: Harper & Row, 1965), p. 66.

11. David Bruce and Robert Lovett, "Covert Operations," Report to President's Board of Consultants on Foreign Intelligence Activities, 1956. See Arthur Schlesinger Jr., *Robert Kennedy and His Times* (New York: Ballatine, 1978), pp. 490–491.

12. Erneido Oliva was the second-ranking military officer of Brigade 2506. He had received training in the United States during the Batista era. He retired with the rank of major general, and was commander of the Washington, D.C., unit of the U.S. National Guard.

13. The Helms-Burton legislation was pushed through Congress, and signed into law by President Clinton in the wake of the Cuban shoot-down on 24 February 1996 of two planes piloted by the Cuban exile group Brothers to the Rescue. The Cuban government claimed that the planes had violated Cuban air space; Brothers representatives denied the charge.

14. Kirkpatrick, "Paramilitary Case Study."

15. See Arthur Schlesinger Jr., "Cuba: Political, Diplomatic, and Economic Problems," Memorandum for the President, 10 April 1961, p. 109.

Epilogue: "John Wayne's" Illusions

Wayne helped articulate the system that could not sustain its mission of a *pax Americana*. The imperial reach led to the postimperial letdown. . . . The strength of Wayne was that he embodied our deepest myth—that of the frontier. His weakness was that it was only a myth. Behind the fantasies of frontier liberation . . . was a reality of conquest. And conquest has a way of undoing the conquerors . . . [But] down the street of the twentieth-century imagination, that figure is still walking toward us—graceful, menacing, inescapable.

> *Garry Wills,* John Wayne's America, *1997*

From the time the CIA headquarters started fabricating an organization or making their own resistance, they proved they did not understand the basic facts: *the opposition has to be from the inside, and it has to grow inside!* The same situation exists today. Nobody from the outside can "save Cuba." The only sensible policy then, and now, would be "hands off Cuba!"

> *Lino B. Fernández, 31 May 1996*

By April 1961, a young, untested U.S. president, new to his job, was already up to his neck in crises connected to the worldwide Cold War then underway.[1] In that atmosphere of threat and apocalyptic rhetoric, there was no way to know for sure which crisis, if any, might spill over its geographical or political boundaries and become a full-fledged nuclear confrontation between the United States and the Soviet Union. Many in the Kennedy administration believed that if the confrontation came at all, it would come in Berlin, in the heart of Europe, which was the only "hot spot" that both sides defined as central to their interests. The arrival of the Berlin Wall in August 1961 would do nothing to dispel this intuition. Few, if any, predicted that the showdown between East and West would occur over Cuba in October 1962. It is important, we believe, not to forget that the decisions

149

and events surrounding the Bay of Pigs invasion occurred in the context of one of the darkest, most frightening periods of the Cold War.

Seen against this background, it is clearer why the principal question most often asked about the failed invasion, virtually from its occurrence to the present, has been: *Who lost Cuba?* Or: Who is the betrayer, the "Judas Iscariot" who, either willfully or inadvertently, committed the unpardonable Cold War sin of losing a virtual colony or protectorate of the United States of America, one located, moreover, closer to Washington, D.C., than Dallas or Los Angeles? And to have lost it, moreover, to the Soviet Union, to the archenemy, and lost it so decisively, so unexpectedly, seemed, in the context of the times, to absolutely *require* a villain, an enemy within, to account for it. "Losing" Eastern Europe after World War II, or "losing" China in 1949—though regrettable, these events were comprehensible. The losses were incurred far from America's shores, in strange and distant lands with which the United States had little or no historical connection.

But the idea of "losing" Cuba to Soviet-oriented communists in what seemed like a virtual giveaway was surreal—like "losing" Cape Cod or Miami Beach—to most Americans, and to the Cuban exiles, America's anti-Castro, anticommunist protégés. It would be, as a Cuban-American colleague once said to us, "like John Wayne backing down from a gunfight with an evil dwarf." That kind of thing just didn't happen. Hence the various "witch hunts" for the betrayers on the losing side. A president was humiliated. Bureaucrats' careers at CIA and in the military were terminated or foreshortened. The *brigadistas* lost their country, as it turned out, for good, and many lost their lives. And the members of the underground resistance unlucky enough to have been captured but lucky enough to have survived, not only lost their country, but were to suffer years, even decades of imprisonment in the country of their birth.

Not one veteran of these events at the Musgrove Conference claimed immunity from having held, at one time or another, one or more of the betrayal theories of the Bay of Pigs. Yet by the conclusion of the conference, not one claimed to believe any of them anymore. We would not claim that the conference documents and discussions accounted for all of the renunciations of the various theories of betrayal at Musgrove. Clearly, some of the participants had long before begun to understand the context and nature of the illusions that had guided their thinking as young people, having felt profoundly betrayed at a moment of supreme importance to their lives. Others had had their eyes opened in the context of preparing for the conference, and in their discussions at the conference. In any event, we think it useful, in conclusion, to summarize some of the transformations that have taken place. We do not claim that the Musgrove Conference is solely responsible for these attributive reversals. But we do believe that the shift in explanation from betrayal by others to illusions held by oneself is important, both for setting the historical record straight, and also because of what we believe it signifies about U.S. relations with Cuba today.

We note, in summary form, the following transformations:

1. *Brigade 2506.* "John Wayne" will totally destroy Castro. Probably Castro and his people will flee at the first sign of a U.S.-backed threat, and the Cuban people will support us.

- 1961: Brigade betrayed by Kennedy
- 1996: *Brigadistas* held illusion of imperial invincibility

2. *Underground resistance.* "John Wayne" will assist the anti-Castro rebels with expertise and weapons, but will encourage the indigenous resistance to pursue its own strategy and timing.

- 1961: Resistance betrayed by the CIA
- 1996: Rebels held illusion of benign paternalism

3. *John Kennedy.* "John Wayne" can overthrow the Cuban government so secretly and easily that its role will remain plausibly deniable.

- 1961: John Kennedy betrayed by the CIA and military
- 1996: John Kennedy held illusion of imperial immunity

4. *CIA professionals.* "John Wayne," at the moment of truth, will not abandon freedom fighters aiming to oust a communist dictator.

- 1961: CIA betrayed by State Department (and by Kennedy)
- 1996: CIA held illusion of anticommunist fraternalism

5. *CIA leadership.* "John Wayne" will never fail to exploit an opportunity to destroy communists, especially in the Western Hemisphere, because of the "need" to bow to the concerns of politicians, whether domestic or foreign.

- 1961: CIA betrayed by Kennedy
- 1996: CIA held illusion of Cold War as war, requiring victory at each stage

6. *Robert Kennedy.* "John Wayne" can carry out an anticommunist counterinsurgency in ways that yield predictable, successful results, on time, according to plan.

- 1961: Robert Kennedy betrayed by the CIA
- 1996: Robert Kennedy held illusion of imperial control

7. *All players*. "John Wayne" and his subordinates can carry out covert action programs aiming to subvert governments in secrecy, by means that are morally dubious, without inducing mutual paranoia and bias in those most intimately involved.

- 1961: Everyone betrayed by someone else
- 1996: All held illusions of betrayal

The film critic Eric Bentley claimed in 1971 that John Wayne (without quotation marks) was the most dangerous man in America because without him, and the mythology of his movies, America's tragic involvement in Vietnam was unthinkable.[2] We are not prepared to claim quite this much for "John Wayne" and the Bay of Pigs. It is worth noting, however, that there are far closer historical connections between the themes of Wayne's most successful films of the 1940s and 1950s and issues related to Cuba, rather than to Vietnam. According to popular North American myth, the United States had liberated Cuba in the Spanish-American War, and had taken care of it ever since. It is also worth meditating on the finding that polls then, and now, indicate that Wayne is—not was, but *is*—America's most popular actor.[3] The analysis of precise connections between Wayne's films and U.S.–Cuban relations in the Kennedy years would seem to be fertile ground awaiting a cultural critic with knowledge of both western movies and Cuba. For us, for now, we are satisfied if "John Wayne" serves as a useful short-hand for a particular set of Cold War illusions that, due to elapsed time, availability of documents, and the courage of the Musgrove participants, can just now be seen for what they were.

Were and *are*, alas. For U.S. policy toward Cuba, as we write in March 1997, may be the last hurrah of "John Wayne's" sway over American foreign policy. The reader will have noted several references in the Musgrove discussions to the Helms-Burton legislation of 1 March 1996—technically called the "Cuban Liberty and Democratic Solidarity (Libertad) Act of 1996." The law allows the United States to arrest and try in U.S. courts U.S. trading partners who choose to trade with Cuba. Not surprisingly, the legislation has been repudiated by all U.S. allies and adversaries alike, and has given rise to legislation in some countries that makes compliance with the Helms-Burton Act unlawful.

The connections made at Musgrove between the Bay of Pigs invasion and the Helms-Burton Act, however, do not involve foreign trading partners. They have rather to do with the paternalistic, intrusive, imperial attitude that is implicit in it. One hardly needs to be a member of the Cuban

Communist Party to sense the potential for causing resentment in virtually every section of the Helms-Burton legislation. Just to take one example, section 3 ("Purposes") lists the following as U.S. motives in making the Helms-Burton legislation the law of the land:

> The purposes of this Act are—
> (1) to assist the Cuban people in regaining their freedom and prosperity, as well as joining the community of democratic countries that are flourishing in the Western Hemisphere;
> (2) to strengthen international sanctions against the Castro government;
> (3) to provide for the continued national security of the United States in the face of continuing threats from the Castro government. . . .
> (4) to encourage the holding of free and fair democratic elections in Cuba, under the supervision of internationally recognized observers;
> (5) to provide a policy framework for United States support to the Cuban people in response to the formation of a transition government or a democratically elected government in Cuba; and
> (6) to protect United States nationals against confiscatory takings and the wrongful trafficking in property confiscated by the Castro regime.[4]

This cannot fail to remind Cubans—and not only Cubans—of the infamous Platt Amendment of 1901, which the Cuban legislature passed, by a margin of one vote, in order to get the U.S. army of occupation to leave. In return, the United States got the right to intervene in Cuba whenever it felt it appropriate to do so—what historian Louis Pérez succinctly calls "an adequate if imperfect substitute for annexation."[5] Even more stunningly apropos of Helms-Burton is the remark of Senator Albert Beveridge during the discussion of the Platt Amendment in the Senate. He asked: "If it is our business, to see that the Cubans are not destroyed by any foreign power, is it not our duty to see that they are not destroyed by themselves?"[6]

The Helms-Burton legislation reminded several participants in the Musgrove Conference straightforwardly of the Bay of Pigs and its tragic result for those on the losing side. On 3 April 1961, Arthur Schlesinger, with assistance from Wayne Smith and others in the State Department, published a white paper simply called "Cuba," the principal purpose of which was to publicize the Kennedy administration's rationale for the upcoming Bay of Pigs invasion.[7] These are its concluding words:

> We are confident that the Cuban people, with their passion for liberty, will continue to strive for a free Cuba; that they will return to the splendid vision of inter-American unity and progress; and that in the spirit of José Martí they will join hands with the other republics in the hemisphere in the struggle to win freedom.[8]

It is bitterly ironic to Cubans of a wide range of political persuasions that this entire paragraph is a euphemism for the arrogance, ignorance, and overall incompetence of the CIA's handling of the Bay of Pigs invasion. As one Musgrove participant put it privately: "'Join hands with the other republics' meant 'handcuff yourself to the CIA.'"

And so we return to the politics of illusion, never having left it, in the case of U.S. policy toward Cuba—to the last hurrah of "John Wayne," to the alliance of small groups of backward-looking (but unseeing) Cuban exiles and U.S. politicians (both Anglo and Cuban) who still seek to liberate Cuba from the outside. We find it instructive that not a single participant at Musgrove believes this is possible. As Lino Fernández said at Musgrove with all the passion and credibility that 17 years in Cuban prisons provides: "Nobody from the outside can 'save Cuba'; the only sensible policy then, as now, is 'hands off Cuba.'"[9] With Lino Fernández and the other Musgrove participants, we submit this as U.S. foreign policy lesson number one from the Bay of Pigs invasion of April 1961: Keep "John Wayne" out of it; keep your hands off Cuba.

Notes

1. Kennedy aide and biographer Theodore Sorensen lists 15 separate crises during the first eight months of Kennedy's presidency, ranging from threatened Soviet interventions in the Congo in February and Laos in March, to the erection of the Berlin Wall in August to the death in a plane crash of UN Secretary General Dag Hammarskjold in September, followed by Soviet demands for a troika to lead the United Nations—one each from the East Bloc, West Bloc, and the nonaligned Third World. Theodore C. Sorensen, *Kennedy* (New York: Harper & Row, 1965), pp. 292–293.

2. Eric Bentley, "The Political Theater of John Wayne," cited in Gary Wills, *John Wayne's America: The Politics of Celebrity* (New York: Simon & Schuster, 1997), p. 12.

3. Wills, *John Wayne's America*, pp. 11–12.

4. U.S. House of Representatives Report 104-468, "Cuban Liberty and Democratic Solidarity (Libertad) Act of 1996" (Washington, D.C.: U.S. Government Printing Office, 1 March 1996).

5. Louis Pérez Jr., *Cuba: Between Reform and Revolution* (New York: Oxford University Press, 1988), p. 186.

6. Albert Beveridge, cited in Pérez, *Cuba*, p. 187.

7. "Cuba," Department of State Publication No. 7171 (Washington, D.C.: U.S. Government Printing Office, 3 April 1961).

8. Ibid., p. 35.

9. Lino Fernández, chapter 1.

Appendix 1:
Maps

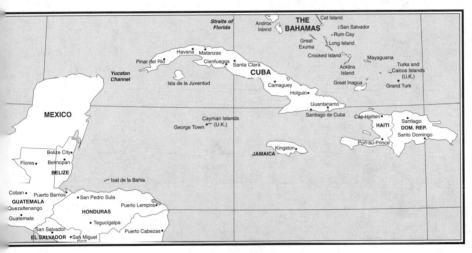

Cuba and Vicinity

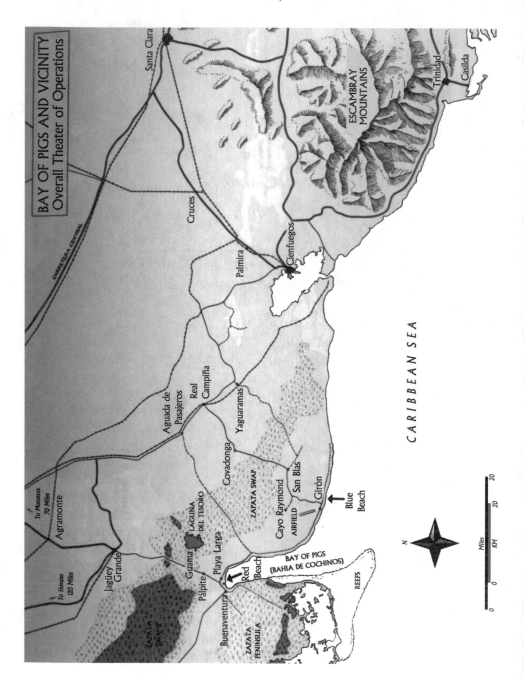

BAY OF PIGS AND VICINITY
Overall Theater of Operations

Appendix 2:
Abbreviations and Acronyms

ACU	Association of Catholic University Students (Agrupacion Católica Universitaria)
AID	Agency for International Development
ALC	Alianza por la Liberación Cubana
CDRs	Committees for the Defense of the Revolution
CEASEN	Center for the Study of National Security Issues
CIA	Central Intelligence Agency
CPC	Communist Party of Cuba
CRC	Cuban Revolutionary Council
CTC	Confederation of Cuban Workers (Confederacion de Trabajadores Cubanos)
DCI	Director of Central Intelligence
DDP	Deputy Director for Plans (of the CIA)
DEFCON	Defense Condition
DGI	[Cuban] General Directorate for Intelligence (Dirección General de Investigaciónes)
DRE	Revolutionary Students' Directorate (Directorio Revolucionario Estudiantil)
EXCOMM	Executive Committee
FEU	Federation of University Students
FEUD	Frente Estudiantil Universitario Democrático
FMLN	Farabundo Martí National Liberation [Front] (Farabundo Martí de Liberación Nacional)
FRD	Revolutionary Democratic Front (Frente Revolucionario Democrático)
FRUS	Foreign Relations of the United States
IG	[CIA] Inspector General
INRA	National Institute of Agrarian Reform
JCS	Joint Chiefs of Staff

KGB	[Soviet] Committee for State Security [Komitet Gosudarstvennoy Bezopasnosti]
LAR	Legión de Acción Revolucionaria
MDC	Movimiento Demócrata Cristiano
MiG	Soviet/Russian fighter planes [named for inventors: A. Mikoyan and M. I. Gurevich]
MRP	Revolutionary People's Movement (Movimiento Revolucionario del Pueblo)
MRR	Movement to Recover the Revolution (Movimiento de Recuperación Revolucionaria)
NSC	National Security Council
OA	Organización Auténtica
OAS	Organization of American States
OSS	Office of Strategic Services
SAC	Strategic Air Command
SAC	Salve a Cuba
SG	Special Group
SGA	Special Group–Augmented
UN	United Nations
UR	Unidad Revolucionaria
WH/4	Western Hemisphere/Region 4 (Caribbean Basin)

Appendix 3:
Chronology of U.S. Decisionmaking Regarding the Bay of Pigs Invasion and Operation MONGOOSE, January 1959–October 1962

1959

1 January: Fidel Castro's 26th of July Movement overthrows the Batista regime in Cuba. In a victory speech from Santiago, Castro states that the new revolution will not be like 1898, "when the North Americans came and made themselves masters of our country."

7 January: The Eisenhower administration formally recognizes the new Cuban government.

19 April: During Fidel Castro's first postrevolution trip to Washington, D.C., he meets with Vice President Richard Nixon for three and a half hours. Soon after the meeting, Nixon becomes a key advocate in CIA efforts to overthrow Castro.

Late October: President Eisenhower approves a program proposed by the Department of State, in agreement with the CIA, to support elements in Cuba opposed to the Castro government while making Castro's downfall seem to be the result of his own mistakes.

11 December: In a memorandum for CIA Deputy Director Richard Bissell, J. C. King, the CIA's head of its Western Hemisphere division, outlines a series of covert and propaganda operations to overthrow Castro. King also proposes that consideration be given to "eliminating" Fidel Castro.

1960

January: The CIA sets up a task force—Branch 4 of the Western Hemisphere Division (WH-4)—to implement President Eisenhower's wish for a more ambitious program directed against the Castro government. Former Guatemala station chief Jacob Esterline is appointed to head the task force, which begins drafting a comprehensive covert plan for presidential approval.

17 March: At an Oval Office meeting with high-ranking national security officials, President Eisenhower approves a CIA policy paper titled "A Program of Covert Action Against the Castro Regime." The president gives authorization to mount an operation to get rid of Castro.

Late March: Richard Bissell selects David Atlee Phillips, a CIA contract employee who until recently had maintained a public relations company in Havana, as chief of propaganda for the Cuba project. Phillips is told that the Cuba project will go by the Guatemala scenario—during the 1954 covert operation against Guatemalan President Jacobo Arbenz, Phillips directed the psychological operations—and that a clandestine rebel radio station, Radio Swan, should be operative within a month. CIA operative E. Howard Hunt, also a veteran of the Guatemala operation, is assigned the position of chief of political action for the project. His primary responsibility is to form a government-in-exile to replace Castro's government following the invasion.

17 May: Radio Swan goes on the air, on schedule. According to the CIA, the station's signal reaches not only its target area of Cuba, but the entire Caribbean as well. The station's programs are taped in studios in Miami, then routed through the Swan transmitter. Also, Bob Davis, the CIA station chief in Guatemala City, receives a message instructing him to build an airport. After getting Guatemalan permission, the agency contracts to have the airport built at Retalhuleu in 30 days for $1 million. The airport is built in 90 days and ultimately costs $1.8 million.

Early July: The CIA transfers exile forces being trained on Useppa Island off the coast of Florida to a camp in Guatemala. Eventually the size of the brigade expands to 1,500 soldiers.

23 July: CIA Director Allen Dulles briefs Senator John F. Kennedy, who is running for president, at Hyannis Port on Cape Cod. The meeting on intelligence matters lasts two and a half hours and includes information on the training of Cuban exiles for operations against the Castro government.

August: Richard Bissell meets with Col. Sheffield Edwards, director of the CIA's Office of Security, and discusses with him ways to eliminate or assassinate Fidel Castro. Edwards proposes that the job be done by assassins handpicked by the American Mafia.

18 August: President Eisenhower approves a budget of $13 million for the covert anti-Castro operation, as well as the use of Department of Defense personnel and equipment. However, the president specifies that, at this time, no United States military personnel are to be used in a combat status.

26 September: During an address before the United Nations General Assembly, Fidel Castro charges that the United States has taken over Swan Island and has set up a very powerful broadcasting station there, which it has placed at the disposal of war criminals.

28 September: The CIA attempts its first drop of weapons and supplies to the internal Cuban Resistance. The air crew tries to drop an arms pack for a hundred men to an agent waiting on the ground. They miss the drop zone by seven miles and land the weapons on top of a dam, where they are picked up by Castro's forces. The agent is caught and shot. The plane gets lost on the way to Guatemala and lands in Mexico.

12 October: The Cuban government nationalizes 382 big businesses including manufacturers of sugar, liquor, beer, perfume, soap, textiles, and milk products, as well as banks.

14 October: The United States issues a fact sheet at the United Nations in response to Castro's accusations before the General Assembly. The paper addresses the issue of Radio Swan by claiming that there is a private commercial broadcasting station on the Swan Islands, operated by the Gibraltar Steamship Company.

20 October: A State Department spokesman announces that U.S. Ambassador Philip Bonsal will be recalled for a prolonged period and that there are no plans to replace him.

21 October: On the eve of a candidates' debate, the Kennedy campaign issues an attack on Eisenhower's Cuba policy and calls for U.S. support for "the non-Batista democratic anti-Castro forces in exile, and in Cuba itself, who offer eventual hope of overthrowing Castro." The statement, drafted by campaign aide Richard Goodwin, states that "thus far these fighters for freedom have had virtually no support from our government."

22 October: During the televised debate, Vice President Richard Nixon, who is fully aware of the anti-Castro activities taking place and being planned, attacks Kennedy's position on Cuba as irresponsible and reckless.

24 October: The Cuban Council of Ministers decrees the nationalization of another 166 U.S. businesses as a response to the aggressive measures of the United States against Cuba.

31 October: CIA headquarters transmits a directive to its senior agent in Guatemala to alter the training regimen from guerrilla warfare to conventional assault tactics. Hundreds of new recruits begin to arrive to build Brigade 2506 up to 1,500 men.

4 November: In the narrowest victory in U.S. history, John F. Kennedy defeats Richard Nixon in the presidential election. Kennedy wins by less than 150,000 votes.

8–9 November: The CIA informs the Special Group of its plans, including a change in the conception of the operation from guerrilla infiltration to amphibious invasion. The Special Group neither approves nor disapproves.

13 November: Young officers revolt in Guatemala. A major grievance is the presence of the Cuban expeditionary force in Guatemala. President Ydígoras calls for U.S. aid in putting down the rebellion, and brigade planes strafe the rebels, helping to end the rebellion.

18 November: CIA Director Dulles and Deputy Director for Plans Bissell visit President-elect Kennedy in Palm Beach and brief him on the plan to overthrow Castro.

29 November: President Eisenhower meets with key aides from the State, Treasury, and Defense Departments, CIA, and the White House. State Department Acting Secretary Dillon expresses the department's concern that the operation is no longer secret but is known all over Latin America and has been discussed in UN circles.

6 December: President Eisenhower meets with President-elect Kennedy and endorses the anti-Castro Cuban operation being planned.

8 December: The CIA Task Force presents its new paramilitary concept to the Special Group. The Special Group authorizes use of special forces to train the strike force, the use of an airstrip at Puerto Cabezas, Nicaragua, and supply missions.

1961

1 January: Recruitment of Cuban exiles for training in Guatemala is greatly stepped up.

3 January: At 1:20 AM the Cuban Ministry of Foreign Relations sends a telegram to the charge d'affaires at the U.S. Embassy in Havana informing him that the total number of personnel at the U.S. Embassy and Consulate should not exceed 11 persons. Further, all other U.S. government personnel "must abandon the national territory" of Cuba within 48 hours of receipt of the telegram.

At 8:30 PM the U.S. Department of State sends a note to the Cuban charge d'affaires advising him of the decision to break diplomatic relations between the two countries and requests that the government of Cuba withdraw all Cuban nationals employed in the Cuban Embassy in Washington as soon as possible.

4 January: The two senior CIA officials in charge of the brigade invasion, Jacob Esterline and Jack Hawkins, prepare a memorandum "to outline the status of preparations for the conduct of amphibious/airborne and tactical air operations against the government of Cuba and to set forth certain requirements for policy decisions that must be reached and implemented if these operations are to be carried out." The concept of the plan is as follows: the initial mission of the invasion force will be to seize and defend a small area. There will be no early attempt to break out of the lodgment for further offensive operations unless and until there is a general uprising against the Castro regime or overt military intervention by the United States forces has taken place.

11 January: The Joint Chiefs of Staff are officially informed and consulted for the first time on the CIA plan for an invasion by a Cuban exile force. As a result, a working committee including representatives of the CIA, State, Defense, and the JCS is created to coordinate future actions on what the Pentagon code-names "Operation Bumpy Road."

25 January: President Kennedy meets with the Joint Chiefs of Staff at the White House. According to a memorandum on the meeting, General Lemnitzer tells the president that in light of the "shipment of heavy new military equipment from Czechoslovakia—30,000 tons or more—clandestine forces are not strong enough. [The United States] must increase the size of this force and this creates very difficult problems. What is required is a basic expansion of plans."

28 January: John Kennedy receives his first CIA briefing as president on the Cuban operation in a meeting attended by Vice President Lyndon B. Johnson, Secretary of State Dean Rusk, Defense Secretary Robert McNamara, National Security Adviser McGeorge Bundy, CIA Director Dulles, Chairman of the Joint Chiefs of Staff General Lemnitzer, Assistant Secretaries Mann (State) and Nitze (Defense), and Tracy Barnes of the CIA.

Late January: A revolt occurs among the Cuban exiles in training in Guatemala. Almost half of the more than 500 men in camp resign.

8 February: In a memo to the president, McGeorge Bundy highlights the divergent positions on the invasion, with Defense and CIA now feeling quite enthusiastic about it. At worst, according to the memo, the invaders would get into the mountains, and at best they think they might get a full-fledged civil war in which the United States could then back the anti-Castro forces openly. The State Department takes a much cooler view, primarily because of its belief that the political consequences would be very grave both in the United Nations and in Latin America.

8 February: At an afternoon meeting of President Kennedy and his top advisers, Richard Bissell of the CIA reports the assessment of the JCS that the CIA plan has a fair chance of success—success meaning ability to survive, hold ground, and attract growing support from Cubans. At worst, the invaders should be able to fight their way to the Escambray and go into guerrilla action. After the State Department representatives point out the grave effects such an operation could have on the U.S. position in Latin America, without careful and successful diplomatic preparation, President Kennedy presses for alternatives to a full-fledged invasion, supported by U.S. planes, ships, and supplies. He also authorizes a small junta of anti-Castro leaders to give the brigade a political facade.

11 February: In a memo to the president, Arthur Schlesinger argues that the "drastic decision" to enact the plan being promoted within the government only makes sense "if one excludes everything but Cuba." Taken in the context of "the hemisphere and the rest of the world, the arguments *against* this decision begin to gain force." He points out that there is no way to disguise U.S. complicity in the plan and "at one stroke, it would dissipate all the extraordinary good will which has been rising toward the new Administration through the world."

17 February: President Kennedy meets with representatives from the State Department, CIA, and Joint Chiefs of Staff. Following a discussion of planning and preparations for the invasion, the president indicates the need for an alternative to a direct invasion—such as mass infiltration—and urges an examination of all possible alternatives. Since the meeting does not result in a decision, the military plan for a D-Day of 5 March is put back until April. Two days later, Richard Bissell responds with a comprehensive opinion paper arguing for the invasion. He addresses the "disposal" problem if the mission is aborted: brigade "members will be angry, disillusioned and aggressive." Bissell concludes by arguing that this is the last opportunity for the United States to bring down Castro without overt U.S. military intervention or a full embargo.

18 February: McGeorge Bundy recommends to the president that the United States should institute a trade embargo first, let internal opposition build for several months, and then launch "Bissell's battalion."

11 March: The CIA presents its "Proposed Operation Against Cuba" to President Kennedy. The paper provides four alternative courses of action involving the commitment of the paramilitary force being readied by the United States. These include the course of action favored by the CIA—the Trinidad Plan. The president rejects the Trinidad Plan as too spectacular, too much like a World War II invasion. He prefers a quiet landing, preferably at night, with no basis for American military intervention. No decision comes from the 11 March meeting.

15 March: After two days of round-the-clock replanning, the CIA presents to President Kennedy three alternatives for the Cuban operation. The first is a modification of the Trinidad Plan, the second targets an area on the northeast coast of Cuba, and the third is an invasion at the Bay of Pigs code-named "Operation Zapata." The president orders modifications of the Zapata Plan to make it appear like more of an inside, guerrilla-type operation.

16 March: The CIA returns with a modified Zapata Plan that envisions a night (as opposed to a dawn) landing and airdrops at first light.

28 March: "What do you think about this damned invasion?" Arthur Schlesinger asks President Kennedy. "I think about it as little as possible," Kennedy responds.

29 March: Arthur Schlesinger notes in his journal that a final decision on the invasion will have to come by 4 April. He feels the tide is flowing against the project. At a meeting in the Cabinet Room he finds the president growing steadily more skeptical. Kennedy asks Bissell: "Do you really have to have these air strikes?" Bissell says his group will work to ensure maximum effectiveness for minimum noise from the air and reassures the president that Cubans on the island will join in an uprising.

30 March: Senator J. William Fulbright, chairman of the Senate Foreign Relations Committee, travels to Florida on *Air Force One* and hands President Kennedy a 3,766-word memorandum on the planned invasion. The memo describes the venture as ill-considered. He also predicts that it will be impossible to conceal the U.S. hand.

Early April: The State and Defense Departments and CIA reach a compromise on the air plan for the invasion. Limited air strikes will be made on D-2 (two days prior to the invasion) at the time of a diversionary landing of 160 men in eastern Cuba. These strikes will give the impression of being the action of Cuban pilots defecting from the Cuban air force and thus supporting the fiction that air support for the invasion force is coming from within Cuba.

4 April: At a meeting at the State Department, President Kennedy polls a dozen advisers on whether to go ahead with the Bay of Pigs invasion. After Senator Fulbright outlines his objections, all vote in favor of moving ahead, with only Secretary of State Rusk noncommittal. After a conference with the president, Secretary of Defense Robert McNamara requests that the JCS reconsider the rules of engagement to ensure that the United States would not become overtly engaged with Castro forces.

5 April: Arthur Schlesinger writes a memorandum for President Kennedy expressing his opposition to the impending invasion. He argues that the invasion force is not strong enough to topple Castro quickly and that the operation will turn into a protracted civil conflict that will lead to pressures to send in the marines, and the United States being branded as an aggressor.

8 April: Jacob Esterline and Jack Hawkins, two of the CIA's leaders of the invasion, call on Bissell and tell him they want to quit. They say that the project is out of control and they can't go on with it. Bissell asks them to stay on, and they do.

10 April: Richard Bissell briefs Attorney General Robert Kennedy on the operation. He rates the chance of success as two out of three and assures Kennedy that even in the worst case the invaders can turn guerrilla.

12 April: At a press conference at the State Department, President

Kennedy rules out, under any condition, an intervention in Cuba by the United States armed forces.

13 April: Project Chief Jacob Esterline sends an urgent cable to Puerto Cabezas, Nicaragua, requesting information on any change in the evaluation of the Cuban invasion force. Col. Jack Hawkins sends back a cable reporting his confidence in the ability of the force to accomplish not only initial combat missions but also the ultimate objective of Castro's overthrow. Richard Bissell ensures that the cable is shown to the president, who reads it the next day. It contributes to Kennedy's decision to go ahead with the invasion.

14 April: From the White House, Kennedy calls Richard Bissell and gives the green light for the preinvasion air strikes. Kennedy asks how many planes will participate and is told 16. " Well, I don't want it on that scale. I want it minimal," Kennedy responds. Bissell reduces the attack force by six planes.

15 April: At dawn eight B-26 planes of the Cuban Expeditionary Force carry out air strikes at three sites to destroy the Castro air capability. Initial pilot reports indicate that 50 percent of Castro's offensive air capability was destroyed at Campo Libertad, 75 to 80 percent at San Antonio de los Baños, and five planes destroyed at Santiago de Cuba. Subsequent photographic studies and interpretations indicate a greatly reduced estimate of the damage.

16 April: At about midday, President Kennedy formally approves the landing plan and the word is passed to all commanders in the operation. Assault shipping moves on separate courses toward the objective area. At 9:30 PM, McGeorge Bundy telephones General Cabell to tell him that the dawn air strikes the following morning should not be launched until planes can conduct them from a strip within the beachhead. Bundy indicates that any further consultation with regard to this matter should be with the secretary of state. At 10:15 PM, General Cabell and Richard Bissell go to Secretary Rusk's office. Rusk tells them he has just been talking to the president on the phone and recommended that the Monday morning air strikes (D-Day) should be canceled and the president agreed. Cabell and Bissell protest strongly, arguing that the ships as well as the landings will be seriously endangered without the dawn strikes. Rusk indicates there are policy considerations against air strikes before the beachhead airfield is in the hands of the landing force and completely operational and capable of supporting the raids. Rusk calls the president and tells him of the CIA's objections but restates his own recommendation to cancel the strikes. He offers to let the

CIA representatives talk to the president directly but they decline. The order canceling the air strikes is dispatched to the departure field in Nicaragua, arriving when the pilots are in their cockpits ready for take-off.

17 April: In early morning, aboard the *Blagar,* CIA agent Grayston Lynch receives a message from Washington: "Castro still has operational aircraft. Expect you to be hit at dawn. Unload all troops and supplies and take ships to sea as soon as possible." On learning that the invading troops will meet resistance in the landing area, due to failure to destroy all of the Cuban air force, the *Blagar* moves in close to shore and delivers gunfire support. Brigade troops commence landing at 0100 hours. Later that morning, the *Houston* comes under air attack and is hit. It goes aground with about 180 men on the west side of the Bay of Pigs—about five miles from the landing beach. At 9:30 AM, the freighter *Rio Escondido* is sunk by a direct rocket hit from a Sea Fury—with ten day's reserves of ammunition on board, as well as food, hospital equipment, and gasoline. All crew members are rescued and transferred to the *Blagar.* Fighting rages throughout the day, with the brigade freighters withdrawing 50 miles out to sea. That evening, President Kennedy discusses the deteriorating situation with his advisers.

18 April: At 2:00 PM, with only about a third of the Cuban pilots at Puerto Cabezas willing to continue flying, Bissell, for the first time, authorizes American pilots to fly combat missions. By the end of the day, the brigade has almost run out of ammunition. In spite of heavy fighting, casualties appear to be few among the invaders. CIA headquarters asks the brigade commander via the *Blagar,* if he wishes to be evacuated. Answer: negative.

At 10:00 PM Adlai Stevenson denies in the UN that the United States is intervening militarily in Cuba and claims the right of the United States to protect the hemisphere from external aggression in the event of an intervention of outside forces. Stevenson goes on to claim that there is no evidence against the United States and that it is not true that the guerrillas have been transported by American-piloted planes.

19 April: At a meeting at the White House that begins just after midnight, the president, Vice President Johnson, McNamara, and Rusk, all in white tie, with General Lemnitzer and Admiral Burke in dress uniform, hear a report on the decline of the invasion force. Burke asks the president to "let me take two jets and shoot down the enemy aircraft." The president says no, reminding Bissell and Burke that he had warned them that he would not commit U.S. forces to combat. At 1:00 AM, the president authorizes one hour of air cover from 0630 to 0730 for the invading brigade's B-26s by six unmarked jets from the carrier *Essex.* The jets are not to seek air combat nor attack ground targets. But, because of the unrealized time differential between Nicaragua and Cuba, the U.S. Navy Combat Air Patrol arrives an hour before the B-26s and fails to rendezvous. Two B-26s, piloted by American CIA contract agents, are shot down and four Americans are lost. After three days of fighting, brigade casualties total 89 killed and 1,197 taken prisoner. Cuba suffers 157 dead.

21 April: At a press conference President Kennedy accepts responsibility for the failed invasion. He says: "I am the responsible officer of the government."

22 April: President Kennedy charges Gen. Maxwell D. Taylor, Attorney General Robert Kennedy, Adm. Arleigh Burke, and Director of Central Intelligence Allen Dulles to investigate why the Bay of Pigs operation failed. The group becomes known as the Taylor Committee.

Late Spring/Early Summer: The CIA's inspector general at the time of the invasion, Lyman Kirkpatrick, conducts a postmortem of the operation and issues a highly critical report based on his findings. The report accuses Bissell and his aide, Tracy Barnes, of "playing [the invasion] by ear" by setting up an "anarchic and disorganized" command structure for the invasion. Kirkpatrick characterizes the planning as "frenzied" and suggests that Bissell misled the president by failing to tell Kennedy that "success had become dubious." The report concludes that "plausible deniability had become a pathetic illusion." Angered at the tone of the report, Bissell receives permission from newly appointed CIA Director John McCone to draft a rebuttal arguing that the operation would have worked if Kennedy had allowed the air strikes to go forward as planned.

13 June: General Taylor submits to President Kennedy the report of the Board of Inquiry. The board concludes:

> A paramilitary operation of the magnitude of Zapata could not be prepared and conducted in such a way that all U.S. support of it and connection with it could be plausibly disclaimed. . . . By about November 1960, the impossibility of running Zapata as a covert operation under CIA should have been recognized and the situation reviewed. If a reorientation of the operation had not been possible, the project should have been abandoned.

However, the board ends its assessment of the failure of the Bay of Pigs invasion with the conclusion that the preparations and execution of paramilitary operations such as Zapata are a form of Cold War action in which the country must be prepared to engage.

4 November: A major new covert action program aimed at overthrowing the Cuban government is developed during a meeting at the White House. The new program, code named Operation MONGOOSE, is to be run by counterinsurgency specialist Gen. Edward G. Lansdale. A high-level inter-agency group, the Special Group–Augmented (SGA), is created with the sole purpose of overseeing Operation MONGOOSE. A memorandum formally establishing MONGOOSE is signed by President Kennedy on 30 November.

1962

18 January: Edward Lansdale outlines "The Cuba Project," a program under Operation MONGOOSE aimed at the overthrow of the Castro government. Thirty-two planning tasks, ranging from sabotage actions to intelligence activities, are assigned to the agencies involved in MONGOOSE. The program is designed to develop a "strongly motivated political action movement" within Cuba capable of generating a revolt eventually leading to the downfall of the Castro government. Lansdale envisions that the United States will provide overt support in the final stages of an uprising, including, if necessary, using military force.

14 March: Guidelines for Operation MONGOOSE are approved by the SGA. Drafted by Maxwell Taylor, they note that the United States would attempt to "make maximum use of indigenous resources" in trying to overthrow Fidel Castro but recognize that "final success will require decisive U.S. military intervention." Indigenous resources would act to "prepare and justify this intervention, and thereafter to facilitate and support it." Kennedy is briefed on the guidelines on 16 March.

10 August: The SGA meets in Dean Rusk's office to decide on a course of action for Operation MONGOOSE following the intelligence collection phase scheduled to conclude in August. The SGA initially chooses a plan proposed by John McCone in which limited actions, including economic sabotage, would be used to force a split between Fidel Castro and "old-line Communists." President Kennedy rejects the SGA's recommendation in favor of a more ambitions plan aimed expressly at overthrowing Castro.

15 October: The CIA discovers Soviet nuclear missile sites being constructed in Cuba. SGA orders the acceleration of covert activities against Cuba. In particular, the group agrees that "considerably more sabotage should be undertaken" and that "all efforts should be made to develop new and imaginative approaches with the possibility of getting rid of the Castro regime."

16 October: Kennedy convenes two top-secret meetings of his highest advisers—a group known as the Executive Committee or EXCOMM—to discuss a U.S. response to the discovery of Soviet missile sites in Cuba.

The SGA convenes in the White House prior to the second EXCOMM meeting. According to Richard Helms's notes, Robert Kennedy expresses President Kennedy's "general dissatisfaction" with progress under the MONGOOSE program. The SGA discusses but rejects several alternatives for eliminating the newly discovered Soviet missile sites in Cuba, including a proposal to have Cuban émigrés bomb the missile sites.

28 October: Under pressure of a U.S. naval blockade, the Soviets agree to withdraw missiles from Cuba.

Appendix 4:
Chronology of Cuban Resistance, January 1959–July 1961

1959

Late January: A group of about 50 Catholic activists open a literacy school at Managua barracks outside Havana to teach literacy to soldiers of the rebel army, organized by Fr. Cavero. Antonio García Crews directs the school.

A group of members of the rebel army, including Cmdr. Humberto Sorí Marín, Manuel Artime Buesa, and Rogelio González Corzo organize the Comandos Rurales at the Agrupación Católica Universitaria in Havana. Many of the comandos had been active in the Legión de Acción Revolucionaria (LAR), an armed group that operated against the Batista regime in Pinar del Río and had affiliates in Havana and Camagüey.

13 February: A revolutionary tribunal presided over by Cmdr. Félix Peña absolves a group of aviators and mechanics of having engaged in the reckless bombing of peasant villages during the struggle again the Batista regime; the government ordered a retrial at which they were found guilty and convicted; Peña died under mysterious circumstances.

Late February: About 50 Comandos Rurales go to the Manzanillo region of Sierra Maestra and, coordinated by Manuel Artime, fan out through the region to teach literacy to peasant families. A radio program, "Trinchera Guajira," is broadcast to the area from Manzanillo.

Late March: The first group of Comandos Rurales is replaced by a second contingent.

April: The literacy school of Camp Managua is closed and organizers are notified that they can no longer teach. In a subsequent visit to the camp they discover that the troops shall be taught Marxist doctrine and that plenty of communist literature is being stacked at the camp's cultural center.

11 May: The University of Havana reopens with a ceremony attended by the top leadership of the revolutionary government.

17 May: The first agrarian reform statute is decreed and the National Institute of Agrarian Reform (INRA) is created to implement the reform.

19 May: Fidel Castro signs the agrarian reform law at La Plata, in the Sierra Maestra; a group of Comandos Rurales attends the ceremony.

Summer: The first few conspiracies against the government begin to take shape; the government moves against the Comandos Rurales, to get them out of Oriente province and away from any contact with agrarian reform and agriculture in general.

August: A conspiracy supported by Dominican dictator Rafael Trujillo is neutralized; the army is purged of all elements identified with the previous regime.

September: The Federation of University Students (FEU) holds elections at the University of Havana; Cmdr. Rolando Cubela defeats Pedro Luis Boitel for the post of secretary general.

October: Disgusted by what he learned in a secret meeting of INRA regional coordinators in Havana, Lt. Manuel Artime resigns as head of the O-22 (Ciro Redondo) agrarian reform sector in Manzanillo, Oriente; later on, Artime will publicize the proceedings of the secret INRA meeting, during which Fidel Castro, Ché Guevara, and Antonio Núñez Jiménez discussed a blueprint for a more drastic plan of agrarian reform, and described the real functioning of the government and its ultimate goals.

Cmdr. René Vallejo receives orders to incarcerate any members of Comandos Rurales still active in Camagüey and Oriente.

21 October: Maj. Huber Matos, chief of the Camagüey garrison, and 30 of his officers are arrested in his headquarters by Fidel Castro and Camilo Cienfuegos.

25 October: Maj. Camilo Cienfuegos and his pilot Luciano Fariñas cannot be accounted for; both presumed lost while returning from Camagüey.

31 October: Manuel Artime leaves Manzanillo.

2 November: The first in a number of clandestine meetings between members of LAR and representatives of Carlos Lorié, who is the liaison with a number of disgruntled rebel army officers. Manuel Artime, Carlos Rodríguez Santana, Emilio Martínez Venegas, and Rafael Rivas Vázquez (for LAR), and Angel Ros Escala and Cmdr. Jorge Sotús (for Lorié), hold subsequent meetings during this month.

November: Manuel Artime travels undercover to Mexico and telegraphic contact is established between "the children of Felipe" and LAR members in Mexico; the Bible is used as source for coded messages; Rogelio González Corzo asks Dr. Lino Fernández to stockpile all the weapons gathered by LAR and to begin to create a network of internal security and rudimentary intelligence.

First Sunday of December: Rogelio González Corzo, Rafael Rivas Vázquez, Carlos Rodríguez Santana, Jorge Sotús, and Sergio Sanjenís meet and agree to structure their ongoing efforts as the Movimiento de Recuperación Revolucionaria (MRR). Angel Ros is designated as secretary general and immediately leaves for the United States to report to Lorié.

Late December: The Movimiento Demócrata Cristiano (MDC) is organized.

1960

First half of January: Artime's letter of resignation is made public, the *Ideario* of the MRR is approved, and a number of people are charged with specific responsibilities; Ricardo Lorié and Manuel Artime are designated to represent MRR outside Cuba; Jorge Sotús and Sergio Sanjenís are in charge of military actions, but there is no military department as such; Alberto Müller and Antonio González Mora are in charge of the student and professional sections, respectively; González Corzo takes care of discipline and control; and Rafael Rivas Vázquez is designated to head the propaganda section.

Second half of January: Manuel Artime publishes a second letter responding to attacks directed against him by Fidel Castro during the program "Ante la Prensa." The MRR professional section distributes copies of Artime's letter, with details of the INRA's secret meeting, to passers-by at a busy intersection in downtown Havana.

Late Winter: Three officers of the rebel army, Joaquín Membibre,

Diosdado Mesa, and Vicente Méndez, take over their post in Camajuaní, requisition all the weapons, and march into the Escambray Mountains; about a dozen small spontaneous uprisings like this occur in Cuba around this time.

February: The 30th of November Movement begins to function, led by David Salvador, secretary general of the Confederation of Cuban Workers (CTC), Pedro Aponte, former Lt. Hiram González, and others.

5 February: Members of the student wing of the MRR organize a demonstration at Central Park in Havana, to protest the visit of Anastas Mikoyan; later on, the leaders of that protest will create the Directorio Revolucionario Estudiantil (DRE), led by Luis Fernández Rocha, Ernesto Fernández Travieso, Antonio García Crews, Alberto Müller, and Juan Manuel Salvat. Virgilio Campanería and Alberto Tapia Ruano brought their Salve a Cuba (SAC) comrades into the new organization; the MRR offers safe haven to Müller and Salvat and spirits them out of the country.

February: Distribution of a proclamation describing the MRR; Ricardo Lorié travels to Mexico to get acquainted with Artime; shortly thereafter, Artime travels throughout Latin America denouncing the revolutionary regime; Cmdr. Higinio "Niño" Díaz is appointed coordinator of the MRR in Oriente; "Una reunión inolvidable" ("An Unforgettable Meeting"), describing the secret INRA meeting, part of a book written by Artime, is widely distributed.

March: Pedro Martínez Fraga coordinates efforts for the creation of the Frente Revolucionario Democrático (FRD) in Cuba; the first few men begin training in Cuba; Cmdr. Plinio Prieto conducts a survey of the Guanayara area in the Escambray Mountains; guerrilla operations begin in Escambray shortly thereafter with three groups led by Cmdr. Evelio Duque, Osvaldo Ramírez, and Capt. Sinesio Walsh, respectively; Cmdr. Plinio Prieto leaves the country.

CIA agents begin to establish contacts with MRR; Carlos Rodríguez Santana conducts a tour of Oriente, to help organize the MRR there.

Former rebel army captain Manuel Beatón and his brother Cipriano launch a guerrilla group in Oriente; they will be captured in June and executed.

4 March: The French freighter *Le Coubre* explodes while unloading weapons and ammunition in Havana harbor.

13 March: MRR propaganda secretary Rafael Rivas Vázquez leaves the country to deliver a report of all the work being done.

19 March: Captain Jorge Sotús and Sergio Sanjenís are arrested and charged with conspiracy; Sotús would escape from jail but was electrocuted while rigging a craft for a raid in Cuba.

April: MRR extends its network to all provinces; there is progress in coordinating the organizations integrating the FRD, especially in Havana and Pinar del Río. MRR emphasizes collaboration with individuals and organizations interested in armed struggle: the 26th of July Movement, Organización Auténtica, Movimiento 30 de Noviembre, the rebel army, Confederation of Cuban Workers, and military intelligence (G-2).

13 April: Communiqué issued by the MDC asking that the government end its provisional status and hold free elections, signed by José Ignacio Rasco and Enrique Villareal.

15 April: MDC activates its clandestine network.

May: Rescate Revolucionario is organized by Lomberto Díaz, César Lancís, Alberto Cruz, Tony Santiago, and others. MRR has contact with them through "Francisco" (Rogelio González Corzo).

2 May: The Frente Estudiantil Universitario Democrático (FEUD) releases a document signed by Juan Manuel Salvat warning the government that it will respond to violence in kind; FEUD will become the Directorio Revolucionario Estudiantil (DRE).

13 May: A meeting takes place of the organizing committee of the Democratic Revolutionary Front (FRD).

19 May: Two small groups arrive at Useppa Island, off of Ft. Myers, Florida, to begin formal military training.

23 May: MDC recesses as a public organization.

31 May: First meeting occurs of national coordinators of organizations composing the FRD in Cuba, including MRR (Rogelio González Corzo), MDC (Enrique Ros), Organización Montecristi (Raúl Villasuso), Triple A (Mario Escoto and José Utrera), and Rescate Revolucionario (Lomberto Díaz); González Corzo is designated military coordinator of FRD.

Late May–early June: "Ojeda" (Lino Fernández) travels to Miami to resolve the issue of a dual MRR that is trying to establish contact with FRD in Cuba on its own, and to discuss ways to coordinate internal struggle and resistance, focused on guerrilla fronts, with external supply and support.

8 June: In San José, Costa Rica, the MRR issues a communiqué denouncing the government leadership and accusing them of betraying the revolution, signed by Manuel Artime, Higinio "Niño" Díaz, Ricardo Lorié, and Michel Yabor.

22 June: Announcement is made of the creation of the FRD in Havana; a document signed by Manuel Antonio de Varona, Manuel Artime, José Ignacio Rasco, Aureliano Sánchez Arango, and Justo Carrillo is released.

25 June: FEUD issues a document asking students to join the struggle against the government in one of the FRD organizations.

June: MRR military coordinator sends a list of 47 geographic points for the clandestine insertion of men and materiel—those outside lack the operational capacity to take advantage of this.

3 July: A group that was training in Ft. Gulick, Panama, travels to Guatemala (Trax) via the Opa-Locka airport.

6 July: "Francisco" (Rogelio González Corzo) is voted national coordinator by the executive committee of the FRD in Cuba.

12 July: The national directorate of the MRR meets to discuss organizational problems and give full powers to "Francisco" to travel to Miami and resolve the matter.

22, 31 July: In two separate meetings, Rogelio González Corzo (MRR) and Enrique Ros (MDC) unsuccessfully try to convince Reinol González, of the Catholic workers movement, to join the FRD; later on, González, Manuel Ray, and others will organize the Movimiento Revolucionario del Pueblo (MRP).

July: The FRD leadership in Cuba realizes the growing estrangement in the visions of the situation between those inside and outside Cuba; the effort to remain coordinated is renewed but communication difficulties continue, and there is lack of control about the type of training that those sent outside are receiving.

August: Cmdr. Plinio Prieto returns; MRR decides to support the Escambray guerrilla groups to alleviate the pressure exerted by the increasing number of regular troops that are encircling the area and denying them access to their peasant base—in what became known as the "first sweep of the Escambray" (August 1960–March 1961).

7 August: Alianza por la Liberación Cubana (ALC) is created by former MRR members: the Organización Auténtica, Cruzada Constitucional, and Frente Anticomunista Cubano.

Mid-August: "Francisco" (Rogelio González Corzo, FRD military coordinator) travels undercover to the United States, to try to coordinate external support and internal action; "Ojeda" (Lino Fernández) replaces him temporarily; MRR intelligence gets hold of sensitive information concerning the mixing of propellant fuels for military purposes and passes this information on to the United States Embassy in Havana; Plinio Prieto is in contact with "Ojeda" regarding plans being made to return Prieto to the Escambray.

Late Summer: Captain Porfirio Reemberto ("El Negro") Ramírez leads a guerrilla troop of DRE militants in Escambray.

September: To alleviate the shortage of supplies, the *Reefer* and the *Wasp* begin to deliver weapons to a point offshore Club Náutico de Marianao; they operate out of a warehouse in Key West; the MRR clandestine network distributes the supplies.

8 September: Carlos Rodríguez Santana dies in an accident in Guatemala, the first casualty of the brigade. The brigade takes his number as its name: Brigade 2506.

15 September: Due to official pressure, the last group of FRD leaders abandons Mexico City to relocate in Miami.

20 September: The countdown to deliver Commander Prieto and his men to the Escambray begins.

29 September: "Ojeda" delivers Cmdr. Plinio Prieto to Cienfuegos, where he rendezvous with OA militants, who deliver him to a point along the road to Cumanayagua to take command of the troops of Capt. Sinesio Walsh in Loma de la Lora; once in camp, Prieto discovers that he can transmit but not receive messages.

4 October: "Ojeda" returns to Cienfuegos with a new transmitter for Plinio Prieto.
　　Unaware that a new transmitter is on the way, Cmdr. Prieto heads back to Cienfuegos to try to secure one on his own and is captured in Cumanayagua.

October: Rogelio González Corzo returns from the United States, unable to establish the necessary coordination for steady supply.

7 or 8 October: "Ojeda" travels to the United States to assess the degree to which the internal resistance can count on this support.

October: Through the southern coast of Las Villas, Evelio Duque receives a modest shipment of 30 M-3 machine guns, five BARs, grenades, ammunition, and equipment.

10 October: Gerardo Fundora leads a guerrilla unit into the hills of Madruga, is captured on 20 October, tried, and summarily executed.

Former pilot and rebel army officer Martín Amodia leads a nine-man guerrilla group into action in Camagüey.

12 October: Prieto is prosecuted under Brief 829 of 1960, together with Porfirio Ramírez, José Palomino, Angel Rodríguez del Sol, Sinesio Walsh, and about a hundred of their followers; the five leaders are executed at dawn, 13 October; the rest of the men are sentenced to between 15 and 30 years; the women receive slightly lighter sentences.

22 October: "Ojeda" meets with Artime in New York following the Kennedy-Nixon debate; Artime is worried about Kennedy's intentions, and is given a detailed briefing of the extent and condition of MRR's military organization and its collaboration with other groups, including those outside the FRD; Artime pledges his best effort to send communication specialists and equipment to guarantee the viability of the resupply.

Late October: MRR military coordinator sends to Manuel Artime: (1) the entire operational blueprint for military actions already planned by FRD in Cuba and for which supplies are necessary, dated 25 October; (2) Order of Battle No. 1, discussing tactical question concerning the operational plan; (3) a description of MRR military cadre and strength in different cities and municipalities of Pinar del Río province, including a series of concluding observations about the desperate shortage of supplies and ammunition with which to carry out the plan; and (4) inventory of MRR strength in other regions of the country.

28 October: Having sent to Miami the plan of military action elaborated by the FRD leadership in Cuba, "Francisco" travels there undercover to press the point that the whole effort depends on a steady supply of materiel and reliable communications.

7 November: 30th of November Movement secretary general David Salvador is arrested.

13 November: MRR leadership decides to continue the support to the Escambray guerrillas; that evening, an MRR party, lead by "Ojeda," waits in vain at the Los Jejenes farm in Pinar del Río for weapons to be dropped—the flight was canceled because of a military revolt in Guatemala.

Late November: There are guerrillas operating in areas other than Escambray: there are four in Pinar del Río, under the leadership of Pastor Rodríguez Roda ("Cara Linda"), the Martínez brothers, Clodomiro Miranda, and Bernardo Corrales, respectively; in the Cárdenas area of Matanzas, Juan A. Montes de Oca led a group that occupied a sugar mill on 17 April 1961; in southern Matanzas, bordering on Havana, are the groups of Erelio Peña, Jorge Gutiérrez Izaguirre (trained in Guatemala), Juan José ("Pichi") Catalá, and Perico Sánchez; in Las Villas, outside the Escambray region in the Sagua la Granda to the Corralillo plains, the guerrilla unit led by former rebel army lieutenant José Martí Campos Linares and his father, Benito Campos ("Campitos"), had been supplied directly by sea by the MRR; a group commanded by Margarito Lanza Flores ("Thondyke") operated in the vicinity of Aguada; in the Escambray proper were the guerrillas under Osvaldo Ramírez, one unit under Cmdr. César Páez, the guerrilla unit of Joaquín Membivre, that of Merejo Ramírez and others—all sharing the problem of an excruciating lack of supplies and ammunition; in Camagüey, there were the guerrillas under Tomás San Gil in the Sierra de Cubitas.

Late December: "Francisco" returns by clandestine means; many of the men who return by established channels belong to the student wing of the MRR, which becomes the DRE; they advance plans for opening new guerrilla fronts in the Escambray and in the Sierra Maestra; reliance on communication specialists trained abroad and on a grid controlled by the CIA create great difficulties and almost total noncommunication among the groups operating as guerrillas in Cuba.

30 December: Hiram González, national military coordinator of the 30th of November Movement, is captured in Havana; sentenced to 30 years, he escaped from prison disguised as a woman; recaptured, he escaped once again and, following an unsuccessful attempt to leave the country, he waited until 1963 in the Uruguayan Embassy until he was allowed to leave Cuba.

31 December: A fire at the Epoca department store in Havana is attributed to sabotage.

1961

January: Acting on his own, Commander "Augusto" (Ramón Ruiz Sánchez, military coordinator of Rescate, and a brother-in-law of FRD general coordinator Tony de Varona) pretends to play the role of FRD military coordinator in Cuba, and tries to replace Cmdr. Evelio Duque with Osvaldo Ramírez; the guerrillas are too busy to bother.

"Augusto" managed to have deliveries sent directly to him, not to the FDR apparatus; "Augusto" utilized messengers, not the radio, to communicate with the Escambray guerrillas; Commander Duque is able to put together seven different columns of between 30 and 60 men each; Osvaldo Ramírez commands an additional (eight) column with considerable autonomy.

4 January: The revolutionary government issues Law No. 923, institutionalizing the practice of applying the death penalty to anyone guilty of arson, terrorism, conspiracy, or armed action against the regime; hundreds would be tried under this statute and condemned to death in the early months of 1961.

11 January: MRR and 30th of November Movement go ahead with plans to launch a common front near Fomento, in Escambray.

18 January: A column of MRR led by "Ojeda" and 30th of November fighters led by Pedro Fraginals march toward Fomento to rendezvous with two 30th of November columns also heading there, but a government task force apprehends 82 participants in Placetas, surrounds the Fomento region, cuts off the highways, and the effort is thwarted.

23 January: MRR and 30th of November fighters elude the government encirclement at the Fomento area by wading down the Falcón River gorge.

26 January: "Ojeda" leads MRR party into the Santa Lucía region, near Sancti Spíritus, to rendezvous with the guerrillas of Merejo Ramírez, but Ramírez had left to avoid encirclement by government troops.

28 January: FRD crisis comes into the open over the inclusion of MRP and other groups in the front, and over the FRD's acknowledged incapacity to influence the design of military plans and their very precarious contact with the men in training in Central America.

Three of Méndez's guerrilla columns join forces, attack the El Jovero outpost, inflict 32 casualties on the militia, and set the barracks on fire.

February: The government dismisses 119 magistrates and judges on grounds of "immoral conduct," to expedite revolutionary justice.

1 February: MRR decides on a new attempt to establish a guerrilla front, this time in the Yaguajay region of northern Las Villas.

6 February: "Ojeda" leads an MRR party toward Yaguajay where 500 peasants await to join the guerrillas.

8 February: "Ojeda" reaches the designated site—where Cmdr. Camilo Cienfuegos had camped during the struggle against Batista. The drop zone was marked and communications were established to agree on the evening of 16 February for a weapons drop. Peasant recruits begin to arrive in the area during the next few days.

14 February: A communications specialist arrives in camp and verifies all the information previously transmitted in a new message, thereby confirming all the details for the operation on 16 February.

16 February: A government contingent of 16,000 police and regular troops have surrounded the area; the aircraft is sighted but does not drop the weapons; "Ojeda" and his communications officer are captured in a jeep on the highway to Zulueta by troops under the command of Félix Torres; about 500 peasants are rounded up and sent to the Santa Clara jail.

3 March: Cmdr. Humberto Sorí Marín arrives in Key West on the *Tejana,* of Unidad Revolucionaria (UR), brought by Tony Cuesta; he is very concerned about what he finds and worried that the invasion date is so near.

11 March: Cmdrs. William Morgan, the only U.S. citizen to earn the rank, and Jesús Carrera are shot for treason.

13 March: Cmdr. Humberto Sorí Marín clandestinely returns to Cuba.

18 March–3 April: The paramilitary underground suffers enormous losses.

18 March: Rogelio González Corzo, Humberto Sorí Marín, Domingo Trueba, Manuel Puig, Nemesio Rodríguez, Rafael Díaz Hanscom, Lito

Riaño, and others are detained during a meeting at a private residence in Miramar. Police had arrived on the scene pursuing a maid escaping from a government dragnet at a nearby residence. The group includes the military coordinators of the groups represented in the FRD.

21 March: Following a meeting at the Skyways Motel, the Consejo Revolucionario Cubano is created to replace the FRD; Dr. José Miró Cardona is appointed coordinator; Manolo Ray, Felipe Pazos, and Raúl Chibás represent the MRP.

27 March: DRE members Virgilio Campanería, Alberto Tapia Ruano, and Tomás Fernández Travieso are apprehended; a large quantity of explosives and ammunition, plus some weapons, are seized; all will be shot on 18 April, except Fernández Travieso, who is a minor.

29 March: Two separate groups linked to OA organizations Triple A and Rescate are apprehended in Havana; they are charged with sabotage, terrorism, recruiting counterrevolutionary elements, and supporting the Escambray guerrillas; some are shot on 18 April.

13 April: Eight tons of weapons are seized in Pinar del Río; Howard Anderson, August McNair, and their Cuban collaborators are apprehended, tried on 18 April under Brief 151 of 1961, convicted, and executed the next day.

14 April: El Encanto department store burns to the ground as a result of a sabotage conducted by MRP and members of the infiltration teams of the brigade.

18 April: Cmdr. Humberto Sorí Marín, former rebel army lieutenant Rogelio González Corzo, Manuel Puig, Eufemio Fernández, Gaspar Trueba, Rafael Díaz Hanscom, and Nemesio Rodríguez—the FRD leaders apprehended on 18 March—are brought to trial, convicted, and executed on 19 April.

15–16 July: Guerrilla leaders meet at El Cicatero, in the Escambray Mountains, to discuss a new plan of action; they elect Osvaldo Ramírez as commander-in-chief of an integrated Cuban liberation army (Ramírez died in combat at Las Aromas de Velázquez on 16 April 1962).

Appendix 5:
Declassified Documents

Contents

Chapter 1: The Anti-Castro Resistance Meets the CIA

Chapter 2: The CIA Calls the Shots

Chapter 3: Kennedy's Attempts to Topple Castro

Chapter 4: Assassination and
the Use of U.S. Military Force at the Bay of Pigs

Chapter 5: Operation
MONGOOSE and the Fate of the Resistance

Chapter 6: Aftermath of the Bay of Pigs Invasion

Dear Luis;   Late August 1960

About your letters prior to 25 August it surprised us and made us laugh to see a letter for Francisco dated August 13. Where is it?

We need urgent information on the following people;

Plinio Prieto; He claims to be the exclusive representative of the sabotage and accion plans for all organizations in Cuba (he told us he has made contact with all of them). He claims to have total and direct support from the American Intelligence Service and says he is capable of supplying all the necessary equipment if he is given the men to execute HIS PLANS.

What is going on with this?

Comandante Diego; claims to be the representative of the entire group, more precisely groups that are in the Escambray, and he claims to be the one who sent Orlando Bosch there.

He wants to enter the MRR in order to help in the Escambray. What is going on with this? From our part we have sent Manduco (Raul knows who he is) who went up, saw what there was and the possibilities. We are planning an ascend of a small and well organized group of ours to take charge of all of that.

We need the supplies once this is accomplished. We will choose detailed marks, whose positions you will receive on time so that we can be supplied with the indispensable materials. Further, we would like a house to be rented in Cayo Hueso so that a boat that we will be receiving shortly as a donation could serve us for that purpose and for other types of provisioning. Give us an answer about this as soon as possible.

According to your predictions the dissidents in Cuba have made an attempt to re-conciliate seeing that they don't have anything here either. The Direccion Nacional rejects any type of agreement with those men at the present time. Lets hope that the same inflexible politics are being pursued outside. We would like the true names of the comrades that are in Cuba to be omitted anytime a message is sent to them, because the risk here is greater every day and in addition we all have our legal "baptism".

We would also like to know if the last communications that we directed to Raul via our friends have arrived, and when, in order to know which is the best way to establish contact with you guys.

Regards to everybody and we hope to see you soon.

Document 1.1   [MRR Strength in Northern Oriente]; letter from Anselmo Mendez (Dr. Andres Cao) [Lino Fernández is second in command] to "Luis," late August 1960.

17-18 October, 1960

Report to Dr. Manuel F. Artime Buesa

Subject: Interviews with Dr. Manuel A. de Varona held by:

      Mr. Luciano Martinez *MRR* "Carlos Roca"
      Dr. Juan Sordo   "Geronimo"

on 17 October at 3:00 PM and the second interview on the 18th at 2 AM.

1.- We violently raised the economic and military crisis that the general and revolutionary work inside of Cuba is experiencing. Heavy criticism was made for the lack of economic help and supply of arms.

2.- He admitted all the criticism and suggested correctly solutions concerning the economic situation and the question of arms.

3.- He offered $200,000.00 monthly for the work inside the island.
The delivery would take place through Dr. Raul Villasuso. (Dr. Raul Villasuso belongs to Justo Carillo's group, and he replaced Mr. Belisario Tellechea as the person in charge of finances in the executive of the FRD in Cuba. Not withstanding, he participated in the interview on the 18th together with Tony).

4.- Concerning the weapons, he informed that two shipments had entered and that we could already count on them. He showed two letters which originated in Cuba, acknowledging the receipt of said shipments. The contact to obtain them would be "Eladio", yet this is not definitive, (on other occasions Tony has mentioned a certain "Augusto" as a military liaison, who according to him has the same authority as "Francisco"). Tony made it clear that the weapons should not be used as instruments for violent attacks or for terrorist acts, but rather purely for military operations.

5.- Tony stated that he was unaware of "Francisco's" appointment as coordinator of the FRD. He said the appointment was a response to an imposition by the "friends" and that "Francisco" was one of Artime's men and not a representative of the FRD. As a solution to this situation he proposed that these two men and Villasuso, on their return to Havana, talk with other organizations to choose a coordinator, who would travel to Miami to receive instructions. He suggested Lomberto Diaz.

6.- He offered economic help for trips and lodging of family members who would like to leave Cuba. Mr. Sosa would resolve these problems abroad.

7.- He referred to an organizational diagram of Havana that an official named Leon, who works directly with him, was working on. He also showed numerous reports of ex-military

men, organized by counties. He claimed he counted on their support. He also asked for military reports, which should be sent to him. (these reports arrive via Rafael Rivas Vazquez with news material for the radio, of course Tony is unaware that he is the person who possesses the reports from Cuba).

Document 1.2   Report to Manuel Artime from MRR group, regarding a meeting in Miami with Dr. Manuel Antonio A. de Varona, 17–18 October 1960.

HEADQUARTERS OF THE F.R.D.

Havana, October 25

PLAN OF OPERATION No. 1

Relation of the organizations that will carry out this plan:

1) Units, groups, and elements of the F.R.D. of the province of Pinar del Rio
2) Units, Groups, and elements of the F.R.D of the province of Havana
3) Units, groups and elements of the F.R.D of the province of Las Villas
4) Units, Groups, and expeditions abroad of the F.R.D.
5) Air support with airplanes of the F.R.D
6) Other groups or elements and related organizations that join the movement.

I- GENERAL SITUATION

a) Enemy Forces- (those of the current government) The enemy forces are made up of the Rebel Army, the Rebel Air Force, The Revolutionary Navy, The Revolutionary Police, and the Militia. The most important nuclei of the Rebel Army are to be found in the barracks of the towns and capitals of the provinces. In the province of Havana the largest and best equipped troops of the Government are in Managua, San Antonio de los Baños, and La Cabaña.
The Revolutionary Police is in charge of order in the towns and cities and its combat power is relative.
The Rebel Air Force has few combat planes in flying condition and very few pilots at this moment; which interferes with them being able to help the land troops in the mountains. (However, rumors exist that the Government has received combat planes from socialist countries.)
The workers' militias, the farmer's militia and all the other militias and similar groups, although they have been very indoctrinated, lack discipline and training
The Government has received many weapons lately, and is distributing them, but needs time to train the militia in their use.

b) Our Forces.

The units, groups, and elements of the F.R.D. and other related elements.
Our men are receiving some arms and ammunition and expects to receive more soon.
Our men have a high morale and receive help and sympathy from a large part of the Cuban people, which sees with horror how communism is destroying the country and its institutions.

II- OUR MISSION

Document 1.3   Military Strength of the FRD in Cuba; report of Rogelio Gonzáles Corzo ("Francisco"), 25 October 1960.

In this initial plan our mission is first to liberate the province of Pinar del Rio, to make it an independent territory in Cuba, to produce uprisings in the north coasts of Las Villas, commando actions in the city of Havana, in conjunction with disembarkations on the south coast of Pinar del Rio, initiating in this way the war of the liberation of Cuba.

III- SPECIFIC ASSIGNMENTS FOR UNITS AND GROUPS

(A) With sufficient lead time one of our forces of two hundred well armed men will be situated in the mountain system of Pinar del Rio, which will operate the length and width of the "Cordillera de los Organos" and the "Sierra del Rosario" coordinated with groups of the plains of the north and south of the province.

(B) The group of the F.R.D. of Guanajay is assigned as an action zone and area of responsibility for the whole municipality.
(C) The group of the F.R.D. of Mariel is assigned the whole municipality, including the corresponding coastal area as their zone of action and area of responsibility.
(D) The group of the F.R.D. in Artemisa is assigned the territory of Artemisa and the corresponding coastal area as their zone of action and area of responsibility.
(E) In the Municipality of Cabañas there will be a group that will have as its zone the territory of "Bahia Honda", including the coastline, bays, and ports.
(F) The group in "Candelaria" is assigned the territory of the municipality and the corresponding southern coastal area as its action zone and area of responsibility.
(G) The group in San Cristóbal is assigned all the municipal territory and corresponding southern coastal areas as its action zone and area of responsibility.
(H) The group in "Consolación del Norte" is assigned all the municipal territory and corresponding coastal areas as its action zone and area of responsibility.
(I) The group at "los Palacios" is assigned all the municipal territory and corresponding southern coastal areas as its action zone and area of responsibility.
(J) There will be three groups in the municipalities of "Pinar del Río": No.1 will fight in the city and outlying neighborhoods; No.2 will fight in the northern part of the municipality; and No.3 will operate in the southern part of the municipaly including the corresponding coastal area.
(K) The group in "San Luis" is assigned the municipal territory and the corresponding coastal area as its action zone and area of responsibility.
(L) The group in "San Juán y Martínez" is assigned all the municipal territory and the corresponding southern coastal area as its action zone and area of responsibility.
(M) The group in Mantua is assigned all the municipal territory and corresponding coastal area.
(N) The group in Guane is assigned all the municipal territory and the north and south coasts of the "Guanacabibes" peninsula.
(O) The group in Viñales is assigned all the municipal territory and the corresponding northern coastal area.

Remark: See Report No.3 for the number of men we can count on.

Document 1.3   continued

HAVANA

The groups, units and elements of Havana will act in commando operations in the key zones of the city, to cut off the functions and movements of the government forces of repression and the normal development of essential activities, producing unrest and weakening control to make sure the government cannot accumulate troops and send them to "Pinar del Río"

LAS VILLAS

The units, groups and elements in the northern coast of "Las Villas" will rise up in arms in the zone of "Corralillo" and "Rancho Veloz" relieving the pressure that the "Escambray" is subjected to today, distracting the forces that are now pressuring our men in this area.

These groups in "Corralillo" and "Rancho Veloz" as long as they keep growing, will be a force with enough offensive power to become strong in the province and carry out big operations.

In their initial phase of this plan they will operate in the highlands of the surrounding mountain ranges, making incursions into the towns and settlements in the action zone, harrying the enemy and creating all kinds of problems.

LANDING ACTIONS

"A" On the south coast of Pinar del Río armed expeditions from outside Cuba will land to reinforce the personnel, materials, troops, and the groups which will be operating in the province.
"B" the landings will coincide with the beginning of operations in the province.
"C" The initial objectives of the expeditions will be in the strategic places closest to the landing points.
"D" After each successful landing a beachhead will be established to provide security for the personnel and materials, making sure that it does not fall into enemy hands.

AIR SUPPORT

Our aviation will be in charge of two principle missions.

(a) Attack the enemy military objectives, such as the Air Base at San Antonio de los Baños, de base at Managua, Guanito, Seboruco, and the concentrations of troops, as well as to support our military operations- but avoiding, in all cases, harm to the civilian population.

Document 1.3   continued

(b) Ensure delivery of provisions to our troops, with transport planes, bringing all kinds of material, especially the most necessary to maintain the course of operations/

COMMON INSTRUCTIONS TO ALL UNITS

1.- Although in this plan action zones and areas of responsibility for each group and/or unit have been fixed, this should not get in the way of neighboring units helping each other when necessary.

2.- The units or groups will help the landings in their respective zones.

DATE AND TIME TO BEGIN EXECUTING THE PLAN

The day and hour will be transmitted to those concerned with this signal- the day "D" will be (date here), and then hour "H" will be (exact time here).

SUPPLIES

a) Delivery of provisions will be maintained, above all arms, ammunition and others to eat and fight.

b) The units will obtain food supplies in their zones, however if the circumstances require food will be supplied.

HEADQUARTERS, COMMAND POSTS, COMMUNICATION

A) There should be a command unit in each group or unit.

B) The superior command, common to all units which participate in this plan, will be exercised by the responsible person of the F.R.D. in the military organization.

C) The command post of the chief of this operation will be installed initially somewhere in the province of "Pinar del Río", which will quickly be made known.

D) To communicate with the command post of their common superior chief, the units will use the means at their disposal.

E) Each unit or group will have its own command post; the command posts will not be fixed, this is to say that they will change from one place to another in the zone depending on the circumstances.

Francisco Gutierrez

Written by ----------------> (Rogelio Gonzales Corso) Co-ord. of the M.R.R.
and of the F.D.R

Document 1.3   continued

VERY SECRET

Democratic Revolutionary Front Commanding Office
Havana, October 27, 1960.

Combat Order N° 1.

Report on our units, organizations and other elements that will fulfill this order.

1)   Units, groups and elements of the DRF in the Province of La Habana.
2)   Units, groups and elements of the DRF in the Province of Pinar del Rio.
3)   Units, groups and elements of the DRF in the Province of Matanzas.
4)   Units, groups and elements of the DRF in the Province of Las Villas.
5)   DRF armed expeditions coming from abroad.
6)   DRF aviation coming from abroad.
7)   Related organizations and elements to cooperate in the execution of this combat order.

I. GENERAL SITUATION

        a)   Enemy forces - (those of the Government).
        The greatest concentrations of enemy forces that have artillery, mechanized troops and aviation, are located in Managua, San Antonio de los Baños, La Cabaña, and on a smaller scale at the Columbia airport. There are also considerable enemy troops in the air-naval base of Mariel and at the Gramma base or camp, located at the Dominica, near Mariel.
        Likewise, the enemy has troops in different places of the operations theater this order refers to.
        Likewise, the enemy has armed a large part of the workers and farmer militia, but these do not yet have sufficient cohesion.
        b)   Our forces are composed of the organizations that appear on the heading of this order and will be reinforced with first class personnel and material in the course of action.

II. OUR MISSION
        a)   According to the Operation Plan (N° 1), our initial mission is to free the Province of Pinar del Rio, to make it Cuba's independent territory; but it is first necessary, before covering the whole Province, to carry out a series of local confrontations and take key points that insure the success of the general operation.
        b)   To guarantee the success of our mission, we must attack the San Julian air base, near Guane military objectives in the most populous towns of the province of Pinar del Rio, and protect the disembarkation process of our expeditions, as well as the landings of our planes.

Document 1.4   Combat Order Number 1 (FRD plan for insurrection, beginning in Pinar del Río province), by Rogelio Gonzáles Corzo ("Francisco"), 27 October 1960.

III. SPECIFIC MISSIONS THAT OUR UNITS, GROUPS AND LIKE ELEMENTS WILL CARRY OUT.

a) Our units, groups and like elements which operate in the Pinar del Rio, Guane, San Juan y Martinez, San Luis, and Mantua districts will combine to attack the San Julian base. This base will be attacked initially with combined forces of machine guns and mortars, then assaulted with rifles and other light weapons fire in coordination with the men the DRF has inside such military base. Simultaneously to the attack, access roads to the town of Guane will be blocked or interrupted, as well as the railroad that joins the city of Pinar del Rio with this town, thus preventing enemy reinforcements by land. The section of the road that joins the La Fe port with San Julian, will be maintained usable, so it can be used by one of our expeditions from abroad which will disembark at La Fe.

Once the San Julian base has been conquered, this airport will be occupied and sustained by our men, to be used as an operation base for our air and land force. In case of enemy air attack, natural shelters of the terrain will be provided and other measures will be taken to prevent enemy planes to cause damage in our ranks.

The surprise factor must be well considered, for which reason all attack preparations must be made with the highest secrecy and the enemy prevented from obtaining such information. It is also important to quickly establish a link with our expeditionary forces disembarking at La Fe and act in coordination with this expedition.

b) Our units, groups and like elements operating in the San Cristobal, Los Palacios, and Consolacion del Sur districts, have as their fundamental mission to protect one of our expeditions disembarking at the Dayaniguas, on the South coast of the Pinar del Rio district, in order to secure and protect the personnel and supplies this expedition brings. Once the expedition has disembarked, they will join it and perform a series of attacks on military objectives located in the most important towns and villages of the region, cutting off communications to the enemy, blocking roads and railroads, and preventing the opposing forces, their militia included, from concentrating and counterattacking at large.

If, under any circumstance, it becomes difficult to remain on the plain, you will go to the mountains, where you will reorganize and later attack by surprise any military objective that is either propitious or favorable. The point is to keep the enemy at "check-mate" and weaken him to defeat.

c) Our forces operating in Guanajay, Artemisa, Candelaria, Mariel and Cabañas, have as their main mission to assault Rebel Army headquarters, police stations, militia headquarters, and to occupy post offices and telegraph stations, telephone centers, city halls and public buildings in general by carrying out a series of flash actions on the plains or getting into the hills when a position is made un-sustainable; but they will get into the hills by falling back in echelons, that is, by groups that will protect each other with their fire, and always resisting the enemy. When in the mountains, they will use the time to get reorganized and make new attacks.

Because they are closest to the province of La Habana, our forces operating in these hills are most exposed to quick enemy counter-attack, for which reason special attention must be put on interrupting the roads and railroads that lead to these hills. It is important to remember that the enemy may mobilize its troops from San Antonio-Alquizar-Artemisa, the Central road, and the railroad. Therefore, besides the blockage, anti-tanks, such as the bazooka and anti-tank mines, must be mobilized, if available, on these tracks.

Document 1.4　continued

Equally dangerous are the roads Guanajay-Mariel, Guanajay-Cabañas, and Artemisa-Cabañas, since enemy forces may receive reinforcement from this zone. These roads must be made impassable for the enemy, not only through blockage; armaments will also be displayed on their dominant points.

In this zone, our forces must adopt a war-movement system, especially if the enemy presented considerable superiority in number in any action; harass as much as possible, to make him spread out and delay his movements. Once this is achieved, our forces will fall back in echelons to more secure positions, where they can reorganize and then continue the attacks.

It must not be forgotten that success of our other forces in the province of Pinar del Rio, greatly depends on the DRF activity in Guanajay, Artemisa, Mariel, Candelaria and Cabañas.

Another very important mission of our forces in the above-mentioned zones, is to prevent the enemy from bringing great contingents to the Western zones of the province and attacking the expeditionary elements of the DRF which will disembark at the previously mentioned places in this order.

d)   The DRF units, groups and like groups of the Habana province will act in accordance with the plan designated for the capital of the Republic and close municipalities, and their sections should be effective and cooperating in conjunction with our elements of the Pinar del Rio province.

e)   Our Matanzas and Las Villas units will do likewise. In these two provinces, activity must start when the Pinar del Rio activities initiate, according to Operation Plan N° 1.

Combat actions in Matanzas and Las Villas will largely contribute to the success of the operations at the war theater at Pinar del Rio province.

f)   Day and time of initiation of activities.

All of our unit and group leaders will be attentive and expect to receive the message in which the date and time to execute this Combat order will be set.

IV. SUPPLIES

Supplies of materials to units will be made as circumstances allow, but war materiel and armaments of all kinds will have preference.

Local resources will be taken advantage of, especially regarding articles for mouth care and food in general.

Each group must develop initiative to gather, within their zone, anything that can be useful to the operations.

V. COMMUNICATIONS.

For communications, trusted messengers will be used. Unit and group leaders will communicate with adjacent and bordering units, and with the common superior of this operation.

The common superior will establish his command post in a place of the Pinar del Rio province, to be made known in time.

Francisco Gutierrez

Copies of this to be distributed as secret to those concerned.

Document 1.4   continued

EXPLANATORY REPORT ON INFORMATION TRANSMITTED TO YOU IN THE
LAST DAYS ABOUT RAFAEL AND THE UNIDAD REVOLUCIONARIA

The communiqué's objective was the following. Various people in Cuba
are taking steps to integrate a new front called Revolutionary Unit. Among these people
are Mr. Rafael (war name) and the ex member of the MRR, Mr. Villasuso, Representative
of Montecristi in Cuba, and Mr. Justo from the Liberation Front. This Revolutionary Unit
has a minimal governing program, and have their regulations, so that, according to them,
the Frente Revolucionario Democratico and other organizations that would agree, would
form a great organization which they would call Unidad Revolucionaria. The signing
organizations would each name a delegate, and in a big assembly would elect a new
executive from this unit, composed of new members, who would recognize Martin Helena
in exile and momentarily, as we attribute the representatives of the F.R.D. in exile.

This was initiated after moving abroad. The organizations that were talked about invoked
on the name of Martin Helena, others from the F.R.D. and from the M.R.R., all of these
without the authorization and behind the backs of the previously mentioned organizations
or people. When I arrived in the country the executive of the F.R.D. met again to consider
this newly created situation, and after several meetings with the delegate of Montecristi, as
member of the executive of the F.R.D. and promoter of the Unidad Revolucionaria, which
considers that the way the unit is being organized created confusion among the militias of
the F.R.D., since the F.R.D. already represents the unit in Cuba. Taking into account that
this was being done without the consent of the F.R.D. and that for the moment it was an
undisciplined act, I urge the representative of Montecristi that this same action should be
made through the F.R.D and not through a new ineffective front, because clandestine
actions can not be operated like political campaigns, which have big delegate assemblies to
name numerous executives that would direct the actions, which I agree with. The
Direccion Nacional committed the same action with our friend Rafael, who presented his
resignation in order to continue the task of creating unity, which he considered to be more
important.

All our friends have been explained that the executive of the F.R.D has always
promoted an effective unity when considering actions and future plans of all organizations
for Cuba, so that the material may be distributed to all organizations from there. So that
the military plans can rely on the different organizations, so that the Ejercito de
Liberacion of the F.R.D. can ask the military of all the organizations in Cuba to integrate
into their ranks. What the F.R.D. does not want is to create confusion among the Cubans,
who are willing to fight for their ideals, by asking for the unity of the small organizations
and by forming big assemblies of delegates in order to delegate new people. And we
mention this because according to the plans of the people of this new unit, since the
F.R.D. had a unit when it was founded, it would be formed of maybe 25 or 30
organizations which would mean 30 delegates in order to form an executive of 9. But now
I ask, should the rest of the organizations, which without exaggerating amount to over 50,

**Document 1.5   Report on Unidad Revolucionaria, by Rogelio Gonzáles Corzo ("Francisco"), 7
January 1961.**

not also name their delegates and vote for a new executive? If this would happen we would be contemplating a political campaign and not an insurrectional fight.
It is because of this that the F.R.D. has created the document for the integration of all the organizations into the F.R.D. In this document we ask for a true unity in the plans for sabotage and in the military plans.

This would imply the recognition of the F.R.D, both in exile and in Cuba, as well as the recognition of the military staff of the Ejercito de Liberacion of the F.R.D.

We truly hope that God help us, not only in creating unity between the organizations, but also in the fight for unity of all those Cubans, who are willing to fight for their ideals, their liberties and their principles.

Francisco

January 7, 1961

Document 1.5   continued

PROGRAM A   <u>FRIDAY 20 JANUARY 1961</u>.

1--- INVASION HYMN
2--- TRINCHERA ON THE AIR, RADIO PERIODICO UNIVERSITARIO.
--- A TRENCH OF IDEAS IS WORTH MORE THAN A TRENCH OF STONE.
--- FOR THE RESCUE OF THE UNIVERSITY'S AUTONOMY.
--- FOR THE RESCUE OF STUDENT DIGNITY.
--- TO RECUPERATE THE BETRAYED REVOLUTION.
--- FOR THE FREEDOM OF OUT FATHERLAND.
--- TRINCHERA RADIO PERIODICO UNIVERSITARIO, AT THE SERVICE OF
   THE DIRECTORIO REVOLUCIONARIO ESTUDIANTIL.
--- DIRECTOR: ALBERTO MULLER, ALREADY IN CUBA.
--- EDITORIAL STAFF: MANUEL SALVAT.

4--- TRINCHERA RADIO PERIODICO UNIVERSITARIO, PRESENTS ITS NEWS
   "ACTUALIDAD" [*CURRENT NEWS*], BY REBECA MILIAN AND ELIO MAS.
--- ATTENTION! AFTER OUR NEWS, WE WILL BROADCAST THE MOST
   RECENT REPORTS ON THE FIGHT IN THE VILLAS AREA.
--- THE AIRPLANES OF THE FRENTE REVOLUCIONARIO DEMOCRATICO
   FLY OVER HAVANA ANY TIME THEY WANT AND AT THE HOUR THEY
   FEEL LIKE. ON THE NIGHT OF TUESDAY THE PLAZA CIVICA AND THE
   CASTILLO DEL PRINCIPE WERE WITNESSES OF YET ANOTHER
   AUDACIOUS AERIAL INCURSION WITH THE CONSEQUENT SHOOTING
   AND THE ALARM OF THE NEIGHBORS.
--- FIDEL CASTRO'S "TRAINED" MILITARY COULD NOT EVEN STRIKE THE
   GHOST AIRPLANE ONCE, WHICH FLEW OVER THE CENTER OF VEDADO
   AS LONG AS IT THOUGHT CONVENIENT.
--- IT IS MOST LIKELY THAT WITHIN THE NEXT FEW DAYS NO PILOT FROM
   FIDEL CASTRO'S AIR FORCE WILL WANT TO FLY, SINCE AFTER THE
   GHOST AIRPLANE'S LAST VISIT, AN AIRPLANE FROM THE CUBAN AIR
   FORCE WAS SHOT DOWN, WHICH COST THE LIFE OF THREE PEOPLE,
   INCLUDING THAT OF A MEMBER OF THE G-2.
--- HOW AWFUL THAT MILITIA IS! EVERY WEEK A GHOST PLANE VISITS
   THEM, AND THE ONLY DAY THEY ARE ABLE TO SET TARGET TO IT,
   THEY SHOOT DOWN ONE OF THEIR OWN PLANES AND KILL THREE
   PEOPLE FROM THEIR OWN FORCES. ALL OF THIS HAS TO HAPPEN IN A
   MILITARY THAT IS PREPARING TO REPEL AN INVASION FROM THE
   PEER.
 --- CUBA'S YOUTH IS CLOSING RANKS WITH THE DIRECTORIO
   REVOLUCIONARIO ESTUDIANTIL. THE YOUNG CUBAN STUDENTS, WHO
   WERE STUDYING AT NORTH AMERICAN UNIVERSITIES AND OTHER

Document 1.6   DRE Radio Broadcast ("Trinchera Radio"), 20 January 1961.

COUNTRIES IN AMERICA, HAVE ABANDONED THEIR BOOKS IN ORDER TO SAY PRESENT AT THEIR COUNTRY'S CALLING.

--- HUNDREDS OF CUBAN STUDENTS HAVE DECIDED THAT THEIR INESCAPABLE DUTY AT THIS MOMENT IS TO COMBAT THE COMMUNIST TYRANNY THAT IS RULING CUBA. THEY HAVE CLOSED RANKS WITH THE D.R.E., IN ORDER TO MARCH HAND IN HAND, TO THE GROUND OF THEIR FATHERLAND AND TO OVERTHROW THE TRAITOR FIDEL CASTRO AND HIS COMRADES OF CUBAN BODY, YET OF FOREIGN SOULS.

--- THE EXAMPLE GIVEN BY THE CUBAN STUDENTS FROM THE UNIVERSITY OF GAINSVILLE, WHO WERE THE FIRST ONES TO TAKE THIS VALIANT AND PATRIOTIC STEP, DESERVES MUCH EMPHASIS.

--- 70,000 CREOLE PINEAPPLES ADORN THE ATLANTIC.
A SHIPMENT OF 70,000 PINEAPPLES ORIGINATING IN CUBA HAD TO BE THROWN INTO THE OCEAN AFTER THE DOCK WORKERS IN MIAMI REFUSED TO UNLOAD ANY SHIPMENT COMING FROM RED CUBA.

--- AND NOW TRINCHERA PRESENTS THE PUBLIC RELATIONS COORDINATOR OF THE DRE IN HIS SECTION TITLED "THE TRUTH ABOUT LATIN AMERICA AND CUBA".

--- AND NOW OUR SECTION "ACTUALIDAD" CONTINUES.

--- ATTENTION! ATTENTION! MORE NEWS ON THE FIGHTS IN THE ESCAMBRAY AREA.

--- THE MILITARY CONTINUES TO TRY TO CONTAIN THE FORCES OF THE LIBERATION ARMY, WHICH ARE OPERATING IN DIFFERENT AREAS IN THE VILLAS PROVINCE. COMMANDERS ALMEIDA, ESCALONA, FELIX DUQUE AND MANUEL PINEIRO ARE IN COMMAND OF THE COMMUNIST FORCES.

--- SEVERAL COMMANDERS ARE JOINING RANKS WITH THE LIBERATION TROOPS. WE HAVE BEEN INFORMED THAT COMMANDER RODRIGUEZ PUENTE, AN OLD FIGHTER AGAINST FULGENCIO BATISTA'S DICTATORSHIP, JOINED THE INSURGENTS WITH THREE HUNDRED MEN UNDER HIS COMMAND.

--- COMMANDER CESAR PAEZ, WHO WAS A PILLAR IN THE CAMPAIGN BROUGHT ABOUT BY THE DIRECTORIO REVOLUCIONARIO 13 OF MARCH, JOINED THE LIBERATION ARMY. WITH THESE COMMANDERS WE NOW HAVE SIX COMMANDERS, WHO HAVE ABANDONED THE RANKS OF FIDEL CASTRO'S RED ARMY, IN ORDER TO JOIN THE DEMOCRATIC FORCES.

--- A FIERCE COMBAT DEVELOPED AROUND YAGUAJAI, WHERE NUMEROUS MILITIAS HAD TO RETREAT AFTER SUFFERING HEAVY LOSSES. THE SOCIALIST POPULIST PARTY'S DELEGATE IN YAGUAJAI, LUIS ALBERTO, INFORMED COMMANDER CARLOS IGLESIAS, HEAD OF THE FOURTH MILITARY DISTRICT OF LAS VILLAS, OF THE DEFEAT SUFFERED BY THE MILITARY IN THAT AREA.

--- ON THE HILLS OF BANAO, CLOSE TO TRINIDAD, THERE WAS A FIGHT WHERE THE COMMUNISTS SUFFERED SUCH HEAVY LOSSES, THAT IT

Document 1.6   continued

WAS NECESSARY TO USE ALL THE MILITARY VEHICLES AND BUSES AT THE DISPOSAL OF THE I.N.R.A. IN ORDER TO TRANSPORT THE WOUNDED.
DESERTIONS HAVE BEEN NUMEROUS AND ORDERS FOR VIOLENT REPRESSION HAVE BEEN GIVEN, IN ORDER TO AVOID THE CONTINUED DEMORALIZATION OF THE CUBAN COMMUNIST MILITARY.

--- THIS IS THE VOICE OF THE DIRECTORIO REVOLUCIONARIO ESTUDIANTIL, WHO INVITES YOU, THE CUBAN STUDENT, TO JOIN OUR FIGHT IF YOU HAVE NOT YET DONE SO. THE EXECUTIVE IN PLENARY OF THE D.R.E IS DIRECTING THE CLANDESTINE FIGHT WITHIN OUR FATHERLAND. FOR GOD AND FOR CUBA JOIN THE DIRECTORIO. CUBA NEEDS YOU.

--- ATTENTION ALBERT MULLER...ATTENTION ALBERT MULLER....RECEIVED MESSAGE FROM EUGENIO...RECEIVED MESSAGE FROM EUGENIO...EVERYTHING IS GOING WELL...EVERYTHING IS GOING WELL.

--- POPULATION OF CUBA, THE FINAL HOUR IS IMMINENT. CUBANS, CLEAN OF EVERY STAIN FROM THE PAST, SOON THEY WILL LIBERATE YOU IN THE FINAL BATTLE IN THE HOMELAND. KEEP THIS NAME IN MIND...FRANCISCO. REMEMBER, ALL OF CUBA SHOULD REMEMBER THIS NAME. FRANCISCO.

--- THE SABOTAGE AGAINST THE COMMUNIST REGIME IN CUBA IS INCREASING. IN THE VICTORY OF LAS TUNAS, HEAVY DAMAGES WERE CAUSED TO THE OFFICES OF THE PARTIDO SOCIALISTA POPULAR. THE ATTACK ON SAID OFFICES WAS BROUGHT ABOUT BY THE BRAVE MEN OF THE RESISTANCE.

--- NUMEROUS FIRES WERE CAUSED IN THE EXTENSIVE ZONE, LOCATED BETWEEN VICTORIA DE LAS TUNAS AND PUERTO PADRE, WHERE VARIOUS CENTRAL SUGAR CANE GROWERS ARE LOCATED. THE MOST AFFECTED PROPERTY WAS THAT OF ARMANDO ESCALONA, WHERE 12,500,000 POUNDS OF CANE WERE BURNT.

--- WE THANK ALL OUR LISTENERS IN CUBA AND LATIN AMERICA FOR THEIR LETTERS OF ENCOURAGEMENT AND SUPPORT THAT THEY HAVE SENT US. WE HOPE THAT THEY CONTINUE TO REPORT TO US AND SEND US SUGGESTIONS THAT THEY THINK WOULD BE OF GENERAL INTEREST.

--- WE ARE BEING INFORMED THAT JOSE FELIPE NAVARRO, WHO WAS ROBERTO CRUZ'S YOUNG INFORMER, DIED IN THE GARAGE OF INFANTA AND SAN RAFAEL, IN HAVANA. (ROBERTO CRUZ WAS THE FIRST TO BE EXECUTED FOR THE ATTACK ON A HYSTERIC WINDBAG KNOWN BY THE NAME OF JOSE PARDO LLADA.)

Document 1.6   continued

La Habana, January 24, 1961.

The Honorable
John F. Kennedy
President of the United States of America
White House, Washington, DC

Dear Mr. President:

"In the long history of the world, only a few generations have been granted the role of defenders of Freedom in their most perilous hours."

One of those hours of maximum danger is Cuba's and America's present hour.

For that reason, we, the Americans who fight today in Cuba against oppression and totalitarianism, students who have risked our lives in the "role of defenders of Freedom" and, having done so twice in a period of less than four years, have lived through intense and unique experiences. From our position of persecution in Cuba, we now address you, Mr. President, as well as the elected president of the United States of Brazil, Mr. Janio Quadros, both representatives of a generation which has also embraced "the role of defender of Freedom," in order to state open and respectfully our opinion about the situation of Cuba and America.

As Your Excellency knows, many diverse problems are converging to provoke in our Latin-American peoples a unique condition which became explosive long ago:

The deficient agrarian structure, weak industrialization, lack of an international integration of marketing, insufficient economic planning, deficient regulation of foreign investment in the economic field; the already grave food deficit, lack of housing and hygiene for a considerable percentage of our population, our society's badly developed organization wherein privileged minorities "peacefully coexist" at present with the dispossessed majorities, pronounced increase in population, still not accomplished racial integration, serious educational problems in the social area; the existence of merely formal dictatorships or democracies, excessive influence of military castes, poor representation of the press regarding the political order; and the perfunctory Latin-American integration, international weakness, barely disguised colonialism which still exists in some regions in the international arena... these are only some of the problems.

This, Mr. President, worsened even more by the disgraces necessarily brought about by tyranny, was Cuba's situation before the first of January of Nineteen Hundred fifty-nine.

So began the long martyrdom of our generation. Many times, with no other weapons than our fists or rocks, Cuban students flung ourselves into battle, along with other groups representing the most diverse social and political tendencies. For some of these groups, the goal was only to overthrow the government and to reestablish the traditional status quo. For us, on the contrary, that was only the first step to a transformation the country was so much in need of.

We wanted to carry out, with the prestige of an immaculate revolution, a development process that enabled all Cubans the full exercise of their rights. We did not deem necessary, nor did we consider

Document 1.7   Letter from Alberto Müller, secretary general of the DRE, to President John F. Kennedy, 24 January 1961 (excerpts). (English translations from the Spanish by Andrew R. Goodridge.)

We have been given the highest of destinies: that of "burning" our best years in the heroic fight for freedom and for the advancement of our country, that of maintaining our dignity and preventing adulteration or mishandling of the people's consciousness.

We will fight alone if necessary, or with the generous help of those who wish to do so, but knowing that this cause depends mainly on Cuba and Cubans.

The country, along with all Latin America, will be greatly indebted to us. In saving Cuba, we will be saving America. The purest principles of our civilization, the principle of "man's rights do not come from any State but from God," are at stake, and we are the ones destined to the battle. Your faith in Cuba, your future in America will depend on the "courage," the blood and death of Cuban youth who were able to say "I will join" in this, our country's fight.

And it is we, Mr. President, those addressing Your Excellency from our oppressed Cuba, with the moral strength gained from fighting a transcendent fight, with the integrity of not having lowered our heads to anyone except God, who express with all due respect, that Cuba's situation may soon be Latin-America's situation, that world destinies are at stake and that therefore, we all must start the great work of returning to our original positions, reviewing them all and rectifying them, if necessary, before it is too late.

In this task, the United States of America has a major role to fulfill. If Latin-American nations, if Cuba, must find by her own hand a moral solution, the United States' will be obliged to cooperate with that solution.

And that will only be true if the US leaders understand that there are no "quick and easy remedies against communism," that its foreign policy must not be based on negative concepts, on "closing the doors to evil before doing good," nor on "giving priority to military solutions over economic and social solutions." If the US leaders understand that these forms of politics quickly make people realize that the help given does not come from the moral obligation, nor from its own needs, but from private foreign goals; if the US leaders understand that their task is that of associating in a friendly manner with all people, respecting their fairest aspirations and with the greatest desire possible for civilization possible, and not bind the people to crusades with goals that lack authentic spirituality.

The role of the US is to prevent communism, disguised as Fidelism, from becoming the expression of the present revolutionary feeling in Latin-America before the unfair situation of delay and misery; and to prevent "that the Andes become the Sierra Maestra of the American Continent"; it is also to be capable of understanding that what, to date, has been called "pan-americanism" has been nothing but a long chain of unfulfilled dreams, of abandoned purposes, of deceptions and frustrations, impositions, and disregard of the people's most legitimate aspirations, which is becoming an empty word for Latin-American youth. We do not see how reciprocity for its help toward the defense of Western principles of freedom and justice could be the insensitivity to the maintenance of conditions that prevent the effective enforcement of freedom and justice in your countries.

Pan-americanism will only make sense if a restructuring of the Inter-American System is accomplished (as Chilean students said in a letter to your predecessor) on the basis of absolute equality and reciprocity, in search of true democratic promotion and Latin-American economic development or integration.

Finally, Mr. President, we want to state that our hope lies with someone like you, who knew how to defend freedom risking his own life during the past World War; who, during the electoral campaign, had the sincerity to say "that the United States would lose prestige in the world" and that

Document 1.7   continued

"the goal of American foreign policy had to be something very different from simply sustaining the present world situation"; who declared in his speech to take office that it was the mission of the United States to "help the people to help themselves"; by your performance as President of North Americans; whose predecessor, so many years ago, speaking in Gettysburg by the tombs of those who "had given their lives for the Nation to live," declared that those who had fallen "had not died in vain" and that "the government of the people, for the people and by the people" would never disappear from earth.

We use this opportunity to reiterate to Your Excellency the highest testimony of our appreciation.

For the National Executive of the Student Revolutionary Directory.

Alberto Müller Quintana
Secretary General

Document 1.7   continued

16 March 1960

A PROGRAM OF COVERT ACTION AGAINST THE CASTRO REGIME

1. Objective: The purpose of the program outlined herein is to bring about the replacement of the Castro regime with one more devoted to the true interests of the Cuban people and more acceptable to the U.S. in such a manner as to avoid any appearance of U.S. intervention. Essentially the method of accomplishing this end will be to induce, support, and so far as possible direct action, both inside and outside of Cuba, by selected groups of Cubans of a sort that they might be expected to and could undertake on their own initiative. Since a crisis inevitably entailing drastic action in or toward Cuba could be provoked by circumstances beyond control of the U.S. before the covert action program has accomplished its objective, every effort will be made to carry it out in such a way as progressively to improve the capability of the U.S. to act in a crisis.

2. Summary Outline: The program contemplates four major courses of action:

    a. The first requirement is the creation of a responsible, appealing and unified Cuban opposition to the Castro regime, publicly declared as such and therefore necessarily located outside of Cuba. It is hoped that within one month a political entity can be formed in the shape of a council or junta, through the merger of three acceptable opposition groups ....
The council will be encouraged to adopt as its slogan "Restore the

Document 2.1   A Program of Covert Action Against the Castro Regime, a draft for President Eisenhower, 16 March 1960 (excerpt).

EYES ONLY
---SECRET-FIED
2

Revolution", to develop a political position consistent with that slogan,
and to address itself to the Cuban people as an attractive political
alternative to Castro. This vocal opposition will: serve as a magnet
for the loyalties of the Cubans; in actuality conduct and direct various
opposition activities; :::
::::::::::::::::::::::::::: (Tab A)

b. So that the opposition may be heard and Castro's basis of
popular support undermined, it is necessary to develop the means for
mass communication to the Cuban people so that a powerful propaganda
offensive can be initiated in the name of the declared opposition.
The major tool proposed to be used for this purpose is a long and short
wave gray broadcasting facility, probably to be located on Swan Island.
The target date for its completion is two months. This will be supplemented by broadcasting from U.S. commercial facilities paid for by
private Cuban groups :::
::::::::::::::::::::::::::: (Tab B)

c. Work is already in progress in the creation of a covert
intelligence and action organization within Cuba which will be responsive to the orders and directions of the "exile" opposition. Such a
network must have effective communication and be selectively manned
to minimize the risk of penetration. An effective organization can
probably be created within 60 days. :::::::::::::::::::::::::::::::::::
:::::::::::::::::::::::::::::::::::

EYES ONLY
SECRET-FIED

Document 2.1   continued

EYES ONLY
SECRET

d. Preparations have already been made for the development of an adequate paramilitary force outside of Cuba, together with mechanisms for the necessary logistic support of covert military operations on the Island. Initially a cadre of leaders will be recruited after careful screening and trained as paramilitary instructors. In a second phase a number of paramilitary cadres will be trained at secure locations outside of the U.S. so as to be available for immediate deployment into Cuba to organize, train and lead resistance forces recruited there both before and after the establishment of one or more active centers of resistance. The creation of this capability will require a minimum of six months and probably closer to eight. In the meanwhile, a limited air capability for resupply and for infiltration and exfiltration already exists under CIA control and can be rather easily expanded if and when the situation requires. Within two months it is hoped to parallel this with a small air resupply capability under deep cover as a commercial operation in another country.

3. Leadership: It is important to avoid distracting and devisive rivalry among the outstanding Cuban opposition leaders for the senior role in the

EYES ONLY
SECRET

Document 2.1   continued

EYES ONLY
SECRET

opposition. Accordingly, every effort will be made to have an eminent, non-ambitious, politically uncontentious chairman selected. The emergence of a successor to Castro should follow careful assessment of the various personalities active in the opposition to identify the one who can attract, control, and lead the several forces. As the possibility of an overthrow of Castro becomes more imminent, the senior leader must be selected, U.S. support focused upon him, and his build up undertaken.

4. :::

5. <u>Budget:</u> It is anticipated that approximately :::::::::::::: of CIA funds will be required for the above program. On the assumption that it will not

EYES ONLY
SECRET

Document 2.1   continued

March 18, 1960

MEMORANDUM OF CONFERENCE WITH THE PRESIDENT
2:30 PM, March 17, 1960

Others present: Vice President Nixon, Secretary Herter,
Mr. Merchant, Mr. Rubottom, Secretary Anderson,
Secretary Irwin, Admiral Burke, Mr. Allen Dulles,
Mr. Richard Bissell, Colonel J. C. King, Gordon
Gray, Major Eisenhower, General Goodpaster

After Mr. Herter gave a brief comment concerning use of the OAS
in connection with the Cuban situation, Mr. Allen Dulles reported
to the President an action plan provided by the "5412" group for
covert operations to effect a change in Cuba.   The first step
will be to form a moderate opposition group in exile.   This will
take about one month.   Its slogan will be to "restore the revolution" which Castro has betrayed.   A medium wave radio station
to carry out gray or black broadcasts into Cuba will be established, probably on Swan Island (south of Cuba, belonging to the
United States), in two months.   Concurrently a network of dis-
affected elements will be established within Cuba.

To a question by the President Mr. Bissell indicated the opposition would probably be located in Puerto Rico.   Mexico would
be better if they could be brought to agree, which is not likely.
Venezuela would be even better, but it is not probable that the
government could permit this.   Mr. Rubottom thought Costa
Rica may be a possibility and this will be explored.

Mr. Allen Dulles said that preparations of a para-military force
will begin outside of Cuba, the first stage being to get a cadre
of leaders together for training.   The formation of this force
might take something like eight months.

The President said that he knows of no better plan for dealing
with this situation.   The great problem is leakage and breach
of security.   Everyone must be prepared to swear that he has not

DECLASSIFIED

E.O. 12958, SEC. 3.6(b)
MR 94-122#2
BY *BBm* DATE 7/31/96

Document 2.2   Memorandum of Conference with the President, 18 March 1960 (minutes of a
meeting regarding Cuba on 17 March, drafted by Gen. Andrew Goodpaster).

heard of it.   He said we should limit American contacts with
the groups involved to two or three people, getting Cubans
to do most of what must be done. Mr. Allen Dulles said that a
group of New York businessmen is being organized as cover for
this activity.   The President indicated some question about
this, and reiterated that there should be only two or three
governmental people connected with this in any way. He understood that the effort will be to undermine Castro's position and
prestige. Mr. Bissell commented that the opposition group
would undertake a money-raising campaign to obtain funds on
their own -- in the United States, Cuba and elsewhere.

Mr. Gray commented that events may occur rapidly in Cuba,
and force our hand before these preparations are completed.

Secretary Anderson stated that Castro is in reality financing
his operations out of the funds of the U. S. companies that are
operating in Cuba.   He suggested that the Administration might
take steps to bring business leaders together with elements
of our government to consider what course the businesses --
which are now being milked of their assets -- should take.   He
said he had received a report that Castro is trying to inflame
Cuban opinion and create an incident against the Americans
which would touch off attacks on Americans in Cuba which might
result in the death of thousands.   The President stated that
once the operation Mr. Douglas had proposed gets started, there
will be great danger to the Americans in Cuba. Mr. Rubottom
said that the "warning phase" of our evacuation plan is already
in effect, and that many Americans are leaving, with almost
no new ones going in.

Mr. Anderson said he thought that if we were to cut the Cubans
off from their fuel supply, the effect would be devastating on
them within a month or six weeks.   There is some question
whether other countries would join in denying fuel oil -- especially
Venezuela.   Mr. Anderson added that if Cuba is to seize the
Nicaro plant or other U. S. Government property, we could not
stand on the sidelines. In reponse to a question by the President,
it was brought out that there is no treaty on this, and that Cuba
of course has the right to confiscate the plant so long as com-
pensation is given. Mr. Rubottom stated that if we wanted to cut

Document 2.2   continued

- 3 -

their trade drastically we could denounce our two trade agree-
ments with them. This would of course cut into the sales
by our manufacturers to the Cubans. Mr. Nixon asked what we
are doing with regard to cutting off new capital, pulling out
private firms and cutting off tourism. Mr. Rubottom said
that much of this is occurring of its own accord.

The President told Mr. Dulles he thought he should go ahead
with the plan and the operations. He and the other agencies
involved should take account of all likely Cuban reactions and
prepare the actions that we would take in response to these. Mr.
Irwin said the main Defense concern is how we would get our
people out. We have contingency planning, but it would involve
military action.   The President said he would like some ground
work laid with the OAS to let the Latin American countries know
that if the Cubans were to start to attack our people in Cuba
we would be obliged to take action.

Mr. Allen Dulles returned to the point made by Mr. Anderson --
that American business in Cuba wants guidance. The President
said we should be very careful about giving this. Essentially
they will have to make their own decisions. Admiral Burke
stated that many of the American firms want to pull out, but do
not want to endanger their people who are there. Mr. Nixon
said he thought we should encourage them to come out. Particularly
if they think they should get out and are simply staying there to
help the U. S. Government, we should disillusion them on that
score immediately.

The President said that at the next meeting he would want to know
what is the sequence of events by which we see the situation
developing -- specifically what actions are we to take.   He said
our hand should not show in anything that is done.   In the mean-
time, State should be working on what we can do in and out of the
OAS. Mr. Nixon asked Mr. Herter whether support was developing satisfactorily within the OAS. Mr. Rubottom's answer indicated
that the situation is not clear.   The President said that, as he saw
it, Castro the Revolutionary had gained great prestige in Latin
America.   Castro the Politician running the government is
now losing it rapidly. However, governments elsewhere cannot

Document 2.2   continued

- 4 -

oppose him too strongly since they are shaky with respect to
the potentials of action by the mobs within their own countries
to whom Castro's brand of demagoguery appeals. Essentially
the job is to get the OAS to support us.

Mr. Gray asked whether OAS support will only be forthcoming
if the Cubans actually attack Americans on the island. Mr.
Rubottom thought that the OAS might be brought to act prior to
such an attack on the basis of Castro being tied up with international communism. The President asked whether we have
to base it on the word "communism" or whether we couldn't
base it on dictatorship, confiscation, threats to life, etc. Mr.
Nixon said he thought the Caracas Resolution was based on the
term "international communism."

Mr. Bissell said he understood the sense of the meeting to be
that work could start on forming the opposition Council and on
other preparations. Mr. Herter said that the radio station is
very important. The President asked that we try to obscure the
location of the radio station.

A. J. Goodpaster
Brigadier General, USA

Document 2.2   continued

SECRET

January 3, 1961
12:30 p.m.

MEMORANDUM OF CONVERSATION WITH MR. DEAN RUSK

I discussed with Dean Rusk the following three matters:

1. The Cuban situation resulting from the note sent through the Embassy in Havana to the effect that our personnel had to be reduced within 48 hours to a total of eleven, including locals. I explained that our Charge d'Affaires in Havana had recommended that the best course for us would be to break off diplomatic relations completely since it would be impossible to carry on in anything like a dignified or effective way with such small staff. I further told him that we had checked with Wadsworth in New York, who had felt that such a break would not interfere with the debate on the charges brought by Cuba against us to begin tomorrow, and I, likewise, checked with Braddock in Havana, who reiterated his recommendation for a clean break and felt that such a break would not jeopardize the situation with respect to the remaining U. S. citizens in Cuba.

I then told Dean Rusk that I thought a decision would be reached this afternoon with respect to breaking diplomatic relations, and that my expectation was that this would be done. He asked if he could have until 3:00 p.m. to report reactions , and that his own impression was that there would be no reaction unless there was a very violent feeling on the part of the President-elect.

Dean Rusk said that he felt he could not give me an answer on this until Friday. It was his impression, however, that Senator Kennedy might feel some embarrassment in going to see the President again, only because of press speculation as to what might be discussed between them, particularly in the light of the situation in Laos and in Cuba.

However,

SECRET

Document 2.3   Memorandum of Conversation with Mr. Dean Rusk (memorandum of conversation by Secretary of State Christian Herter, 3 January 1961).

- 2 -

However, he would be seeing Senator Kennedy personally on Friday, and would then communicate with me.

3. I mentioned that the Portuguese Foreign Minister in Paris and again the Portuguese Ambassador here had expressed the hope that Burke Elbrick might be allowed to stay on in Portugal as Ambassador. As in previous similar cases, I explained that I was passing this along as an item of information without any personal comment, but merely for Mr. Rusk's information.

Christian A. Herter

S:CAHerter:ms

Document 2.3   continued

February 8, 1961

T̶O̶P̶ ̶S̶E̶C̶R̶E̶T̶

MEMORANDUM FOR

     THE PRESIDENT

When you have your meeting this afternoon on Cuba, I think
you will find that there is a divergence of view between State
on the one hand and CIA and Defense on the other. Defense
and CIA now feel quite enthusiastic about the invasion from
Guatemala -- at the worst they think the invaders would get
into the mountains, and at the best they think they might get
a full-fledged civil war in which we could then back the anti-
Castro forces openly. State Department takes a much cooler
view, primarily because of its belief that the political consequences would be very grave both in the United Nations and
in Latin America. I think they will urge careful and extended
diplomatic discussions with other American states, looking
toward an increasing diplomatic isolation of Cuba and the
Dominican Republic before any drastic action is taken. This
divergence of view has not been openly and plainly considered
in recent task force discussions, as I understand it. Therefore, you are quite likely to hear it in quite fresh form this
afternoon.

Dick Goodwin has been in on most of the Cuban discussions,
and he and I join in believing that there should certainly not
be an invasion adventure without careful diplomatic soundings.
We also think it almost certain that such soundings would confirm the judgment you are likely to hear from State.

                         McG. B.

                    T̶O̶P̶ ̶S̶E̶C̶R̶E̶T̶

Document 3.1 Memorandum from the President's Special Assistant for National Security
Affairs (McGeorge Bundy) to President Kennedy, 8 February 1961.

TOP SECRET

February 9, 1961

MEMORANDUM OF MEETING WITH THE PRESIDENT
ON CUBA - February 8, 1961

Present: Messrs. Rusk, Berle, Mann, Bohlen, McNamara, Nitze,
Barnes, W. P. Bundy, Haydn Williams, Dulles, Bissell,
McG. Bundy

The meeting opened with an account by Mr. Bissell of the current
plan for launching the troops from Guatemala. He reported that
the JCS, after careful study, believed that this plan had a fair
chance of success -- "success" meaning ability to survive, hold
ground, and attract growing support from Cubans. At the worst,
the invaders should be able to fight their way to the Escambray
and go into guerrilla action. If the troops are to land in top form,
the operation should not be delayed, at the longest, beyond March 31,
and the decision to land for it must be made before D minus 21.

Secretary Rusk stated that without careful -- and successful --
diplomatic preparation such an operation could have grave effects
upon the U. S. position in Latin America and at the U. N.   Mr.
Berle said that it would be impossible, as things stand now, to
avoid being cast in the role of aggressor.   Both Mr. Rusk and
Mr. Berle believed that no present decision on the proposed
invasion was necessary, but both made clear their conviction
that U. S. policy should not be driven to drastic and irrevocable
choice by the urgencies, however real, of a single battalion of
men.

The President pressed for alternatives to a full-fledged "invasion,"
supported by U. S. planes, ships and supplies. While CIA doubted
that other really satisfactory uses of the troops in Guatemala
could be found, it was agreed that the matter should be carefully
studied. Could not such a force be landed gradually and quietly
and make its first major military efforts from the mountains --
then taking shape as a Cuban force within Cuba, not as an invasion
force sent by the Yankees?

TOP SECRET

SECRET

Document 3.2   Memorandum of a Meeting with the President, minutes of a meeting on Cuba
drafted by McGeorge Bundy, 9 February 1961.

The State Department envisioned a long and complex effort to
win support and understanding -- from other American States
for a strong line against Castro -- the Dominican Republic
thrown in. Mr. Berle believed that the President's own
authority and leadership would be needed in making the U. S.
view understood both at home and abroad. The President
asked that the State Department prepare a clear statement
of the course it would recommend, and meanwhile he urged
all concerned to seek for ways in which the Administration
would make it clear to Latin Americans that it stands squarely
for reform and progress in the Americas.

The only new action authorized at the meeting was the organization of a small junta of anti-Castro Cuban leaders, to be
supported by a larger Revolutionary Council. This junta will
have a strong left-of-center balance, and it will be a response
to the urgent demands of the troops in Guatemah for a sense of
political direction and purpose. Its members will be selected
for their ability, among other things, to join the landing force.

McG. Bundy

Document 3.2 continued

February 11, 1961

MEMORANDUM FOR THE PRESIDENT

As you know, there is great pressure within the government in
favor of a drastic decision with regard to Cuba.

There is, it seems to me, a plausible argument for this decision
if one excludes everything but Cuba itself and looks only at the pace
of military consolidation within Cuba and the mounting impatience
of the armed exiles.

However, as soon as one begins to broaden the focus beyond Cuba
to include the hemisphere and the rest of the world, the arguments
against this decision begin to gain force.

However well disguised any action might be, it will be ascribed to
the United States.   The result would be a wave of massive protest,
agitation and sabotage throughout Latin America, Europe, Asia and
Africa (not to speak of Canada and of certain quarters in the United
States).   Worst of all, this would be your first dramatic foreign
policy initiative.   At one stroke, it would dissipate all the extraordinary good will which has been rising toward the new Administration
through the world.   It would fix a malevolent image of the new Administration in the minds of millions.

It may be that on balance the drastic decision may have to be made.
If so, every care must be taken to protect ourselves against the
inevitable political and diplomatic fall-out.

1. Would it not be possible to induce Castro to take offensive action
    first?   He has already launched expeditions against Panama and
    against the Dominican Republic.   One can conceive a black oper-
    ation in, say, Haiti which might in time lure Castro into sending

Document 3.3   Memorandum from the President's Special Assistant (Arthur Schlesinger Jr.) to
President Kennedy, 11 February 1961.

2.

a few boatloads of men on to a Haitian beach in what could be portrayed as an effort to overthrow the Haitian regime. If only Castro could be induced to commit an offensive act, then the moral issue would be clouded, and the anti-US campaign would be hobbled from the start.

2. Should you not consider at some point addressing a speech to the whole hemisphere setting forth in eloquent terms your own conception of inter-American progress toward individual freedom and social justice? Such a speech would identify our Latin American policy with the aspirations of the plain people of the hemisphere. As part of this speech, you could point out the threats raised against the inter-American system by dictatorial states, and especially by dictatorial states under the control of non-hemisphere governments or ideologies. If this were done properly, action against Castro could be seen as in the interests of the hemisphere and not just of American corporations.

3. Could we not bring down Castro and Trujillo at the same time? If the fall of the Castro regime could be accompanied or preceded by the fall of the Trujillo regime, it would show that we have a principled concern for human freedom and do not object only to left-wing dictators.

If the drastic decision proves necessary in the end, I hope that steps of this sort can do something to mitigate the effects. And, if we do take the drastic decision, it must be made clear that we have done so, not lightly, but only after we had exhausted every conceivable alternative.

as:gs   Arthur Schlesinger, jr.

TOP SECRET

Document 3.3   continued

p. i.

(

THE WHITE HOUSE

WASHINGTON

March 15, 1961

~~TOP SECRET~~

MEMORANDUM FOR

THE PRESIDENT

Subject: <u>Meeting on Cuba, 4:00 PM, March 15, 1961</u>

CIA will present a revised plan for the Cuban operation. They have
done a remarkable job of reframing the landing plan so as to make
it unspectacular and quiet, and plausibly Cuban in its essentials.

The one major problem which remains is the air battle. I think
there is unanimous agreement that at some stage the Castro Air
Force must be removed. It is a very sketchy force, in very poor
shape at the present, and Colonel Hawkins (Bissell's military brain)
thinks it can be removed by six to eight simultaneous sorties of
B-26s. These will be undertaken by Cuban pilots in planes with
Cuban Air Force markings. This is the only really noisy enterprise that remains.

My own belief is that this air battle has to come sooner or later,
and that the longer we put it off, the harder it will be. Castro's
Air Force is currently his Achilles' heel, but he is making drastic
efforts to strengthen it with Russian planes and Russian-trained
pilots.

Even the revised landing plan depends strongly upon prompt action
against Castro's air. The question in my mind is whether we cannot solve this problem by having the air strike come some little
time <u>before</u> the invasion. A group of patriotic airplanes flying
from Nicaraguan bases might knock out Castro's Air Force in a
single day without anyone knowing (for some time) where they came
from, and with nothing to prove that it was not an interior rebellion
by the Cuban Air Force, which has been of very doubtful loyalty in
the past; the pilots will in fact be members of the Cuban Air Force
who went into the opposition some time ago. Then the invasion
could come as a separate enterprise, and neither the air strike nor

DECLASSIFIED
US ARCHIVIST (NLK-79-122)
By [signature] NARS, Date 12/14/82

~~TOP SECRET~~

**Document 3.4   Memorandum from the President's Special Assistant for National Security
Affairs (McGeorge Bundy) to President Kennedy, 15 March 1961.**

- 2 -

the quiet landing of patriots would in itself give Castro anything to take to the United Nations.

I have been a skeptic about Bissell's operation, but now I think we are on the edge of a good answer. I also think that Bissell and Hawkins have done an honorable job of meeting the proper criticisms and cautions of the Department of State.

McGeorge Bundy

Document 3.4   continued

SECRET

THE WHITE HOUSE
WASHINGTON

March 15, 1961

MEMORANDUM FOR THE PRESIDENT

SUBJECT: Cuba

   1.   Free elections statement.   Tom Mann, on further consideration, has backed away from the idea of a demarche on free elections.
He argues that the risk is too great that Castro might accept the
challenge, stage ostensibly free elections, win by a large majority
and thereafter claim popular sanction for his regime.   Mann points
out that a genuinely free election requires more than freedom of
balloting; it requires freedom of press and assembly for some
months prior to the election.   Without such prior freedom from
intimidation, the election itself will not be genuinely free, even with
OAS supervision of the actual voting process.

I agree with this view.   It does seem to me that setting up free elections as a test might give Castro an opportunity to put on a show and
recover prestige.

   2.   White Paper.   I am at work on a White Paper on Cuba.   I
wonder, however, whether we should not consider issuing at the same
time a White Paper on the Dominican Republic.   This would emphasize
the fact that our opposition is to dictatorship in principle and not just to
dictatorships which expropriate US business.   Tom Mann agrees that
it might be a good idea to issue a simultaneous White Paper on the
Dominican Republic.

If you agree, let me know, and I will get someone at State to start
putting the material together.

DECLASSIFIED
PUBLISHED IN FRUS 1961-63
vol X   ccc • 50m
By MMK NARA Date 4/1/96

SECRET

**Document 3.5   Memorandum from the President's Special Assistant (Arthur Schlesinger Jr.) to
President Kennedy, 15 March 1961**

2.

3. Cuban policy. I thought your response to the proposals submitted last Saturday was absolutely right. The trouble with the operation is that the less the military risk, the greater the political risk, and vice versa. It seems to me that the utilization of the men under conditions of minimum political risk is clearly the thing to aim at.

I had the impression that the military aspects of the problem had received more thoughtful attention than the political aspects. It did not seem to me that the political risks had been adequately assessed or that convincing plans had been laid to minimize them. For example, it was not clear that anyone had thought through the question of our public response if the operation should be undertaken. Do we take the public position that it is a spontaneous Cuban enterprise? Do you say in your press conference, for example, that the US had nothing to do with it? Do we swear this in the United Nations? What happens then when Castro produces a couple of prisoners who testify that they were armed, trained and briefed by Americans? Do we continue to deny this? or change our original story?

It would seem to me absolutely essential to work out in advance a consistent line which can hold for every conceivable contingency. Otherwise we will find ourselves in a new U-2 imbroglio, with the government either changing its story midstream or else clinging to a position which the rest of the world will regard as a lie.

I should add that there seems to me a slight danger of our being rushed into something because CIA has on its hands a band of people it doesn't quite know what to do with. When you were out of the room, Allen Dulles said, "Don't forget that we have a disposal problem. If we have to take these men out of Guatemala, we will have to transfer them to the US, and we can't have them wandering around the country telling everyone what they have been doing." Obviously this is a genuine problem, but it can't be permitted to govern US policy.

Arthur Schlesinger, jr.

Document 3.5 continued

TOP SECRET

26
April 1961

MEMORANDUM FOR: General Maxwell D. Taylor

1. Following is the text of a precedence EMERGENCY cable sent to Col. Jack Hawkins (USMC) at Puerto Cabezas on 13 April 1961 by the Project chief:

(a) Please advise EMERGENCY precedence if your experiences during the last few days have in any way changed your evaluation of the Brigade.

(b) For your information: The President has stated that under no conditions will U. S. intervene with any U. S. forces.

2. Following is the text of Col. Hawkins' reply of the same day:

(a) My observations the last few days have increased my confidence in the ability of this force to accomplish not only initial combat missions but also the ultimate objective of Castro's overthrow.

(b) Reference (Paragraph 1 above) arrived during the final briefing of the Brigade and Battalion commanders. They now know all details of the plan and are enthusiastic. These officers are young, vigorous, intelligent and motivated with a fanatical urge to begin battle for which most of them have been preparing in the rugged conditions of training camps for almost a year. I have talked to many of them in their language. Without exception, they have utmost confidence in their ability to win. They say they know their own people and believe after they have inflicted one serious defeat upon opposing forces, the latter will melt away from Castro, who they have no wish to support. They say it is Cuban tradition to join a winner and they have supreme confidence they will win all engagements against the best Castro has to offer. I share their confidence.

Document 3.6 Memorandum for General Maxwell D. Taylor, 26 April 1961 (text of emergency cable traffic of 13 April 1961 between Jacob Esterline, CIA head of the Bay of Pigs operation, and Col. Jack Hawkins, the latter reporting from the Brigade 2506 debarkation area in Puerto Cabezas, Nicaragua).

-2-

(c) The Brigade is well organized and is more heavily armed and better equipped in some respects than U. S. infantry units. The men have received intensive training in the use of their weapons, including more firing experience than U. S. troops would normally receive. I was impressed with the serious attitude of the men as they arrived here and moved to their ships. Movements were quiet, disciplined and efficient, and the embarkation was accomplished with remarkable smoothness.

(d) The Brigade now numbers 1,400; a truly formidable force.

(e) I have also carefully observed the Cuban Air Force. The aircraft are kept with pride and some of the B-26 crews are so eager to commence contemplated operations that they have already armed their aircraft. Lt. Col. George Gaines (USAF) informed me today that he considers the B-26 squadrom equal to the best U. S. Air Force squadron.

(f) The Brigade officers do not expect help from U. S. Armed Forces. They ask only for continued delivery of supplies. This can be done covertly.

(g) This Cuban Air Force is motivated, strong, well trained, armed to the teeth, and ready. I believe profoundly that it would be a serious mistake for the United States to deter it from its intended purpose.

J. C. KING

Distribution:
  Copy #1 - General Taylor
  Copy #2 - Mr. Allen W. Dulles
  Copy #3 - Mr. Richard M. Bissell, Jr.
  Copy #4 - Col. J. C. King
  Copy #5 - Mr. J. D. Esterline

Document 3.6   continued

TOP SECRET   March 11, 1961

MEMORANDUM OF DISCUSSION ON CUBA, March 11, 1961

NATIONAL SECURITY ACTION MEMORANDUM NO. 31

The President directed that the following actions be taken:

1. Every effort should be made to assist patriotic Cubans
in forming a new and strong political organization, and in conjunction with this effort a maximum amount of publicity buildup should be sought for the emerging political leaders of this
organization, especially those who may be active participants
in a military campaign of liberation. Action: Central
Intelligence Agency.

2. The United States Government must have ready a white
paper on Cuba, and should also be ready to give appropriate
assistance to Cuban patriots in a similar effort. Action:
Arthur Schlesinger in cooperation with the Department of State.

3. The Department of State will present recommendations with
respect to a demarche in the Organization of American States,
looking toward a united demand for prompt free elections in
Cuba, with appropriate safeguards and opportunity for all
patriotic Cubans. Action: Department of State.

4. The President expects to authorize U. S. support for an
appropriate number of patriotic Cubans to return to their homeland.
He believes that the best possible plan, from the point of view of
combined military, political and psychological considerations,
has not yet been presented, and new proposals are to be con-
certed promptly. Action: Central Intelligence Agency, with
appropriate consultation.

                                        McGeorge Bundy

                              DECLASSIFIED
TOP SECRET   E.O. 11652, Sec. 3(E) and 5(D) or (E)
                              NSC 8/19/75 NLK-75-403
Copy 11 of 12.   By MEP   NARS, Date 8/29/75

Document 4.1   Memorandum of Discussion on Cuba, 11 March 1961/National Security Action
Memorandum No. 31 (draft by McGeorge Bundy regarding Bay of Pigs invasion).

TOP SECRET

15 March 1961

REVISED CUBAN OPERATION

1. Political Requirements: The plan for a Cuban operation and the variants thereof presented on 11 March were considered to be politically objectionable on the ground that the contemplated operation would not have the appearance of an infiltration of guerrillas in support of an internal revolution but rather that of a small-scale World War II type of amphibious assault.   In undertaking to develop alternative plans and to judge their political acceptability, it has been necessary to infer from the comments made on the earlier plan the characteristics which a new plan should possess in order to be politically acceptable.   They would appear to be the following:

a.   An Unspectacular Landing: The initial landing should be as unspectacular as possible and should have neither immediately prior nor concurrent tactical air support.   It should conform as closely as possible to the typical pattern of the landings of small groups intended to establish themselves or to join others in terrain suited for guerrilla operations. In the absence of air support and in order to fit the pattern, it should probably be at night.

TOP SECRET

TS-176622
Copy _1_

Copy 4 list

Document 4.2   Revised Cuban Operation (a memorandum prepared in the Central Intelligence Agency, 15 March 1961).

b.   A Base for Tactical Air Operations: It was emphasized that
ultimate success of the operation will require tactical air operations
leading to the establishment of the control of the air over Cuba.   In
order to fit the pattern of revolution, these operations should be
conducted from an air base within territory held by opposition forces.
Since it is impracticable to undertake construction of an air base in
the rainy season and before any air support is available, the territory
seized in the original landing must include an air strip that can
support tactical operations.

c.   Slower Tempo: The operation should be so designed that
there could be an appreciable period of build up after the initial landing
before major offensive action was undertaken.   This would allow for
a minimum decent interval between the establishment and the
recognition by the U.S. of a provisional government and would fit
more closely the pattern of a typical revolution.

d.   Guerrilla Warfare Alternative: Ideally, the terrain should
not only be protected by geography against prompt or well-supported
attack from land but also suitable for guerrilla warfare in the event
that an organized perimeter could not be held.

- 2 -

TS#176622

Document 4.2   continued

2.   Alternative Areas: Five different areas, three of them on the mainland of Cuba and two on islands off the coast, were studied carefully to determine whether they would permit an operation fitting the above conditions. One of the areas appears to be eminently suited for the operation. All the others had to be rejected either because of unfavorable geography (notably the absence of a suitable air strip) or heavy concentrations of enemy forces, or both. The area selected is located at the head of a well protected deep water estuary on the south coast of Cuba. It is almost surrounded by swamps impenetrable to infantry in any numbers and entirely impenetrable to vehicles, except along two narrow and easily defended approaches. Although strategicall isolated by these terrain features, the area is near the center of the island and the presence of an opposition force there will soon become known to the entire population of Cuba and constitute a serious threat to the regime. The beachhead area contains one and possibly two air strips adequate to handle B-26's. There are several good landing beaches. It is of interest that this area has been the scene of resistance activities and of outright guerrilla warfare for over a hundred years.

3.   Phases of the Operation:

a.   The operation will begin with a night landing. There are no known enemy forces (even police) in the objective area and it is anticipated that the landing can be carried out with few if any casualties

- 3 -   TS #176622

Document 4.2   continued

TOP SECRET

and with no serious combat. As many supplies as possible will be
unloaded over the beaches but the ships will put to sea in time to be
well offshore by dawn. The whole beachhead area including the air
strips will be immediately occupied and approach routes defended.
No tanks will be brought ashore in the initial landing. It is believed
that this operation can be accomplished quite unobtrusively and that
the Castro regime will have little idea of the size of the force
involved.

    b.   The second phase, preferably commencing at dawn
following the landing, will involve the movement into the beachhead
of tactical aircraft and their prompt commitment for strikes against
the Castro Air Force. Concurrently C-46's will move in with gas
in drums, minimal maintenance equipment, and maintenance
personnel. As rapidly as possible, the whole tactical air operation
will be based in the beachhead but initially only enough aircraft
will be based there plausibly to account for all observable activity
over the island.

    c.   In the third phase, as soon as there is adequate protection
for shipping from enemy air attack, ships will move back into the beach
to discharge supplies and equipment (including tanks). It must be

TS #176622

Document 4.2   continued

presumed that counter attacks against the beachhead will be

undertaken within 24 to 48 hours of the landing but the perimeter

can easily be held against attacks along the most direct approach

routes.   The terrain may well prevent any sizeable attacks

(providing the enemy air force has been rendered ineffective) until

the opposition force is ready to attempt to break out of the beach-

head.

      d.   The timing and direction of such offensive action will

depend upon the course of events in the island.   At least three

directions of break out are possible.   Because of the canalization

of the approaches to the beachhead from the interior, a break out

will require close support by tactical air to be successful unless

enemy forces are thoroughly disorganized.   The opposition force

will have the option, however, of undertaking an amphibious

assault with tactical air support against a different objective area

if it should seem desirable.

      4.   Political Action: The beachhead area proposed to be occupied is

both large enough and safe enough so that it should be entirely feasible to

install the provisional government there as soon as aircraft can land safely.

Once installed, the tempo of the operation will permit the U.S. Government

TS #176622

Document 4.2   continued

TOP SECRET

to extend recognition after a decent interval and thus to prepare the way for

more open and more extensive logistical support if this should be necessary.

5.   Military Advantages:

a.   This is a safer military operation than the daylight landing

in force originally proposed. The landing itself is more likely to

be unopposed or very lightly opposed and the beachhead perimeter

could be more easily held.

b.   There are no known communications facilities in the

immediate target area. This circumstance, coupled with the plan

for a night landing, increases the chance of achieving surprise.

c.   By comparison with any of the known inaccessible parts

of the Oriente Province the objective area is closer to rear bases

for air and sea logistical support.

d.   The plan has the disadvantage that the build up of force

can be only gradual since there is virtually no local population from

which to recruit additional troops and volunteers from other parts of

Cuba will be able to infiltrate into the area only gradually.

6.   Political Acceptability: The proposal here outlined fits the three

conditions stated in paragraph 1 above for the political acceptability of a

paramilitary operation. The landing is unspectacular; no tactical air support

will be provided until an air base of sorts is active within the beachhead area;

- 6 -

TOP SECRET   TS #176622

Document 4.2   continued

the tempo of the operation is as desired; and the terrain is such as to minimize the risk of defeat and maximize the options open to the opposition force.

a. It may be objected that the undertaking of tactical air operations so promptly after the landing is inconsistent with the pattern of a revolution. But most Latin American revolutions in recent years have used aircraft and it is only natural that they would be used in this case as soon as the opposition had secured control of an air strip. Wherever in the island a paramilitary operation is attempted and whatever its tempo, command of the air will sooner or later have to be established, and aircraft will have to be flown into a beachhead to enable this to be done. Sooner or later, then, it is bound to be revealed that the opposition in Cuba has friends outside who are able and willing to supply it with obsolescent combat aircraft. This revelation will be neither surprising nor out of keeping with traditional practice.

b. An alternative way to handle this problem would be to make a few strafing runs against the Castro Air Force some days before the landing and apparently as an opposition act unrelated to any other military moves.

- 7 -

TOP SECRET　　　　　　TS #176622

Document 4.2　continued

7. Conclusion: The operation here outlined, despite the revision

of concept to meet the political requirements stated above, will still have a

political cost. The study over the past several months of many possible

paramilitary operations makes perfectly clear, however, that it is impossible

to introduce into Cuba and commit to action military resources that will have

a good chance of setting in motion the overthrow of the regime without paying

some price in terms of accusations by the Communists and possible

criticism by others. It is believed that the plan here outlined goes as far as

possible in the direction of minimizing the political cost without impairing

its soundness and chance of success as a military operation. The alternative

would appear to be the demobilization of the paramilitary force and the return

of its members to the United States. It is, of course, well understood that

this course of action too involves certain risks.

Document 4.2   continued

May 10, 1996

COVERT OPERATIONS AGAINST THE CASTRO GOVERNMENT OF CUBA
January, 1960 - April, 1961

COMMENTS

by

COLONEL JACK HAWKINS, U. S. MARINE CORPS (RET.)

QUESTION: What were the duties and responsibilities of Colonel Hawkins in the Central Intelligence Agency Cuba Project?

In early 1960, the CIA began preparations for the possible landing of a small force of Cuban exiles in Cuba. In late summer, a request was sent to the Marine Corps for the services of an officer experienced in amphibious warfare to assist with the project. In response, the Commandant of the Marine Corps assigned me to the CIA on a temporary basis and I reported for duty on September 1, 1960.

In the Cuba Project, I served as Chief of the Paramilitary Staff, reporting directly to the Chief of the Project, Mr. Jacob Esterline. The paramilitary staff included an average of twenty-four officers, six military and the remainder CIA personnel.

The paramilitary staff was responsible for the organization, training and equipment of the infantry force and preparing plans for landing it in Cuba. The training of the force was accomplished by Army Special Forces personnel under the direction of an Army officer of the paramilitary staff.

The responsibility of the paramilitary staff for air preparations and operations was limited to submitting recommendations to the Deputy Director Plans, Mr. Bissell, concerning air support required for the Cuba Project. A separate air staff responsible directly to Mr. Bissell was responsible for all air matters.

I had no command authority other than to exercise control and direction of the paramilitary staff.

1

Document 4.3   Covert Operations Against the Castro Government of Cuba, January 1960–April 1961 (comments by Col. Jack Hawkins in a letter to James G. Blight, 10 May 1996, excerpt).

QUESTION: Why, on the day before the scheduled first strike
against Castro's air force, did the President reduce the number
of participating aircraft from sixteen to eight?

     Mr. Bissell was informed by the President on that fateful
day that he wanted the number of aircraft reduced to the minimum.
Without consulting me or the Chief of the Cuba Project, Mr.
Esterline, Mr. Bissell suggested reducing the number from sixteen
to eight. The President agreed.

     It is reasonable to believe that the President was influenced
to make such a decision by the Secretary of State, Mr. Rusk, who
had consistently opposed all air operations.

     Mr. Bissell made a fatal error in volunteering a fifty
percent reduction in the power of the first strike without consulting his staff.

     Had he consulted me, I would have recommended that he take
the position that a full-force attack was absolutely essential
and , if that could not be allowed, the concept of landing the
force in Cuba should be abandoned. Such a recommendation on my
part would have been consistent with everything I had said, orally
and in writing, throughout the many months of planning.

     After the reduced-force first surprise attack was made, our
aerial photography revealed that half of Castro's air force had
escaped destruction and the runways of the three military airfields had not been sufficiently cratered to prevent air operations.
He had eight aircraft left, including B-26 bombers, Sea Furies
and three T-33 jets. These posed a deadly threat to the landing.
They had to be knocked out. But now the element of surprise was
lost and we might not catch them all on the ground again.

11

Document 4.3   continued

QUESTION: Why, only a few hours before the night landing was to begin, did the President cancel the air strike which was scheduled to be made at dawn in an effort to eliminate Castro's remaining eight military aircraft? What was the reaction of the CIA?

As might be expected, news of the first air attack on 15 April traveled far and fast. At the United Nations, Ambassador Adlai Stevenson, a leading political power of the Democratic Party and one-time presidential candidate, who had not been informed about the operation, denied United States participation. It was widely reported in the media at that time that when he learned the truth he was outraged and made strong protests to President Kennedy, saying that this affair was too embarrassing politically both to the President and to him. I feel sure that Mr. Stevenson's influence, undoubtedly reinforced by Mr. Rusk, had much to do with the cancellation.

I was at the CIA operations center when Mr. Esterline, the Cuba Project Chief, informed me of the cancellation at about 10 pm, only three hours before the landing was to begin. I was appalled. I went immediately to the telephone and called Mr. Bissell who was at the State Department and urged him in the strongest terms to explain to the President that we were going to have a disaster and persuade him to reverse the decision..

In that conversation with Mr. Bissell, I predicted that the ships would be attacked by air the next morning and some, or possibly all, of them would be sunk. I said also that if I had known of this decision just an hour or two earlier I would have strongly recommended that the ships be ordered to retire from the area without landing troops. But now the ships were already at the beaches and it was too late.

After this conversation, Mr. Bissell and General Cabell, the Deputy Director of the CIA, spoke to Mr. Rusk about the situation. Mr. Rusk telephoned the President, who had left Washington for the Virginia countryside, and told him that the CIA wanted to reinstate the air strike, but that he, Rusk, recommended that the decision to cancel remain unchanged. Neither Mr. Bissell nor General Cabell spoke to the President although Mr. Rusk offered them that opportunity.

The Cuban Brigade was doomed.

The troops landed successfully during darkness. When morning came, Castro's remaining eight fighters and bombers attacked and continued the attack all day. Unloading of the ships was impossible. Two of them were sunk and the remaining had to flee from the area at top speed to save themselves. One of our LCI control boats, armed with twelve 50 caliber machine

12

Document 4.3   continued

guns, shot down three of the attacking planes, but two Sea
Furies and three T-33 Jets were left. They were enough to
defeat the entire operation.

The CIA plan approved by the President provided for forty
B-26 sorties to destroy Castro's eighteen military aircraft
and crater the runways of the three military airfields.
President Kennedy's last minute cuts reduced the number of
sorties to only eight, a reduction in force applied of 80%.

These cuts sealed the fate of the landing and left the
Brigade ashore without support or supplies. The Brigade was
not driven from the beachhead. The troops simply ran out of
ammunition and had to surrender.

The United States found itself in a world-wide public
glare of embarrassment for what appeared to be a ridiculous
failure. It would have been better to forget about "plausible
deniability" and do whatever was required to win the objective
of overthrowing the communist government of Cuba. Then, if
we felt embarrassed, it would be after winning, not after
losing.

And the nuclear missile crisis soon to follow would never
have occurred.

13

Document 4.3   continued

NSC Meeting, Saturday, April 22nd

There were some thirty-five people at the NSC meeting on Cuba. Again Bob Kennedy was present, and took the lead as at the previous meeting, slamming into anyone who suggested that we go slowly and try to move calmly and not repeat previous mistakes.

The atmosphere was almost as emotional as the Cabinet meeting two days earlier, the difference being that on this occasion the emphasis was on specific proposals to harrass Castro.

Document 5.1 Notes on the 478th Meeting of the National Security Council (prepared by Undersecretary of State Chester Bowles, 22 April 1961).

-5-

On two or three occasions I suggested that the greatest mistake we could make would be to pit the United States
with its 180 million people in a contest against a Cuban
dictator on an island of 6 million people. I stressed that
while we are already in a bad situation, it would be a mistake for us to assume that it could not disintegrate further
and an almost sure way to lose ground was to reach out in
ways that would almost surely be ineffective and which would
tend to create additional sympathy for Castro in his David
and Goliath struggle against the United States.

These comments were brushed aside brutally and abruptly
by the various fire eaters who were present. I did think,
however, that the faces of a few people around the table
reflected some understanding of the views I was trying to
present, notably Dick Goodwin, Ted Sorensen (which is
surprising), Arthur Schlesinger, and above all Jerry
Weisner.

The President limited himself largely to asking questions -- questions, however, which lead in one direction.

Document 5.1   continued

-6-

I left the meeting with a feeling of intense alarm, tempered somewhat with the hope that this represented largely an emotional reaction of a group of people who were not use to set backs or defeats and whose pride and confidence had been deeply wounded.

However, I felt again the great lack of moral integrity which I believe is the central guide in dealing with tense and difficult questions, particularly when the individuals involved are tired, frustrated, and personally humiliated.

If every question in the world becomes an intellectual exercise on a totally pragmatic basis, with no reference to moral considerations, it may be that we can escape disaster, but it will certainly be putting the minds of the White House group to a test when it becomes necessary to add up the components, large and small on the plus or minus side of a ledger and when the minds that are attempting to do this are tired, uneasy, and unsure, the values and the arithmetic are unlikely to reflect wise courses.

Document 5.1   continued

SECRET

Cuba ?

July 8, 1961

MEMORANDUM FOR MR. RICHARD GOODWIN

SUBJECT: Cuban Covert Plan

Analysis of this plan shows that it envisages (a) "an island-wide
resistance organization responsive to Agency direction"; "internal
assets under close Agency control and direction"; (b) "support and
guidance to those anti-Castro groups who are revealed to have a
potential for clandestine operations"; and (c) "primary operations
bases" in the US.   In short, what is intended is a CIA underground
formed on criteria of operational convenience rather than a Cuban
underground formed on criteria of building political strength sufficient
to overthrow Castro.

Despite the pretense of political impartiality, the effect of these CIA
specifications is obviously to favor those groups most willing to accept
CIA identification and control, and to discriminate against those groups
most eager to control their own operations.   I.e., the plan discriminates in favor of mercenaries, reactionaries, etc., and discriminates
against men of independence and principle.   Thus these criteria eliminate the Manuel Ray group; yet I can find nowhere in the documents
any explicit exclusion of pro-Batista people.

Leaving aside the moral merits of this discrimination, the practical
effect is to invest our resources in the people least capable of generating
broad support within Cuba.   The Agency fails to confront the key problem: i.e., that those most capable of rallying popular support against
the Castro regime are going to be more independent, more principled
and perhaps even more radical than the compliant and manageable
types which CIA would prefer for operational purposes.

My recommendation is that you stop this paper in its present form and
demand that it be recast to make political sense.   The key is the

DECLASSIFIED
PUBLISHED IN FRUS 1961-63
vol X   doc # 319
By MMK   NARA. Date 4|19|96

SECRET

Document 5.2   Memorandum from the President's Special Assistant (Arthur Schlesinger Jr.) to
the President's Assistant Special Counsel (Richard Goodwin), 8 July 1961.

SECRET

2.

statement that our covert activity "should be viewed only as the covert contribution to any national program designed to bring about the eventual replacement of the Castro government." This is correct; and there follows from it (a) that our covert activity should encourage the spread of the political sentiments within Cuba most likely to rally support for Castro's overthrow (which means, for example, Ray rather than Batista), and (b) that our covert activity should harmonize with our basic national policy of rescuing the Cuban Revolution, as set forth in the White Paper.

It is a fallacy to suppose that clandestine activity can be carried out in a political vacuum.

Arthur Schlesinger, Jr.

SECRET

Document 5.2 continued

THE WHITE HOUSE
WASHINGTON

EYES ONLY FOR THE PRESIDENT

November 1, 1961

MEMORANDUM FOR THE PRESIDENT:

I believe that the concept of a "command operation" for Cuba, as discussed with you by the Attorney General, is the only effective way to handle an all-out attack on the Cuban problem. Since I understand you are favorably disposed toward the idea I will not discuss why the present disorganized and uncoordinated operation cannot do the job effectively.

The beauty of such an operation over the next few months is that we cannot lose. If the best happens we will unseat Castro. If not, then at least. we will emerge with a stronger underground, better propaganda and a far clearer idea of the dimensions of the problems which affect us.

The question then is who should head this operation. I know of no one currently in Cuban affairs at the State Department who can do it. Nor is it a very good idea to get the State Department involved in depth in such covert activities. I do not think it should be centered in the CIA. Even if the CIA can find someone of sufficient force and stature, one of the major problems will be to revamp CIA operations and thinking -- and this will be very hard to do from the inside.

I believe that the Attorney General would be the most effective commander of such an operation. Either I or someone else should be assigned to him as Deputy for this activity, since he obviously will not be able to devote full time to it. The one danger here is that he might become too closely identified with what might not be a successful operation. Indeed, chances of success are very speculative. There are a few answers to this:

     (1) Everyone knowledgeable in these affairs -- in and out of government -- is aware that the United States is already helping the underground. The precise manner of aid may be unknown but the fact of aid is common knowledge. We will be blamed for not winning Cuba back whether or not we have a "command operation" and whether or not the Attorney General heads it.

EYES ONLY FOR THE PRESIDENT

Document 5.3   Memorandum from the President's Assistant Special Counsel (Richard Goodwin) to President Kennedy, 1 November 1961.

EYES ONLY FOR THE PRESIDENT

- 2 -

(2) His role should be told to only a few people at the very top with most of the contact work in carrying out his decisions being left to his deputy. If that deputy is someone already closely identified with the conduct of Cuban affairs then it would appear as if normal channels are being followed except that decisive attention would be given to the decisions which came through those channels. There are probably three or four people who could fulfill this criterion.

This still leaves a substantial danger of identifying the Attorney General as the fellow in charge. This danger must be weighed against the increased effectiveness of an operation under his command.

RNG

Richard N. Goodwin

EYES ONLY FOR THE PRESIDENT

Document 5.3   continued

SECRET

19 January 1962

MEMORANDUM FOR: The Director of Central Intelligence

SUBJECT: Meeting with the Attorney General of the United
                  States Concerning Cuba

    1. I attended a meeting on Cuba at 11:00 A. M., today
chaired by the Attorney General. Others present were:

        Brig. General E. S. Lansdale (OSD)
        Major James Patchell (OSD)
        Brig. General William H. Craig (JCS)
        Mr. ▮▮▮▮▮▮▮ (CIA)
        Mr. George McManus (CIA)
        (The Department of State was not represented
        although invited.)

    2. The Attorney General outlined to us "How it all started",
findings as they developed, and the general framework within
which the United States Government should now attack the Cuban
problem. Briefly, these were the main points:

    (a) After failure of the invasion, the United
         States Government became less active on
         the theory "better to lay low".

    (b) Over the months the complexion of the
         refugee flow changed (i.e. upper classes
         out first, then middle classes -- drop-
         ping to lower middle class, etc.) which,
         he stated, indicated a strong feeling of
         opposition to Castro within Cuba.

    (c) Progress in Cuba toward a police and Com-
         munist state was more rapid during this
         period than that made by any country in
         Eastern Europe in an equivalent period of
         time. Because of the rapidity of advance,
         immediate action on the part of the United
         States Government was necessary.

**Document 5.4   Memorandum for the Director of Central Intelligence (John McCone); Subject:
Meeting with the Attorney General of the United States Concerning Cuba, 19 January 1962.**

- 2 -

(d) With these factors in mind, the Attorney
General had a discussion at the White House
during the autumn of 1961 with the President, the Secretary of Defense, and General
Lansdale. The Secretary of Defense assigned
General Lansdale to survey the Cuban problem,
and he (Lansdale) reported to the President,
the Secretary of Defense, and the Attorney
General (in late November) concluding:

   (1) Overthrow of Castro regime was
   possible

   (2) Sugar crop should be attacked
   at once

   (3) Action to be taken to keep Castro
   so busy with internal problems
   (economic, political, and social)
   that Castro would have no time for
   meddling abroad especially in
   Latin America.

DETAIL: United States Government was precluded from destroying
the current sugar crop (1) we were late and overly
optimistic and (b) "the assets of the United States
Government were not as great as we were led to believe".

(e) Accordingly, a solution to the Cuban problem
today carries "The top priority in the United
States Government -- all else is secondary --
no time, money, effort, or manpower is to be
spared. There can be no misunderstanding on
the involvement of the agencies concerned nor
on their responsibility to carry out this job.
The agency heads understand that you are to
have full backing on what you need."

(f) Yesterday (18 January 1962), the President
indicated to the Attorney General that "the
final chapter on Cuba has not been written" --
it's got to be done and will be done.

(g) Therefore, the Attorney General directed
those in attendance at the meeting to address

Document 5.4   continued

SECRET

- 3 -

themselves to the "32 tasks" unfailingly
(see program review - The Cuba Project
dated 18 January 1962). He said, "It is
not only General Lansdale's job to put the
tasks, but yours to carry out with every
resource at your command."

3. The Attorney General inquired about the progress in
establishing a refugee interrogation center at Miami and was
informed that this would be in operation by 15 February 1962 --
the target date. With respect to interrogating the back-log
of Cubans in the U. S. A., we agreed that we would attack this
problem by getting at the more recent arrivals first. The
Attorney General was informed that one could not relate, in
time, the establishment of an interrogation facility with the
placing of agents in Cuba -- in other words, a body of information would have to be developed by intensive interrogation of
many sources over a period of time.

4. It was General Lansdale's view that there were several
tasks among the "32" outlined upon which action could be taken
without awaiting this detailed intelligence information. He
noted, for example, the defection of top Cubans as being within
the immediate capabilities of the CIA.

                                    Richard Helms
                            Chief of Operations, DD/P

Document 5.4   continued

T ~~UNCLASSIFIED~~   Doc # ⑨ₐ

20 February 1962

Program Review
by Brig. Gen. Lansdale

THE CUBA PROJECT

The Goal. In keeping with the spirit of the Presidential memorandum of 30 November 1961, the United States will help the people of Cuba over-throw the Communist regime from within Cuba and institute a new govern-ment with which the United States can live in peace.

The Situation. We still know too little about the real situation inside Cuba, although we are taking energetic steps to learn more. However, some salient facts are known. It is known that the Communist regime is an active Sino-Soviet spearhead in our Hemisphere and that Communist controls inside Cuba are severe. Also, there is evidence that the repres-sive measures of the Communists, together with disappointments in Castro's economic dependency on the Communist formula, have resulted in an anti-regime atmosphere among the Cuban people which makes a resistance program a distinct and present possibility.

Time is running against us. The Cuban people feel helpless and are losing hope fast. They need symbols of inside resistance and of outside interest soon. They need something they can join with the hope of starting to work surely towards overthrowing the regime. Since late November, we have been working hard to re-orient the operational concepts within the U.S. government and to develop the hard intelligence and operational assets required for success in our task.

The next National Intelligence Estimate on Cuba (NIE 85-62) promises to be a useful document dealing with our practical needs and with due recognition of the sparsity of hard facts. The needs of the Cuba project, as it goes into operation, plus the increasing U.S. capability for intelligence collection, should permit more frequent estimates for our guidance. These will be prepared on a periodic basis.

Premise of Action. Americans once ran a successful revolution. It was run from within, and succeeded because there was timely and strong political, economic, and military help by nations outside who supported our cause. Using this same concept of revolution from within, we must now help the Cuban people to stamp out tyranny and gain their liberty.

On 18 January, the Chief of Operations assigned thirty-two tasks to Departments and Agencies of the U.S. government, in order to provide a realistic assessment and preparation of U.S. capabilities. The Attorney General and the Special Group were apprised of this action. The answers received on 15 February provided the basis for planning a realistic course of action. The answers also revealed that the course of action must con-tain continuing coordination and firm overall guidance.

The course of action set forth herein is realistic within present opera-tional estimates and intelligence. Actually, it represents the maximum target timing which the operational people jointly considered feasible. It aims for a revolt which can take place in Cuba by October 1962. It is a

Excluded from
automatic regrading:
DoD Dir 5200.10
does not apply.

This document contains____pgs
Copy No. _4_ of _1_ copies

Partially Declassified/Released on _Oct 4 1994_
under provisions of E.O. 12356

Document 5.5   The Cuba Project, a program review by Brig. Gen. Edward Lansdale, 20 February 1962.

UNCLASSIFIED
TOP SECRET
SENSITIVE

series of target actions and dates, not a rigid time-table. The target dates
are timed as follows:

Phase I, <u>Action</u>, March 1962. Start moving in.

Phase II, <u>Build-up</u>, April-July 1962. Activating the necessary operations inside Cuba for revolution and concurrently applying the vital political,
economic, and military-type support from outside Cuba.

Phase III, <u>Readiness</u>, 1 August 1962, check for final policy decision.

Phase IV, <u>Resistance</u>, August-September 1962, move into guerrilla
operations.

Phase V, <u>Revolt</u>, first two weeks of October 1962. Open revolt and
overthrow of the Communist regime.

Phase VI, <u>Final</u>, during month of October 1962. Establishment of new
government.

<u>Plan of Action</u>. Attached is an operational plan for the overthrow of
the Communist regime in Cuba, by Cubans from within Cuba, with outside
help from the U.S. and elsewhere. Since this is an operation to prompt
and support a revolt by the people in a Communist police state, flexibility
is a must for success. Decisions on operational flexibility rest with the
Chief of Operations, with consultation in the Special Group when policy
matters are involved. Target actions and dates are detailed in the attached
operational plans, which cover:

  A. Basic Action Plan Inside Cuba

  B. Political Support Plan

  C. Economic Support Plan

  D. Psychological Support Plan

  E. Military Support Plan

  F. Sabotage Support Plan

  G. Intelligence Support Plan

<u>Early Policy Decisions</u>. The operational plan for clandestine U.S.
support of a Cuban movement inside Cuba to overthrow the Communist
regime is within policy limits already set by the President. A vital decision,
still to be made, is on the use of open U.S. force to aid the Cuban people in
winning their liberty. If conditions and assets permitting a revolt are
achieved in Cuba, and if U.S. help is required to sustain this condition, will
the U.S. respond promptly with military force to aid the Cuban revolt? The
contingencies under which such military deployment would be needed, and
recommended U.S. responses, are detailed in a memorandum being prepared
by the Secretaries of State and of Defense. An early decision is required,
prior to deep involvement of the Cubans in this program.

UNCLASSIFIED
TOP SECRET
2

Document 5.5   continued

/ August 1962

COVERT ACTIVITIES

William K. Harvey, CIA Representative for Operation Mongoose, states:

I. SITUATION:

A. The purpose of this plan is to outline the action which would be required by the Central Intelligence Agency to fully implement course of action "b" in General Lansdale's memorandum to the Special Group (Augmented) dated 25 July 1962.

B. The intelligence estimate for the period of this plan is contained in the National Intelligence Estimate 85-2-62.

C. For the purpose of this plan the following assumptions are made:

1. Conclusion #D of the National Intelligence Estimate 85-2-62 is invalid. (This assumption is not in our opinion valid, but this operational plan is not a valid plan for the overthrow of the Castro-Communist government unless this assumption is made.)

2. Soviet troops will not be present in Cuba in force.

3. Passive resistance can be changed to active resistance through aggressive, provocative propaganda plus aggressive small-scale open resistance and through fortuitous circumstances existing at the time. It cannot be manipulated on a "time table" basis.

II. MISSION:

"Exert all possible diplomatic, economic, psychological, and other pressures to overthrow the Castro-Communist regime without overt U.S. military commitment"

TOP SECRET

SENSITIVE

Document 5.6   Covert Activities, drafted by William K. Harvey, CIA Representative for Operation MONGOOSE, 7 August 1962 (excerpts).

TOP SECRET

for aerial re-supply, infiltration, and leaflet flights. Initially estimate five per month increasing to fifteen per month by January 1963. By the end of 1963 this requirement could substantially increase.

    b. Support for CIA air program per existing arrangements.

   4. Personnel:

      Limited numbers of qualified personnel may be required to provide specialized instruction in CIA training programs, specialized support in connection with the CIA maritime program, and to provide communications support.

B. From USIA and Federal Communications Commission:

    Assistance in the establishment of the Radio Free Cuba transmitter.

VI. POLICY APPROVALS REQUIRED:

    The following policy approvals are required to implement the foregoing program:

    A. Authority to initiate and conduct aggressive psychological warfare operations including calling for work stoppages, slow-downs, sabotage, and other forms of militant mass action and widespread overt resistance.

    B. Authority to establish and operate a medium wave transmitter by Radio Free Cuba.

    C. Authority to conduct propaganda balloon launching.

    D. Authority to conduct overflights of Cuba for leaflet dropping.

    E. Authority to conduct major sabotage operations targeted against Cuban industry and public utilities, i.e., refineries, power plants, transportation, and communications.

    F. Authority to use U.S. Navy submarines for infiltration/exfiltration.

    G. Authority to use non-Cuban contract personnel to strengthen teams being infiltrated.

UNCLASSIFIED

SENSITIVE

Document 5.6   continued

TOP SECRET

H.   Authority to train CIA recruited Cubans on DOD bases using DOD instructors and support facilities.

I.   Authority to overfly Cuba for re-supply/infiltration/exfiltration missions using U.S. contract air crews or USAF crews.

J.   Authority to separate trained Cuban officers and enlisted men from the U.S. Armed Services to permit them to join an exile sponsored group of "Cuban Freedom Fighters."

K.   Authority to utilize Guantanamo Naval Base for operational purposes.

VII.   ESTIMATED COST TO CIA:

A.   The total number of CIA personnel assigned full-time to Operation Mongoose would have to be increased to at least 600.

B.   Estimated Budget:

Fiscal Year 1963 - $40,000,000

Fiscal Year 1964 - $60,000,000 (exclusive of reimbursement for DOD support which it is felt should be on a non-reimbursable basis.)

10

TOP SECRET

SENSITIVE

Document 5.6   continued

SECRET

16 October 1962

MEMORANDUM FOR THE RECORD

SUBJECT: MONGOOSE Meeting with the Attorney General

1. At 2:30 this afternoon, the Attorney General convened in his office a meeting on Operation MONGOOSE consisting of General Lansdale and Colonel Patchell, General Johnson of the Joint Staff, Robert Hurwitch of State (vice Ed Martin who was unable to attend), Hewson Ryan of USIA, and the undersigned.

2. The Attorney General opened the meeting by expressing the "general dissatisfaction of the President" with Operation MONGOOSE. He pointed out that the Operation had been under way for a year, that the results were discouraging, that there had been no acts of sabotage, and that even the one which had been attempted had failed twice. He indicated that there had been noticeable improvement during the year in the collection of intelligence but that other actions had failed to influence significantly the course of events in Cuba. He spoke of the weekly meetings of top officials on this problem and again noted the small accomplishments despite the fact that Secretaries Rusk and McNamara, General Taylor, McGeorge Bundy, and he personally had all been charged by the President with finding a solution. He traced the history of General Lansdale's personal appointment by the President a year ago. The Attorney General then stated that in view of this lack of progress, he was going to give Operation MONGOOSE more personal attention. In order to do this, he will hold a meeting every morning at 0930 with the MONGOOSE operational representatives from the various agencies (Lansdale, Harvey, Hurwitch, Ryan, and General Johnson).

3. The Attorney General spoke favorably of the sabotage paper which had been presented by General Carter this morning to the meeting of the Special Group (Augmented). He obviously did not like the earlier memorandum, since he felt it showed no "push" in getting on with the acts of sabotage.

4. When asked for my comments, I stated that we were prepared to get on with the new action program and that we would execute it aggressively. I pointed out, however, that the objective of Operation MONGOOSE would have to be determined at some point since the Cubans

SECRET

Document 5.7   Memorandum for the Record by Richard Helms, CIA Deputy Director for Plans; Subject: MONGOOSE Meeting with the Attorney General, 16 October 1962.

SECRET

- 2 -

with whom we have to work were seeking a reason for risking their lives in these operations. I retailed my conversation with the young Cuban from the DRE who pointed out that they were willing to commit their people only on operations which they regarded as sensible. I defined "sensible" in Cuban terminology these days as meaning an action which would contribute to the liberation of their country, another way of saying that the United States, perhaps in conjunction with other Latin countries, would bail them out militarily. My point was specifically echoed by Hewson Ryan. The Attorney General's rejoinder was a plea for new ideas of things that could be done against Cuba. In passing, he made reference to the change in atmosphere in the United States Government during the last twenty-four hours, and asked some questions about the percentage of Cubans whom we thought would fight for the regime if the country were invaded.

5. The meeting concluded with the reaffirmation by the Attorney General of his desire to hold a meeting each day, beginning tomorrow. He said that these meetings might later be changed to every other day when and if he finds a daily get-together is not necessary. The meetings are to last no more than one-half hour.

> Richard Helms
> Deputy Director (Plans)

Distribution:
  Original - Mr. Elder for the DCI and DDCI
    1 cc - Chief, TFW
    1 cc - DD/P

SECRET

Document 5.7 continued

Memorandum for the Record ~~by the Chief, Western Hemisphere~~　　　　4

~~Division, Directorate of Plans,~~ Central Intelligence Agency

Washington, April 23, 1961.

SUBJECT　　　　First Meeting of General Maxwell Taylor's Board
of Inquiry on Cuban Operations Conducted by CIA

TIME AND PLACE: 1400-1800 hours, 22 April 1961, Quarters Eye

PARTICIPANTS : Study Group Members

　　　　General Maxwell D. Taylor
　　　　Attorney General Robert Kennedy
　　　　Admiral Arleigh Burke
　　　　Allen W. Dulles

　　　　Department of Defense

　　　　Major General David W. Gray
　　　　Colonel C. W. Shuler
　　　　Commander Mitchell

　　　　CIA Personnel

　　　　General C. P. Cabell
　　　　C. Tracy Barnes
　　　　Colonel J. C. King
　　　　Jacob D. Esterline
　　　　[name not declassified]
　　　　Colonel Jack Hawkins

1. After a discussion of procedural matters, it was decided that
all papers and documents stemming from the inquiry would be retained
by General Maxwell Tayler. Colonel J. C. King, Chief, Western
Hemisphere Division, was designated recorder of the first meeting.

Document 6.1　Memorandum for the Record, The First Meeting of General Maxwell Taylor's
Board of Inquiry on Cuban Operations Conducted by CIA (minutes taken by Col. J. C. King,
Chief Western Hemisphere Division of CIA's Directorate of Plans, 22 April 1961, excerpts).

government. Beyond that, we had an overt phase, wherein the provisional government was recognized after its people had gone into Cuba. Here a military logistic advisory group would assist the volunteer Cuban forces in providing sustained logistic support, and then following the stabilization of the new government with diplomatic representatives re-entering Cuba, it envisaged the establishment of a military aid program through DOD. I have omitted mention of the fact that we had a U.S. Army field-type hospital set up and ready to go to Vieques.

GENERAL TAYLOR - How did you figure on evacuating casualties?

GENERAL GRAY - We could get them out by air.

MR. BISSELL - We thought that we could do this after H/4.

GENERAL GRAY - We also had a War Room set up in the Joint Staff area with all messages exclusive from the Joint Chiefs of Staff to Admiral Dennison and the task force commander, or from them to me. Though the messages from Washington had to be relayed to the Cuban expeditionary forces' shore through these channels and it was cumbersome, I don't think that you could say the operation failed because of organization.

GENERAL TAYLOR - Don't you think that withholding all this from the staff was an impediment?

GENERAL GRAY - I don't think so, but it took a lot of the time of the Joint Chiefs of Staff.

ADMIRAL BURKE - There are always a lot of delays involving anything from a half hour, to one to three hours; and these delays, mostly due to communications, could be fatal. If we had had a naval commander of the task force there, he could have made instantaneous decisions. I found myself writing a message to my naval task group commander, telling him what to do if he was under fire from the beach. What in the hell was I doing writing this in Washington?

GENERAL GRAY - I don't say that this was the way to do it, but I don't think that you could say that faulty organization defeated the operation.

Document 6.1   continued

ADMIRAL BURKE - I agree with that.

GENERAL GRAY - If we had had an interdepartmental setup, charged with the responsibility of coming up with a concept and with an over-all national plan, and then had presented it in writing each time to the President, I think there would have been less confusion as to just what was approved at the end of this operation.

MR. BARNES - That couldn't have been achieved because of the way this operation developed. Though we had a fairly definitive plan in Trinidad, after that we just couldn't do it as we kept changing our plan because of political considerations and changes in the ground rules.

ADMIRAL BURKE - That's where we made a mistake I think. We should have drawn up a paper stating our concept, our mission, our tasks, our requirements, the status of the plan, etc. The way this developed, General Gray had to come to me with all sorts of questions. For example, what we could use the carriers for? Whereas if we were working under an agreed concept, he would not have had to do so.

MR. BISSELL - Many actions that came up involved the political considerations of importance. For example, at one time in the operation, a decision was made to authorize Navy jets to give protection to our B-26s when they came in to give close ground support, at least for a limited period of time. This involved a high-level decision and also amounted to a reversal of the policy that had been made that no U.S. forces would be overtly engaged. It's hard for me to see how this could have been worked out in advance.

GENERAL TAYLOR - It depends on what you mean by the use of the word "concept". I don't think that any changes were actually made in the concept.

ADMIRAL BURKE - That task which Bissell just discussed was laid on after we were told that the carriers would get out of there so that Castro's air force would the decision was made to launch aircraft was pretty late.

- 19 -

Document 6.1   continued

GENERAL GRAY - If we had had an agreed-on national plan, it would have forced us to different conditions for our rules of engagement, and to different employment of our tactical air. I think that the rules of engagement should have been in the over-all plan, and not in our plan, or CIA's plan, or CINCLANT's plan.

GENERAL TAYLOR - How is it possible to keep from tying the hands of our military men by these political considerations?

GENERAL GRAY - By having all the departments participate in the planning from the very beginning.

 - And by having this over-all plan signed as approved by the President.

GENERAL GRAY - Once we got the State Department in on the agreed tasks, I was surprised in that Braddock took care of every one of them. Until then, it had been difficult to get them to do anything. Another mistake, lies in the fact that we said at the beginning we should have war-gamed this operation, yet when it got to be an approved plan, the CIA was going flat out, racing the clock, and I found that it was impossible to stop them even for a day in order to do this.

GENERAL TAYLOR - What factors caused this rush?

GENERAL GRAY - First, we were trying to beat the rainy season. Second, there was also the matter of the jets. We'd had information that the Cuban jet trainees in Czechoslovakia were coming back.

- Also the President of Guatemala told us to get out of the country by early March, and we had about 1400 men there.

GENERAL GRAY - American newsmen were also getting into the act. (At this point, there was some discussion over a message that Admiral Burke received from McGeorge Bundy in regard to the reception and interrogation party at Vieques. This was terminated when General Taylor declared:) -

GENERAL TAYLOR - As far as I know, this Vieques business is now a concern of the Joint Chiefs of Staff and the CIA.

MR. DULLES - I don't think that you should get mixed up in that.

(Following this, there was some discussion on this position of the

- 20 -

Document 6.1 continued

personnel and equipment of the Cuban Expeditionary Force. At the
end of this discussion, General Taylor stated:) -

GENERAL TAYLOR - For our own purposes, it would be useful to
screen these people and get the best of them somewhere near here
where we could interview them.

(At 1618 hours, ████████, one of the American contract pilots,
entered the room, accompanied by ████████.)

GENERAL TAYLOR - We're trying to find out what can be done to
improve operations of this type in the future.

████████ - I'm prepared to answer questions from a resume
which I have.

████████ - Your resume has not been circulated.

(At this point, ████████ read from a resume which he had prepared,
a copy of which will be made available for the file. Among his
pertinent observations was that sufficient preparation had not been
made for effective target study by the B-26 pilots; also that
they were not permitted to use napalm on the B-26s which the Planners
had considered to be an extremely useful munition. He felt that as
a recompense, they had been authorized to employ 8 B-26s rather than
5 B-26s on the initial strike, although there were 14 B-26s available
operationally for launch.)

████████ - Why weren't all of the operational aircraft
launched?

████████ - Permission was not given by Headquarters.

MR. DULLES - On D-2? There's another reason for that, which
I will go into later.

(████████ then stated that debriefing of the crews after the first
air strike on the 15th showed that at most, only fifty per cent of
the enemy's air capability had been destroyed. The strike was
rescheduled for Sunday, and napalm called for again, and again
permission for its use was refused. He also stated that while he
was getting constant calls for air protection on the beachhead on
the 17th of April, Headquarters confused the issue by a call for
further requirements for airfield targets, and in the
resulting confusion, three or four critical hours were lost.)

Document 6.1   continued

Eventually, he said we wound up with split forces, trying to cover both the beachhead and enemy airfields. ▓▓▓▓ stated that the plan as he knew it, had been changed a 180 degrees, in that they were originally supposed to use 100 per cent of their operational capability for strikes at the enemy airfields in an effort to neutralize Castro's air force, and also to hit his microwave communications.)

▓▓▓▓▓ - What were your orders on D-Day morning?

▓▓▓▓ - We were ordered to put two aircraft each on the two airfields near Havana, and one aircraft each on the airfields near Guantanamo. However, the order to go from 5 to 8 aircraft came in late and it pushed the crew briefing so that they did not have proper target study before the mission. After D-Day it was obvious they had not destroyed the enemy's air capability and there was uncertainty from there on in on the location of the Cuban Air Force's aircraft. The enemy were "turning around" their aircraft in a very short time at their airfields.

GENERAL TAYLOR - What was your "turn around" time?

▓▓▓▓ - We had 7 1/2 hours between our times over target which usually amounted to about 30 minutes. About 2 of this 7 1/2 hours was spent on the ground and the rest in flying to and from the target area. We had very good ground maintenance, and armament people.

MR. KENNEDY - Were these Americans or Cubans?

▓▓▓▓ - These were mainly Americans though we did have some Cubans. The Americans were greatly influenced by General Dossiter, who had pulled these people into the operation and who had excellent control over them.

(▓▓▓▓ stated that he had felt exactly what Castro had put into words, that the first air attack only served to make Castro angry and also gave him time to rally his forces.)

GENERAL TAYLOR - You mean the pause after the D-2 air strikes until the actual landings?

▓▓▓▓ - Yes.

(▓▓▓▓ then stated that some of his crews had reported ragged naval air cover over the beachhead area. There had been some

- 22 -

Document 6.1   continued

confusion as to whether the cover was friendly or enemy, inasmuch as there had been reports that Castro's air force was using MIGs.)

GENERAL TAYLOR - Did they have U.S. Navy aircraft over the beachhead?

ADMIRAL BURKE - Only in the later stages of the operation.

GENERAL CABELL - Permission was given for them to cover the beachhead area for one hour at dawn of D/2.

GENERAL TAYLOR - Did you debrief all of these crews?

▓▓▓▓▓ - Not all of them. I started off with the B-26 pilots and then went to the C-54 and C-46 crews as they could report more because of the nature of their piloting operations. I debriefed them for the purposes of intelligence.

(▓▓▓▓▓ then stated that in his opinion the erratic reports of naval intervention may have served as an asset in the air battle, but as far as the Cuban Volunteer Force was concerned, we had given them something and then had taken it back. A complete cover by naval air was never established.)

MR. KENNEDY - Had you or these pilots expected to have this aid or cover?

▓▓▓▓▓ - We were never briefed so.

MR. KENNEDY - Did you ever expect it by inference? Were you ever told that you would NOT get it?

▓▓▓▓▓ - I don't think they ever definitely said that they would NOT get it to the pilots.

MR. KENNEDY - Did you expect such aid?

▓▓▓▓▓ - No Sir.

MR. BISSELL - On the early morning mission of D/2, the pilots were briefed to expect naval air protection. They might have expected that protection after that.

ADMIRAL BURKE - Do you know if they were briefed that they would get naval air cover for one hour after dawn on D/2?

▓▓▓▓▓ - Yes Sir.

(At this point, ▓▓▓▓ went back to reading points from his prepared resume. He pointed out that if they had not had the assurance of naval air cover over the area on the morning of D/2, they would not

Document 6.1   continued

have put American crews in the aircraft. That morning, the 19th, because of lack of Cuban crews, they had scheduled four American B-26 crews. One American crew was shot down that morning, and one was chased off by T-33s. The commander of the second element of the B-26s tried to contact the naval aircraft and when he could not, he elected not to penetrate the coast and he turned back from his mission when he was 35 miles out to sea. One ▓▓▓▓▓▓▓ ▓▓▓▓▓▓▓▓▓▓ crewmember observed another American crew in a B-26 go into the sea after it was shot down at 1200 ZULU during the period when they had been promised naval air cover.)

MR. DULLES - Did any of your people see any MIGs?

GENERAL CABELL - They've already said that they would have liked to authenticate that, but they couldn't, that it remained only conjecture.

(At this point, ▓▓▓▓▓▓ stressed one point very emphatically, that he thought that one lesson that could be learned was in regard to the inability of the Cuban crews to do an effective job under tough combat conditions. He pointed out that when the going was easy and morale was high, they did a good job, but that by the end of the operation, when things were very difficult, it had been almost impossible to get them into the air at all.)

GENERAL TAYLOR - Why was this naval air cover only to be over the beach for this one special hour?

ADMIRAL BURKE - They didn't want them to be over the beachhead area for a long time, picked up and attributed to the United States. However, because of the serious troubles the landing forces were in, they did want them over the area at first light to protect this first air strike.

▓▓▓▓▓▓ - One of our pilots reported that on the road west of Blue Beach that there were an estimated 20 large Russian tanks, and some 50 to 60 trucks. Three of our B-26s made passes on the trucks before they could stop and have the men climb out.

GENERAL TAYLOR - When was this?

▓▓▓▓▓▓ - On D/1, I think.

MR. BISSELL - That was Tuesday afternoon.

- 24 -

Document 6.1   continued

- If we hadn't hurt them badly, they would have
moved right on down into the landing area.

MR. KENNEDY - Could you tell where the fighting was going on?
(At this point, ███, at the chart depicted where targets had
been seen at points above Blue, Green, and Red Beaches.)

██████ - They moved in tremendously quickly into the area.

GENERAL TAYLOR - Where did they report that flak from?

██████ - They reported flak from all around the area.
The Cubans seemed to have excellent coverage and seemed to know
what they were doing.

GENERAL TAYLOR - How were the aircraft directed? From the
ground by radio?

██████ - No, this wasn't possible as the communications
went down with the ship that was sunk. They did land an aircraft
on the strip and try to do some controlling with their radio. We
then tried to have other aircraft land, but the Cuban pilots' fuel
control procedures were bad and they had to turn back.

MR. KENNEDY - You say then that you did not find the Cuban
pilots to be very good?

██████ - No. When the chips were down and the going was
tough, they found excuses NOT to do the job.

MR. KENNEDY - What percentage would you say did do their job?

██████ - I'd say that not over 35 per cent of them did.

██████ - In our early missions, we had some Cuban crews
making as many as three passes over heavily defended targets.

██████ - That was in the early days when they smelled
victory. When the going got tough, we had trouble even getting
them into the aircraft. On D/2, it took us several hours to get
some of their crews in the aircraft, and then they aborted the
mission.

ADMIRAL BURKE - When our pilots were over the beachhead on the
morning of D/2, they couldn't find any enemy infantry at all.

MR. KENNEDY - Can you tell us where the fighting took place?

- 25 -

Document 6.1   continued

███████ - I'm getting int) an area I really cannot answer.

MR. KENNEDY - You say that they had tanks and trucks west of
Blue Beach?

███████ - Cn D-Day morning, there were Cuban tanks
hitting our troops on Red Beach.

GENERAL TAYLOR - Were there any attempts made at marking lines
by smoke or other means? How did your aircraft know that they were
not hitting your own troops?

███████ - On our missions in the beachhead area, we were
preoccupied with heavy equipment targets. We did not try to put
any fire on troops. We always had heavy equipment targets when we
were in the area.

MR. KENNEDY - How long did our people last on Red Beach?

███████ - It only seemed to be a matter of hours. The DZs
where we dropped by C-46s did not seem to be compromised, so there
was spasmodic fire in one or two areas. I don't think they knew
that we were going in there.

MR. DULLES - I'd like to get more clear your statement on
confusion in regard to orders. I didn't think that you had any
question at all in regard to going after airfields on D/2.

MR. BISSELL - We did get authority the previous night to strike
airfields at dusk, even though we knew that our aircraft were heavily
committed. As I recall, we authorized strikes at airfields at dusk
that night.

MR. DULLES - That mission was not carried out.

MR. BISSELL - That's correct Sir. The crews were tired by
then, and the ones that did go in, could not identify the San Antonio
targets in the haze.

███████ - Our orders to execute the strikes were so different
from what we had been told that we would do, that when I saw the orders
that we were calling off the war, I really thought we were trying to
lose it intentionally, though I didn't say anything aloud in regard
to this.

(███████ left the conference room at 1700 hours, and General Taylor
called an executive session of the committee at this time. The
general meeting adjourned at 1701.)

- -26 -

Document 6.1   continued

THE WHITE HOUSE
WASHINGT·
April 24, 1961

Some Preliminary Administrative Lessons of the Cuban Expedition

The main large-scale lessons of Cuba have been drawn by the President in his address to the editors. The present paper is designed to be useful in assessing internal weaknesses which can be avoided in the future. The causes of the failure of this operation are essentially military, and only secondarily political, though the consequences are almost all political and only slightly military. This is a kind of operation in which it is not easy, at best, to get good judgment. In this case there were evident complications. What is set down below implies no criticism of particular individuals; if that were the object the writer would begin with himself; the importance of these points is that they do not reflect personal failure as much as weaknesses in the situations which men found themselves placed. These can all be repaired.

First: There was a new Administration. With the best will in the world, communication and understanding are uncertain in the early days of a new Administration. In the Cuban case, men with doubts did not press them home -- and this is as true of men who favored the operation as of those who opposed it. The former did not insist on proper strength, and gave ground on many politically touchy elements they initially wanted; the latter did not insist upon their general doubts, accepting as significant such modifications as their reservations obtained. There were many reasons for this restraint, but respectful unfamiliarity with a new President was an important element.

Second: This operation necessarily required a very high degree of secrecy, and secrecy makes deliberation difficult. Plans were not held in hand to be read and reread, but distributed and collected at meetings in order to keep them secure. Outside the CIA and the Joint Staff, no close study was given to the details of the military plan; the efforts of others were limited to questioning in meetings.

Third: Neither CIA nor the Joint Staff was a reliable military counselor in this instance. Both were persuaded of the deep urgency of action against Castro, and neither was confident of the determination of the President or his nonmilitary advisers. Thus in a measure both became advocates of action, and there was no countervailing military concern for caution. Usually -- and especially in a democracy -- the pressure for military engagement comes from above down to the military,

Document 6.2   Some Preliminary Administrative Lessons of the Cuban Expedition (draft by McGeorge Bundy, Special Assistant to the President for National Security Affairs, 24 April 1961).

- 2 -

and military staffs think more of ensuring victory than ensuring action. In this case the reverse, unhappily, seems to have been the case. Moreover, the Joint Chiefs themselves were not close to the operation and may have felt constrained from the closest possible comment by the fact that another agency was in charge. It may be doubted whether they would have approved this operation for their own execution. CIA, on the other hand, had no true military staff of its own at a senior level. One important element in this unusual posture of military advocacy against senior political reluctance is that the preparation of the operation had been directed in an earlier administration. Thus what one President had seemed to approve had to be advocated de novo to another.

Fourth: Particularly important was the failure to estimate accurately the proficiency of the Castro forces. The responsibility for this failure must be shared outside the intelligence services. No one seems to have drawn the proper moral from abundant evidence of purges, foreign advice, and massive remilitarization. Castro's military effectiveness was put in the future, not the present -- but without evidence that now seems persuasive. Hope was the parent of belief.

Fifth: For nearly all of those engaged in deliberation, as distinct from advocacy, this operation received far too little time. Men to whom the President had a right to look for independent and personal counsel did not find the time to reach judgments based on careful evaluation. (An honorable exception here is Mr. Schlesinger, who carefully and repeatedly pressed his doubts.) Time was a serious pressure against adequate consideration at every stage.

Sixth: In the pressure of argument about the pros and cons of the operation, those between the Administration and the Cuban force failed to communicate adequately to either one the full views and feelings of the other. Thus the President repeatedly emphasized that he wanted a landing that would be quiet, and that could readily, and in a measure successfully, convert itself into guerrilla operations. This does not appear to have been seriously communicated to the Cubans, or planned for in any thoughtful way. The swamp to which survivors have fled is most unlikely to be a safe hideout. The advocates of the operation did not really believe, in their hearts, in the usefulness of the guerrilla option, but they did not share the disbelief with the President, or seriously communicate his quite opposite view to the Cubans.

At the same time the Cubans had expectations -- and strong ones -- of which the President was inadequately informed. They counted

Document 6.2   continued

heavily, as did the U. S. planners, on complete removal of enemy air,
and they must always have assumed that the Navy would do it if necessary.
They assumed that supplies were a certainty, not a chancy business.
They were certainly told not to expect direct U. S. intervention, but
we must suppose that they did not deeply accept this warning; the
messages received in the last agonies show the hope of active help, and
no notion whatever of a skillful move to the bush.

Seventh: A quite excessive emphasis was placed, in the end, on the
need to do "something" with the Guatemala force. It had to get out of
Guatemala (though even this "necessity" seems less than complete in
retrospect -- further hospitality could perhaps have been bought),
and it seemed impossible to keep it as a real force in being elsewhere
(though this also could have been done). Thus there seemed to be a
prospect of losing an excellent weapon which could never be reconstituted,
and of receiving heavy criticism from refugees and Americans for appeasing
Castro. All those who have wrongly believed that Castro was ready to
fall at a touch would surely have been noisy in complaint. Even in
retrospect this course does not seem a good one, and surely the brigade
could have been kept alive, and tripled in strength, if that had been the
firm decision of the government -- though this would have involved real
strains with many friendly countries. But even disbanding the brigade,
with all its consequences, would have been better, at least in the short
run, than what happened.

Eighth: The moments of decision were not always isolated and treated
with the gravity they deserved. Certain special circumstances contributed
to this result, but it remains urgent that both the President and all his
advisers watch closely for points of no return -- even partial or interim
decisions can strongly change the shape of the problem and so become
decisive.

Ninth: This whole operation raises the great question whether there can
be such a thing as large-scale covert activity in a society like ours.
Many of the hopes of those who concurred in this enterprise were pinned
to the notion that it could be a quiet one. The very wide distance between
this notion and what really happened is not to be explained by any particular
minor specific failures of security or tactical planning. It appears to be
an inescapable conclusion that in peacetime conditions the United States
cannot do things on this scale in private.

Tenth, and most important: In prolonged balancing and rebalancing of
marginal elements of this operation, all concerned managed to forget --
or not to learn -- the fundamental importance of success in this sort of effort.

Document 6.2   continued

- 4 -

Limitations were accepted that should have been avoided, and hopes
were indulged that should have been sternly put aside.   Many of the
lesser mistakes or failures listed above can be explained largely by
the failure to recall this basic rule.

*   *   *   *

The morals of those failures are readily drawn: First, the President's
advisors must speak up in council.   Second, secrecy must never take
precedence over careful thought and study.   Third, the President and
his advisors must second-guess even military plans.   Fourth, we
must estimate the enemy without hope or fear.   Fifth, those who are
to offer serious advice on major issues must themselves do the
necessary work. Sixth, the President's desires must be fully acted on,
and he must know the full state of mind of friends whose lives his
decisions affect.   Seventh, forced choices are seldom as necessary
as they seem, and the fire can be much hotter than the frying pan.
Eighth, what is and is not implied in any specific partial decision
must always be thought through.   Ninth: What is large in scale must
always be open, with all the consequences of openness.   Tenth: Success
is what succeeds.

Document 6.2   continued

~~CONFIDENTIAL~~

May 3, 1961

MEMORANDUM FOR THE PRESIDENT

SUBJECT: Reactions to Cuba in Western Europe

    1.   I spent the period April 22-May 3 in Western Europe, first attending a conference of West European political and intellectual figures at Bologna, Italy, and then spending a few days in Paris and in London.   I made a special point of trying to check reactions to the Cuban debacle -- and also of setting forth (especially to key politicians and journalists) the key facts of the Cuban situation.

In Paris, I had conversations with Pierre Mendes-France; Jean Monnet; Jean-Jacques Servan-Schreiber (L'Express); Raymond Aron; M. Jeanneny, the Minister of Production; M. Baraduc, the chief information officer of the Quai d'Orsay; as well as with Ambassador Gavin, Ambassador Finletter, Cecil Lyon, and the American correspondents Cy Sulzberger, Joe Alsop, Don Cook and Art Buchwald.

In London, I talked with publishers or editors of the Spectator (Ian Gilmour and Bernard Levin); New Statesman (Paul Johnson and Norman Mackenzie); Economist (Donald Tyerman); Observer (David Astor, John Pringle, Edward Crankshaw and leading staff people); Sunday Times (Frank Giles and Nicholas Carroll); Daily Herald (John Beavan); Daily Telegraph (Michael Berry and Maurice Green); Evening Standard (Charles Wintour): Sunday Telegraph (Peregrine Worsthorne); plus a luncheon with the diplomatic correspondents of the London papers and the Manchester Guardian.   Among Labour MPs, I saw Hugh Gaitskell, Denis Healey, Richard Crossman, Roy Jenkins, George Brown, Woodrow Wyatt.   Among members of the government, I saw David Ormsby-Gore, Ian Macleod, Reginald Maudling, Lord Hailsham, Sir Edward Boyle.   I also saw Sir Frank Lee of the Treasury; Bob Boothby, Hartley Shawcross and Gladwyn Jebb, all of whom are now independent members of the House of Lords; Lord Lambton, a right-wing Tory MP; Sir Isaiah

~~CONFIDENTIAL~~

Document 6.3   Memorandum from the President's Special Assistant (Arthur Schlesinger Jr.) to President Kennedy; Subject: Reactions to Cuba in Western Europe, 3 May 1961).

CONFIDENTIAL

2.

Berlin and William Deakin of Oxford; and the American corre-
spondents Drew Middleton (New York Times) and Herman Nickels
(Time). I also consulted closely, of course, with Ambassador
Bruce and members of his staff.

I list these names to make clear the kind of opinions on which this
report is based. I believe that in both Paris and London I saw a
fairly representative cross-section of the political community. My
impression of sentiment in these countries has been supplemented by
my talks in Bologna with people from all over Western Europe and
by the reports of American correspondents and diplomats.

I should add that I encountered everywhere what can only be described
as a hunger for a rational explanation of the Cuban operation. I found
this among left and right alike; among Americans as well as Europeans;
among American Embassy officials (and even CIA representatives) as
well as among American newspaper correspondents. The available
stories had left most people baffled and incredulous. They could not
believe that the U. S. Government had been quite so incompetent,
irresponsible and stupid as the bare facts of the operation suggested,
and they listened sympathetically and gratefully to a more balanced
and complete account.

The apparent decision to keep our own diplomatic personnel in ignorance
about the background of the Cuban operation seems to me especially unfortunate and unnecessary (though there may be considerations here of
which I have no knowledge). The State Department appears to have
sent out no instructions to American Embassies how to explain what
happened in Cuba. As a consequence, our Ambassadors remain in the
dark. If the Foreign Secretary of the state to which they are assigned
asks them what really went on, they are forced to mouth official gener-
alities or to confess ignorance or to rely on Scotty Reston or Time.
This matter could easily have been remedied, in my judgment, if the
State Department had sent out a simple instruction to our Embassies.
I attach as Appendix A to this report the copy of a cable I sent to
Mr. Rusk on this point from Rome.

    2.   Reactions to the debacle: short-term. The first reactions to
Cuba were, of course, acute shock and disillusion. For some months
nearly everybody in Western Europe, and especially perhaps the demo-

Document 6.3   continued

3.

cratic left, had been making heavy emotional and political invest-
ments in the new American administration.   Everything about this
administration -- the intelligence and vision of the President, the
dynamism of his leadership, the scope and generosity of his policies,
the freshness of his approach to the cold war -- had excited tremendous anticipation and elation.   The new American President in three
months had reestablished confidence in the maturity of American
judgment and the clarity of American purposes.   Kennedy was considered the last best hope of the West against communism and for
peace.

Now, in a single stroke, all this seemed wiped away.   After Cuba,
the American Government seemed as self-righteous, trigger-happy
and incompetent as it had ever been in the heyday of John Foster
Dulles.   "Kennedy has lost his magic," one person said to me.
"It will take years before we can accept the leadership of the Kennedy
Administration again," said another.   Friends of America warned
me not to underestimate the gravity of the damage: "Make sure that
our people in Washington understand how much ground we have lost"
(Drew Middleton); "It was a terrible blow, and it will take a long, long
time for us to recover from it" (Lord Boothby).

I should add that nearly all the reactions I encountered expressed sorrow
over the decision to invade rather than over the failure of the invasion.
"Why was Cuba such a threat to you?   Why couldn't you live with Cuba,
as the USSR lives with Turkey and Finland?"   I had expected to find
more people on the right who would complain over our failure to send
in the Marines; but I found only one -- Lord Lambton, a Tory MP who
is a bitter critic of Macmillan's, a great friend of Joe Alsop's and an
advocate of fighting everywhere -- in Laos, Kenya, Cuba, etc.   Other
Tory MPs -- Lord Hailsham, for example -- said that in their view
US intervention would have been a great error and would only have con-
verted Cuba into another Ireland, Cyprus or Algeria.   David Ormsby-
Gore, in making this point, added that British intelligence estimates,
which he said had been made available to CIA, were that the Cuban
people were still predominantly behind Castro and that there was no
likelihood at this point of mass defections or insurrections.

    3.   Reactions to the debacle: long-term.   The severity of the
original shock should not, however, be allowed to overshadow certain

Document 6.3   continued

4.

factors on the other side. The fact is that the new administration made an enormously good impression up to Cuba and in so doing built up a fund of good will which, though now somewhat dissipated, is by no means entirely destroyed. One evidence of this is the eagerness of people on the left -- Mendes-France, Servan-Schreiber, even Dick Crossman and the New Statesman people -- to hear the American side of the case.

Reactions within the British Labour Party are perhaps symptomatic. Hugh Gaitskell was rueful but philosophical. "It was a great blow," he said. "The right wing of the Labour Party has been basing a good deal of its argument on the claim that things had changed in America. Cuba has made great trouble for us. We shall now have to move toward the left for a bit in order to maintain our position within the Party." But he asked what he could do to help, suggested people to whom I should talk and even made an appointment himself for me to see the editor of the Daily Herald. Denis Healey, the 'shadow' Foreign Secretary, was somewhat more bitter. "I've staked my whole political career on the ability of the Americans to act sensibly," he said. He felt badly let down by the Administration but again was perfectly ready to listen to an account of how things had actually happened. Farther to the left, Dick Crossman said, "You really have got off very lightly. If this had taken place under Eisenhower, there would have been mass meetings in Trafalgar Square, Dulles would have been burned in effigy, and the Labour Party would have damned you in the most unequivocal terms. But because enough faith still remains in Kennedy, there has been very little popular outcry, and the Labour Party resolutions have been the bare minimum. You've got away with it this time. But one more mistake like this, and you will really be through."

Conservatives were, on the whole, even more willing to find excuses for the Cuban policy. A number of people, both on the right and the left, remarked consolingly on the shortness of popular memories. Algeria, of course, was immensely helpful in driving Cuba from the front pages.

Over the longer term, in short, I think we have suffered a serious but by no means fatal loss of confidence in our intelligence and responsibility. This can be easily recouped if we seem to return to more intelligent and responsible ways in the future. However, it will all go rather quickly if we embark once more on a course which Europeans regard as ill-considered, impetuous and reckless.

Document 6.3   continued

CONFIDENTIAL

5.

4. Dangers for the future. To sum up, Cuba is forgivable as
an aberration but is greatly feared as forecasting future directions of
US policy. It has created, for example, a vague fear in people's
minds that the Kennedy Administration is bent on a course of subversive
and paramilitary warfare. This fear has been heightened by what some
Europeans regard as an unfolding pattern of events since Cuba, all
seeming to foreshadow policies of military or paramilitary intervention:
the "our patience is not limitless" speech; the emphasis on training for
guerrilla warfare; the appeal to the press not to print stories about US
unconventional warfare projects; the rumors of CIA support for the
Algiers generals; the Presidential offer to intervene in France; the
intimations of possible US intervention in Laos; the huddles with Nixon,
Hoover, MacArthur, etc., interpreted in Europe as an effort to gather
national support for, at the very least, a US invasion of Cuba. A number
of people seriously believe, on the basis of newspaper stories from Washington, that an American invasion of Cuba is a distinct and imminent
possibility. An Observer editor said to me, "If Cuba were just an
accident, all right. But everything since Cuba suggests that the Kennedy
who launched that invasion was the real Kennedy -- that all his talk about
'new methods' of warfare and countering guerrillas represents his real
approach to the problems of the cold war -- that he thinks the West will
beat communism by adopting communist methods and transforming itself
into a regimented paramilitary society on the model of the Soviet Union."
Several people said, "It's not Cuba that worries me; it's the aftermath."

The reported Washington obsession with guerrilla warfare has roused
particular concern. Press stories have given high quarters in England
and France the impression that the U. S. Government suddenly regards
counter-guerrilla activity as the key to victory in the cold war. The
attached piece from the Times expresses British feeling on this matter.
Several people elaborately pointed out to me that guerrilla warfare can
not be isolated from the political battle; that no force, however trained in
counter-guerrilla technique, can clean up a guerrilla situation if the countryside sticks with the guerrillas; that the decisive question therefore is how
the peasants feel. I was reminded that the guerrillas have been defeated
in only two places since the war -- in the Philippines, because Magsaysay's
reform program won back the countryside; and in Malaya, because the
British were able both to mobilize the Malayans against the Chinese and
to offer independence -- and that these examples show that politics, not
combat methods, is the secret of success against guerrilla movements.

CONFIDENTIAL

Document 6.3   continued

CONFIDENTIAL

6.

The new tone of urgency in Washington has a somewhat shrill ring
in many European ears.   The Europeans to whom I talked believe
that the fight against communism is still a matter for the long haul;
they are much more impressed by the Alianza para el Progreso than
by the training camps for anti-guerrilla warfare; and they hope for a
return to the main lines of US foreign policy as set forth in the months
before Cuba.   I should add that nothing would do more to reestablish
confidence in the U. S. Government than a visible shake-up and
subordination of CIA.   As the Algerian affair showed, CIA is going to be
blamed for everything, especially so long as it continues to operate under
its present management.   People are eager to believe that the President
was misled by bad advice in the matter of Cuba, but they are also eager
to be reassured that he will not continue to get the same bad advice in
the future.

Arthur Schlesinger, jr.

cc: Mr. Bundy
     The Attorney General
     Mr. Sorensen
     Mr. Goodwin

CONFIDENTIAL

Document 6.3   continued

Appendix A ~~SECRET~~

To: RUSK

From: SCHLESINGER

In connection with instructions to embassies concerning Cuba you may wish to consider following points:

1. New administration inherited plan for overthrow of Castro regime through operations involving not only anti-Castro Cubans but US Navy and Air Force.

2. New administration rejected proposed US intervention and killed original plan.

3. This decision left question whether to disband or assist anti-Castro Cubans trained to return to homeland.

4. Administration saw no obligation to protect Castro from Cuban patriots who felt he had sold out Cuban Revolution. In view moreover of supposed bad effect in Latin America of total cancellation, the administration decided, all senior officers involved concurring, that effort should be made at mass infiltration of exiles back into Cuba.

5. This was not repeat not an invasion though so played by press. Difficulties were obviously underestimated.

6. This operation in no way comparable to Hungary or Suez. If US had intervened, obviously Castro would be through. US government stuck resolutely to determination against military intervention. US role was to lend sympathy and limited support to group of liberal Cubans.

7. Remedial measures are under way to repair malfunctioning services.

~~SECRET~~

Document 6.3 continued

Index

About the Book

The defeat of the attempted April 1961 invasion of Cuba at the Bay of Pigs (Playa Giron) was one of the worst foreign-policy disasters in U.S. history. Since then, explanations of the event have emphasized betrayal by one U.S. agency or another, seeking to assign blame for the "loss" of Cuba. With the benefit of new documentation, however—from U.S. government and Cuban exile sources—as well as the first-hand accounts of key participants, *Politics of Illusion* shows the current mythology to be just that.

Based on an innovative series of meetings that brought together former CIA officials, former anti-Castro Cuban operatives, a former high-ranking Soviet official, and others who were directly involved in the events—nearly all speaking on the record for the first time—this critical oral history demonstrates that all of the anti-Castro parties were guilty of illusions, to one degree or another. Blight and Kornbluh provide a thorough and perceptive context for the discussions held at the meetings, transcripts of the actual sessions, a selection of the main documents discussed by the participants, and a discussion of the implications of the participants' conclusions for current U.S.-Cuban relations.

James G. Blight is professor of international relations at Brown University's Watson Institute for International Studies. His extensive work on Cuba includes *Cuba on the Brink: Castro, the Missile Crisis, and the Soviet Collapse;* he has also written extensively on the recent history of U.S. foreign policy. **Peter Kornbluh** is senior analyst at the National Security Archive, a nongovernmental research facility located at George Washington University. His publications include *The Cuban Missile Crisis* and *The Iran Contra Scandal: A Declassified History.*